100+ WORDS
I'VE NOT LIVED
WITHOUT
A MEMOIR IN WORDS

A VERY BUELLER BOOK

WHAT OTHERS ARE SAYING

100+Words I've Not Lived Without

The amusing title took me in and I began a wordsmithing journey. I was quickly engaged by the relatable stories and personal anecdotes that comprised this page-turner! Many words were familiar, but many others were headscratchers that were entertaining and fundamentally educational. The stories established clear connections to the application/meaning. The robust timeline provided a poignant context to me—as I believe it will for anyone—who enjoys a trip down memory lane! This book shows that good communication allows for fundamental relationships that bring people together while providing shared moments of understanding.

—Newton Brown
Director of Administration, BNSF, Springfield Division

As an educator and cognitive trainer, I think *100+Words I've Not Lived Without* is a brilliant approach to learning vocabulary and understanding the power of words! The engaging stories will inspire families to create their own 100+ Word type books with their children.

—Carol Brown Ed.D
Ex. Director and Educational Specialist/Cognitive Developmental Therapist @ Equipping Minds

Whether you're a seasoned grammarian who closely scans copy with an editor's eye, or a casual reader eager to learn new things with a few laughs, this book is for you. Using wit, humor and plenty of anecdotes, Timothy L. Price takes you on a grammatical journey that is sure to bring a smile to your face — and several new words to your vocabulary.

—Chuck Green
Writer, editor, & journalist – University of Nebraska-Lincoln

This is a delightful exploration of how words frame our lives. Personal character and wit develop through lifelong memories. My dad always told me, "Words have meaning. Choose your words wisely."

—Jana Belcher
Recruitment Coordinator – Randall University

100+ Words I've Not Lived Without is a witty & winsome collection of unique words that Timothy Price ensconces in brief anecdotal stories, which help readers learn the meaning of the term in context. Intended for home schoolers and all logophiles, this is a clever and informative book, including a measure of the word's usage through the years. Readers will enjoy a delightful read and gain a better vocabulary.

—**Lemke Steve**
Provost at New Orleans Baptist Theological Seminary

Timothy L. Price's latest publication, *100+ Words I've Not Lived Without*, offers an entertaining, yet informative, education about terms most of us might have heard, but never had a clear definition on. As a former English-Lit. teacher, I can envision ways this volume could be used to stimulate students' curiosity about the origin of language. I welcome it as a useful resource.

—**Gloria Gibbons**
Retire English Teacher – Oklahoma

For both experienced logophiles and novice lovers of words, Timothy L. Price's autobiographical *100+ Words I've Not Lived Without* is a delightful, informative, and provocative read. It is a vocabulary treasury for novice and expert logophiles alike. Price's accounting for words he cherishes in the form of a memoir invites inveterate lovers of words to reflect on events, persons, or books that occasioned their acquisition of an expanding lexicon.

—**Ardel Caneday**
Ret. University of Northwestern Professor of New Testament & Greek

Timothy L. Price delivers up a candy bowl of words, each one a singular treat that sparkles with understanding and nuance. Timothy breathes life into the meaning and subtext of these delicious terms. He tells personal and family stories about his encounters with such gems as caterwauling, shtick, and farding, reminding readers of the elasticity of our language, along with the power and satisfaction that comes from coloring our thoughts with just the perfect word.

—**Rick Brown**
Writer at Kearney Hub and Yard Light Media

This book is utterly unique. It attests to wordsmanship and gives us a new way to enjoy a memoir. Turn the page, you get a new word. Then you find its roots and how it impacted the author's life. Innovative!

—Jim Backens
Metro Omaha Board Member - Nebraska Writers Guild

100+ Words is a fascinating book! It will be considered "light" reading, as in literary desert. The place words have filled in Timothy L. Price's journey unfolded in a way that is stimulating, challenging, and educational. This is the perfect book to curl up with when you are fed up with fluff and drivel—but it isn't *The Brothers Karamazov*.

—Jon Zens
Editor of Searching Together, author of *Don't Be Called Leaders*

As a "word guy," I love the trivia about the origins of seemingly small but magnificent little parts of our English language. Timothy L. Price hit upon a brilliant formula to teach us word meanings and the etymology behind 100+ words. He weaves them into our memory through the delightful narrative of his colorful life.

—Andrew Pudewa
Founder and Director of Institute for Excellence in Writing

100+ Words I've Not Lived Without is a fun book and quite literally a play on words. Any logophile or historian would enjoy it. It's a quick read, and a great peek into Timothy L. Price's upbringing. I can see where he became an author and logophile and historian himself! Fun read, I highly recommend it!

—Amanda Campbell
Co-Host - goathomeschoolingpodcast

Timothy L. Price has done a remarkable job developing a truly unique and exciting piece of literature. He assembled an expansive list of words and definitions, many of which are obscure or are "victims" of malapropism. This literary work provides a fun way to expand one's understanding and vocabulary, which certainly has been the case for me. Abounding with fascinating stories, vivid illustrations, and a touch of humor, Price has gifted us with an extremely practical work. I highly recommend his "Very Bueller Book". You'll not be disappointed!

—Larry Middendorf
Christian Business Men's Connection (CBMC), Lincoln, NE

Copyright © 2024 by Timothy L. Price

All rights reserved. No part of this publication may be duplicated, distributed, or transmitted in any form by any means, including photocopying, recording, or other electronic or mechanical methods unless written permission from the publisher has been acquired—brief quotations embodied in critical reviews and other specific noncommercial uses permitted by copyright law.

First edition May 2024

Names: Price, Timothy L., author.
Title: 100+ words I've not lived without: a memoir in words / Timothy L. Price.
Description: [Kearney, Nebraska] : [Blue Thumb Productions, an imprint of Ekklesia Press], [2024]

| Includes bibliographical references and index. | Audience: Young adult.

Identifiers: ISBN: 979-8-9905782-9-6

Subjects: LCSH: Price, Timothy L.--Anecdotes. | English language--Glossaries, vocabularies, etc. | Verbal ability. | Vocabulary--Social aspects. | Vocabulary--Study guides. | Lexicology. | Self-culture. | LCGFT: Autobiographies. | Etymological dictionaries. | Thesauri (Dictionaries) | BISAC: YOUNG ADULT NONFICTION / Biography & Autobiography / Literary. | LANGUAGE ARTS & DISCIPLINES / Public Speaking & Speech Writing. | HUMOR / Topic / School & Education.

Classification: LCC: PE1680 .P75 2024 | DDC: 420.71--dc23

For permission requests, write to:
Blue Thumb Productions
C/O Ekklesia Press
2110 30 th Ave. #16
Kearney, NE 68845

TABLE OF CONTENTS

The Great-Aunt Everyone Loved—1973 9
Go Look It Up—1973 11
Nouns Don't Have To Insult—1974 13
A Three-Letter Word That Pops—1974 15
An Old-Fashioned Drama Queen—1974 17
A Book Corner In The Eye–1975 19
A Lacerating Tongue—1976-83 21
The Sound Of Complaining—1978 23
What The Leaves Tell You–1978-80 25
The Stuff You Learn At Church—1979-83 27
Long-Term Training That Sticks—1979-83 29
Clouds That Spread Disease—1979-83 31
Skin-Tone Talk Without Racism—1979-83 33
Checked Out Before Graduation—1984 35
What Musical Appreciation Can Teach You—1984 37
You're In The Army Now—1984-87 39
A Drill Sgt. Taught More Than Push-Ups—1984-87 41
Words We Reduce The Infinite By—1987-89 43
Take Religion Out Of Its' Context—1987-89 45
Elixir Salesman In Another World—1987-89 47
Beware Of Mixtures—1987-89 49
A Stinky Word That Is Funny—1989-92 51
Traditions Of Respect—1989-92 53
Getting Put In Someone Else's Place—1992 55
Leave It To An Interior Designer—1989-92 57
Anger Is Sometimes Hysterical—1993 59
Any Which Way You Can—1994-01 61
A Store By Another Description—1994-01 63
From The Mouths Of Foreign Speakers—1995-98 65
A Tune Worthy Of A Word—1995-99 67
Now Negative Isn't Negative—1997 69
A Precipitously Increasing Identifiability—1998 71
Cat And Mouth Characters—1998 73
Pop-Culture Education—1999 75
The Great Divergence—1999 77

Management Shenanigans—2001	79
Hollywood's Anthropomorphism—2001	81
Verbal Bombast And Piano Lessons—2001-06	83
Does Yiddish Always Insult—2001-06	85
The Dialectics Of Antithesis—2002	87
A Great Responsibility—2003	89
Movie Vocabulary For $100—2003	91
Son Of Poseidon—2003	93
Continuing To Soak Up Understanding—2003	95
An Allegory That'd Stop A Clock—2003-04	97
The Sunny Side Of French—2003-06	99
Reality That Doesn't Have To Be—2003-09	101
A Dressed-Up Conundrum—2004	103
The Effusiveness Of Arranged Words—2004	105
Yiddish For The Mouths Of Goyim—2004	107
Music Isn't Just Music—2004	109
Beat A Different Drum—2005	111
Supplementary Support—2005	113
Verbal Flamboyance—2005	115
Unseen Blindness—2005	117
Old-World Mystique—2005	119
Self-Evident At Mere Statement—2006	121
What A Pooka Never Said—2006	123
Shattering Empty Veneration—2006	125
Challenging The Status Quo—2006	127
Beatle Words Instead Of Music—2006	129
Asceticism That Doesn't Fool Anyone—2006	131
Words Not To Be Confused With Drugs—2006	133
Fellow Exiles—2006	135
New Words From Regressive Therapy—2007	137
Approaching The Line Of Unnecessariness—2007	139
It Rhymes With Calliope—2007	141
Some Words Are Too Superlative—2007-11	143
Exactitude And Creative License—2007-11	145
Cartoons More Than Entertain—2007-11	147
A Well-Scripted Period Piece—2008	149
Lineal Validity—2008	151
The Parallax Of Dialogue And Movies—2008	153
When One Card Takes Down The House—2008	155

Eloquence: Three Stooges' Style—2008	157
Substance Over Imagination—2009	159
Definitely Hard To Miss—2009	161
Words That Are Far Between—2009	163
Beyond What It Is Called—2009	165
Powerful Words That Impact—2010	167
Censoring In Other Words—2010	169
Vaccinating For Diseases In Intellect—2011	171
If Only A Pill Could Do That—2011	173
Big Words Still Have Practical Use—2011	175
Incongruous Terminology—2012	177
Period Stories Accent Creativity—2012	179
With Help From My Friends—2012	181
Footnotes And Scripting—2012	183
Tension All Around Can Be Comedic—2012	185
Serious Critique That Is Funny—2013	187
Lighting It Up According To French, 2013	189
A Commercial Flop That Was Great—2013	191
Late-In-Life Impact—2013	193
Green Spaces Speak—2013	195
Reading To Wait Patiently At Sam's Club—2014	197
A Nice Word For Negative Implications—2014	199
The Unexplainableness In French—2014	201
The Mystique Of A Mystic—2014	203
How Britishisms Enrich English—2014	205
Intermission Words After The Fact	207
A Real-Life Forrest Gump—2014-18	211
Another Look At Servile Terminology—2015	213
Words That Slow Reading Down—2016	215
The Ignorant View Of Communism—2017	217
The Mouse That Roared—2017	219
From The Minds Of Budding Authors—2018	221
Random Foray In The Dictionary—2018	223
Be An Autodidact—2020	225
Two Can Be Right—2021	227
Conversations Of Biblical Proportion—2023	229
Breakfast Over Words—2023	231
Glossary Of Terms	233
Index	239

A tribute:
To my mother: Karel Ida (Geary) Price
You've often wondered aloud if you did well as a mother.
This book wouldn't have happened without you being the
mother you were. I've grown to see the value you brought
to the table, which wasn't minimal. Thank you!

Thanks to:
Duvon McGuire – If you hadn't come along, this book might not have
seen the light of day for many more years. You listened, and then acted
upon the question, "what would it take for you to finish well?"
Thank you! So many never hear a person's heart in what they say.

FOREWORD

"Wise men speak because they've something to say; fools because they have to say something." —Plato

"A word fitly spoken is like a jewel set in gold or a painting in a frame of silver" —Solomon

Timothy (Tim) L. Price is an exceptional writer. He's a wordsmith *par excellence*. I met Tim years ago when a mutual friend, Jon Zens of Searching Together, introduced me to his publishing company. Over the years, our friendship grew, and I became deeply impressed with Tim's work and writings.

Besides the scholarly articles Tim uploads for all to read, his books *The Coming Caesars, The Labyrinth of the World -and- Paradise of the Heart*, and *The Diluted Church* prove Tim's ability to make language a tool for enlightenment. *100+ Words I've Not Lived Without* reveals the genius behind Tim's wordplay.

This book is autobiographical and educational. But most importantly, it is transformational. By reading it, you'll discover the power of words and how they can shape one's life. The book's layout is eye-catching, but the design is more for your understanding than your eyes.

Take time, as I have, to read the chapters and learn the words. Learn more than just the *meaning* of the words; learn from Tim the *life* lessons behind each word and phrase. Tim has permitted me to share a medical diagnosis he received a few years ago: early-onset dementia. The early symptoms forced Tim to leave his full-time Purchasing Agent and Inventory Control job. But these issues haven't stopped Tim from fulfilling his Kingdom's destiny. Since his diagnosis, Tim has accomplished more than most men do in a lifetime.

Tim continues to advance the Kingdom of Christ through his writings. He's a blessing to all who are privileged to read his books. If one must write, it's best done with brevity, clarity, and verity. Tim Price does it better than most. *100+ Words I've Not Lived Without* will clearly and succinctly help lighten your path in life as you see how God has lit Tim's through the power of words.

—Wade Burleson
President, Istoria Ministries
August 2023

INTRODUCTION

Undoubtedly, it takes a village to make anyone who they are—both for good and evil. Even though I am obscure on the national or international stage, the substance of what has been put into my life is of meteoric value, as is what's been given you. I believe that we, the common folk of society, are devaluated for the cliché, salacious, and supposedly vogue in a comparative, starstruck, pro-affluence attitude that permeates the culture in which we live. Instead of each realizing our uniqueness and value, we are taught that only certain people are unique and even fewer deserve mention.

What would happen if we could take the optimal from each and every person and synergize it into a collective that would enrich all while celebrating the value and distinctiveness of each person? What a novel thought.

Memoirs are generally reserved for and about hoity-toity people—or whoever fathoms their influence and the intrigue of their life to be salient to the masses. This trend minimizes the magnitude of obscurity's infinite texture. I've often wonder what makes a person tick. We will never know about many folks because we're not allowed to ever see.

Like any other memoir, this one serves dirt, admits ignorance, names names, and attempts to be positive but honest about a few sketches that have made up a goodly part of my life. There is no attempt to slam anyone, even though some stories don't reflect positively on specific people. It's about the lessons learned and either parabolic or anecdotal nostrums that presented words to me. Some think memoirs are self-serving. Possibly, this could be true in my case as well. You will have to be the judge of that.

My motivations in this effort are to offer tributes those who have given me what I have and highlight various sources, people, and things that have been part of my perennial education. I hope many readers will decide to view the movies or pick up books mentioned herein. The personal stories merely serve as dessert because many are funny and engaging to my mind.

Each word will be accompanied by a *working definition*. These are not exhaustive but more tailored to how I use the words or came to know their use. I am in no way replacing Noah Webster. My point is that it is fun to enjoy anecdotal stories and share my learning at the same time. I hope many of the words shared here will stick with you and that your own learning might be enjoyable.

The book is arranged by date or the approximation thereof—thus reading like the chronology of any typical memoir. In 80 percent of the cases, I can recall the exact place and situation of being awakened to a term. Another feature of this volume is that 75 percent of the words featured are not in SAT preparatory programs I've researched.

A Word About Church:
My relationship with what people *call* church would be appalling to most were I to regale them all with the my experiences. Even so, my sharp references to it have not take away my dependence on God and what I have learned on the rocky road of mankind's religious institutionalism. So please don't be offended.

A Special Feature:
Another book feature is the icon guide on the right side of the lead page of each section. This detail indicates under what general influence I learned the word in that feature. Such paints a case that learning is and can be an extensive involvement beyond any formal situation. I think we far overplay one type of education—though very important—and underplay the notion that learning should be a part of our daily lives as a continuum.

Still, further features are a graph at the bottom of each section. This feature is what is known as an Ngram. This aspect reflects computational linguistics, which, among other things, results in statistical analysis. Google has been a leader in this field of study by scanning and cataloging everything in print or transcripts from the past 500 years. The value is seeing how words come and go in usage. Another feature is the Gunning-Fog index, is formula that generates to a grade level between 0 and 20. It calculates the level of education needed to comprehend the text. Only 10 features read below the 10th grade, by that measure. In the back will be an index of subject, vocabulary, collateral vocabulary and content a reader can quickly resource where they read something in this book. I've tried to employ the notions of John Amos Comenius with visual aids and graphical presentation to make reading more engaging.

Be a Learner:
Learning should be straightforward. However, I've come to realize many people learn and absorb information differently. One could take this book purely as a vocabulary study. Since the words are connected to stories, I feel they will be easier to understand and more memorable because they are delivered in anecdotal format. I hope that whomever reads this book will be encouraged to learn by listening to what occurs in their surroundings. Next, we ought to be disciplined enough to secure a working understanding, for ourselves, of how the unfamiliar can become a valuable part of our own vocabulary.

A great vocabulary opens doors and sets you apart in engaging and interesting ways. People will ask about your university or educational background before they know anything else about you simply because of your word choices. Word power is truly dynamic for anyone. People judge books by their covers and people by their appearances or how well-spoken they are. I hope you enjoy this book and grow in your ability to communicate.

—Timothy L. Price

THE GREAT-AUNT EVERYONE LOVED
—— 1973 ——

`Gunning-Fog Index: 10.6`

Growing up, Lola Mast was one of my favorite relatives on my mother's side. She was my mother's maternal aunt. She lived in Gibbon, Nebraska. Her husband, Arthur Mast, was an old-school blacksmith like you might see in a Western or in a modern living history museum.

They were an interesting couple. They were exceptionally focused upon all their own kin plus as many of the extended family's children of the in-laws, outlaws, and shirt-tail cousins. Lola was my mother's favorite aunt. Lola was a source of solace and balance in the wickedly imbalanced world of my mother's up bringing. It is no stretch to say Lola was everyone's favorite.

Lola always had something engaging for all the kids to do. She made everyone feel special—not by utilizing hollow, politically-correct attempts at "even-handedness." She was totally genuine in her own way. She was an extraordinarily optimistic person and found it difficult to be negative even in concern to the most negative of people; even family members, of which there were a couple prime examples.

Lola and Arthur took us kids to the Happy Jack Chalk Mine in Scotia, Nebraska; or Pioneer Village (a museum) in Minden, Nebraska; or down to Bird City, KS, for the Mast Family reunion, which has continuously gathered for more than 75 years. Lola and Art were travelers, campers, and socializers on the grandest scale. I remember as far back as 1973. We visited Aunt Lola in Gibbon, Nebraska, and she brought out what she called her "feely-meely bag." She encouraged us kids to **filch** for a treat. She was still doing this when my kids came along, and I introduced them to her at her senior-care living place in the 1990s.

`filch`

THE GREAT-AUNT EVERYONE LOVED

Filch is an interesting word that, in most definitions, happens to be negative. Undeterred, this cheerful woman found a positive, figurative application for it. This verb originates from Middle English *filchen*, which meant to attack and take booty. You can be assured we "took booty" from Aunt Lola's feely-meely bag. In English, this word means to steal or pilfer something of minor value.

I like this word because of the memories attached to it and because it is uncommon. Though filch has a negative implication, the figurative, as my aunt used it, is thoroughly acceptable. You could filch a kiss from an unsuspecting spouse or your three-year-old grandchild. It's a great descriptive. You can use this word in speech or writ, and in comedic or creative form, to season up what you have to say. I use it on occasion because it is unusual. I use it always remembering Lola and Arthur, who were tremendous people for all of us kids.

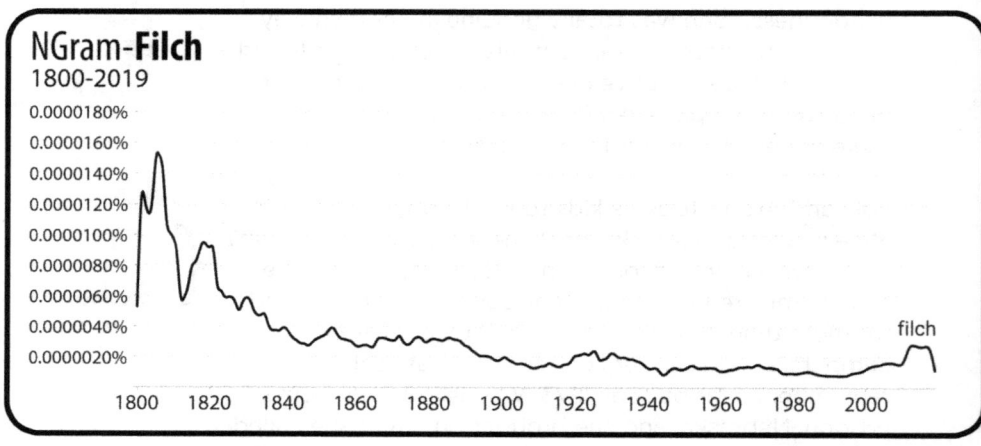

GO LOOK IT UP
1973

`Gunning-Fog Index: 10.72`

As you will read in subsequent pages, I grew up in a family awash in great vocabulary and the determination to use it for all its worth. One always knew where they stood because everyone in the family spoke their minds. In such an environment, just any word would not do. One had to be articulate. Dialogue and conversation were always seasoned by the extreme and diverse.

I remember my mother, Karel Ida (Geary) Price, often using words we did not know as children. The answer? "Go look it up," she'd tell us. To her eight-year-old son, she wasn't unkind or lazy in her involvements as a mother. My direct family had a hands-on approach to learning. Another guiding principle was that no one was going to do something for you.

Such ideals may seem foreign, even harsh, in a modern era. No one has to do much of anything to become appraised of information today. It is my opinion that they are just as quickly divested of such *information* if they were ever an actual repository of it in the first place. It seems that knowledge today is more a collection of trivia that is never closer than some electronic device. Such an arrangement is appalling. In most cases, once electronic devices are unavailable or deactivated, the same will be true of their user's *knowledge*.

I became aware of the term **pablum**, which originated as a trademarked name. I had

păb´yə-ləm

brothers, Stephen and David, who were four and six years my junior. I remember a dried cereal my mother referred to as pablum, which she fed them as babies. This time period would have been around 1973. By the mid-1980s, I learned another use of this word in its proper spelling: *pabulum*. Looking it up! The noun *pabulum* came from the Latin

GO LOOK IT UP

word *pascere*, which means "to feed." In modern English, this word means "a light food, usually a slurry that is easy to absorb"—hence the use of it in describing baby food. An additional meaning would be more figurative, simplistic, or referring to something being intellectually insipid.

I like the figurative definition and have often used it because it is expressive. I have commonly thought that what is served up in churches and the educational system is a pabulum aimed at the lowest common denominator walking through the door. This would be over and against material that would challenge all.

Not everyone is a Phi Beta Kappa, nor do they need to be. But I don't think it is a stretch to say that many people fail to live up to their potential. It is my conclusion that this is so largely because we are commonly fed pabulum from many sources: church, education, and the media.

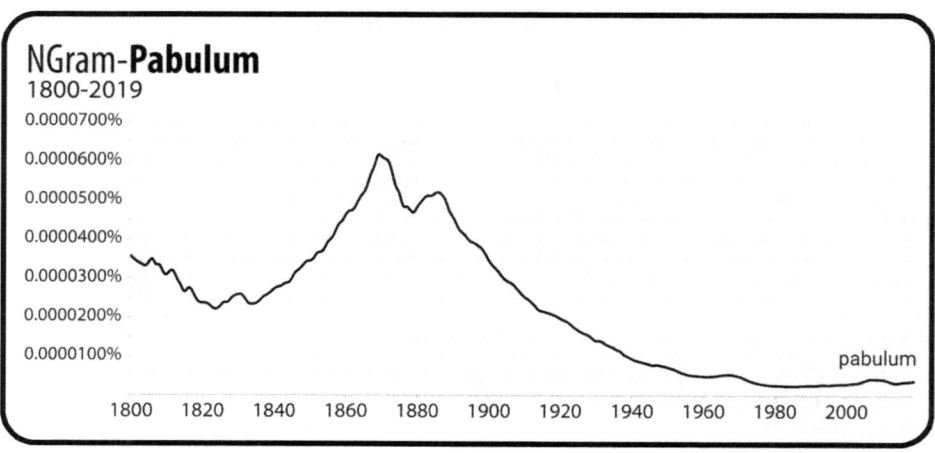

NOUNS DON'T HAVE TO INSULT
1974

`Gunning-Fog Index: 10.82`

My father, James Gail Price, was a peaceable man of fewer words. He was by no means simple, just quieter than most of my other relatives. Yet, he also contributed to my love and understanding of words. On weekends, as early as 1974, I used to go down to our family's furniture plant to work with my dad. The Prices had the largest upholstery plant west of the Mississippi.

My father was an artisan. I grew up in a family whose paternal side were all upholsterers. My great-grandfather literally came to Omaha in the early 1900s with $5 in his pocket. Such stories are not just a well-worn folk legend. Great-grandpa James Everett Price walked across a frozen Missouri River before all the dams existed. At some point, he set up in the upholstery trade. My grandfather and his brother followed suit. My dad and his two brothers also followed in that same enterprise until the mid-1990s.

Dad always was particularly descriptive in his disapproval of people or situations. I don't think he meant to be "judgmental," as folks are acculturated to think these days. His acuteness in feelings were often revealed through word choice. I remember his use of the word **cretin**, which was not a common occurrence. He might have been disgusted with the handling of something or someone's lack of performance in a job at the shop—our family's colloquialism for the furniture factory.

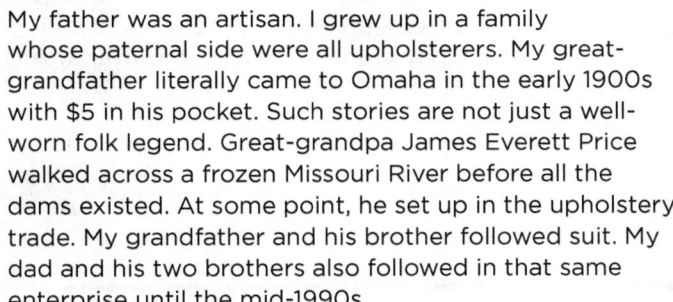

Cretin is most commonly used today as an insult regarding someone who is slovenly, obtuse, or mind-numbingly slow—a half-wit, or even a moron. The noun's derivation is French and German. Initially, it was a medical term to describe a particular deformity, the

NOUNS DON'T HAVE TO INSULT

details of which have been lost to history. One form of the word (*crestin* in French-Swiss dialect) derisively described Christians who apparently appeared odd to their neighbors. Cretin is a colorful noun, not to be confused with Cretan—a native of the Island of Crete.

Today's culture is down on insults—as perhaps they ought to be. Yet, we have words in the language that classify for a reason. One can be colorful in the way they describe someone or their actions. One must be careful with a word such as cretin so as not to be cruel in its usage. An anecdotal story, an allegory, or a poem would be great applications for this word.

I don't think I ever heard my father insult someone by name-calling or even describing their lack of acumen to their face. My father had more class than that. Having said as much, he did share—or let slip—his assessment of various things. Whether his approach was a fault or negative proclivity is above my pay grade. His usage, however, wasn't lost on me.

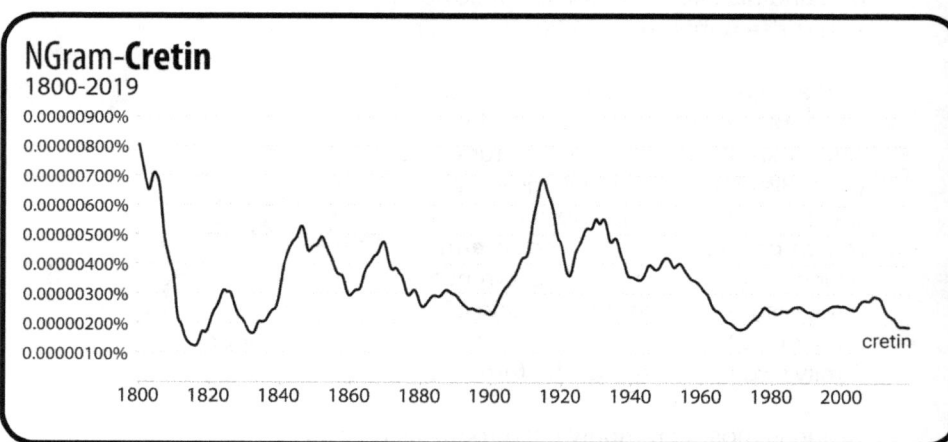

A THREE-LETTER WORD THAT POPS
1974

`Gunning-Fog Index: 11.73`

I've been surrounded by outspoken people my entire life. This isn't necessarily a negative thing. There is nothing wrong with speaking out of conviction or sureness. Today, we live in an era of timidity and tentativeness about everything. Moreover, the culture around us has been brainwashed into political correctness because no one wants to be seen as "arrogant" or "negative."

My maternal grandfather, who we called *Uncle Geary*, which I shall explain later, was one of those who was acutely direct. He often gave unlacquered thoughts because it suited his underlying *modus operandi* of goading people in tease. He knew that many were thin-skinned, even in those days, and he took pleasure in regularly pushing their buttons to demonstrate the fact. You don't get potato chips when you hit the button for a candy bar—we need to remember that. In the larger perspective, he was a good man, assiduously able in craft and fortitude. But he had a way of expressing things that would have drawn a firestorm among today's cultural attitudes of hyper-sensitivity.

I remember him using the word **fop** in one of his many unlacquered moments in 1974: describing a person in the family. In his mind, he wasn't "calling a name," as it might be thought today. He was merely drawing attention to how these people held themselves. Descriptions can be subjective, but if the shoe fits, a word used to describe it isn't wrong. If an ace is an ace of spades, what's wrong with referring to as such?

fŏp

Fop is an interesting little word. This noun originated in Middle English, though lexicographers and etymologists are unclear of the exact origins. Some say the original word was *fob*. In today's English, fop refers to a man who

A THREE-LETTER WORD THAT POPS

is obsessively concerned about the way he looks or appears. The implied meaning is vanity and silliness.

What is interesting about the word *fop* is that it is seen as negative, whereas the synonym "metrosexual" means the same thing and is seen as a positive if not a badge of honor. This example clearly identifies the cliché-ish nature of politically-correct thinking and how word choice changes over the years. I fail to see how two words meaning the same thing can be bad in one case and stupendously acceptable in the other. A pig isn't less so because you put him in a costume.

We can use the word *fop* without offending through the literary device of simile and indirect usages. We can use it in speech because its enunciation is percussive, arresting, and somewhat comedic. I like this word because it's not engineered by a mindless social game of seeming politeness.

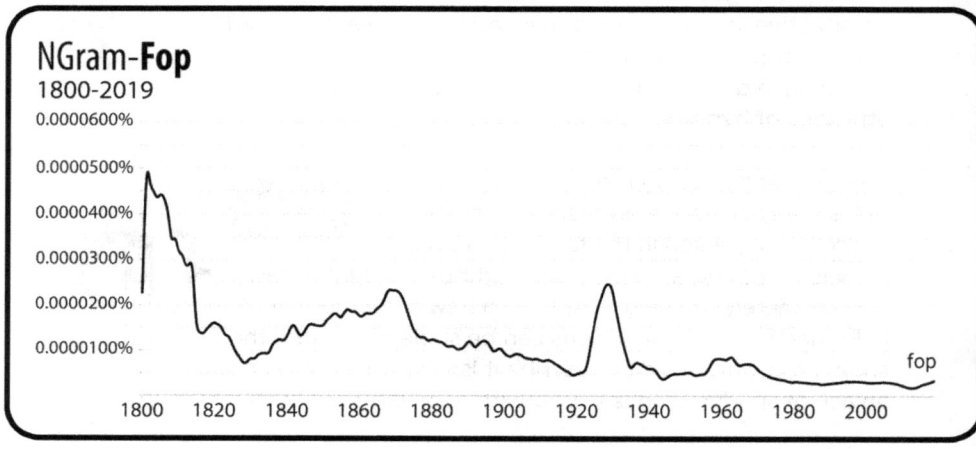

AN OLD-FASHIONED DRAMA QUEEN
1974

Gunning-Fog Index: 9.98

I think almost every fellow enjoys an action movie. War movies are one of my indulgences. First, they often retell the little stories that fill in the broad strokes of history. They bring alive personages and happenings that may otherwise be unknown.

My wife, Pam, and I love movies like *Defiance* or *Amen!*, or *The Night of the Generals* because they are inextricably tied to some level of verifiable heroism. We know Hollywood takes artistic license with facts and dialogue. Even so, such renditions still illume a cavern of history. If a story is compelling, one can pursue it further in books that lend more accuracy.

Growing up, my next-door neighbor, Norbert Nelson, related a story of working for General George S. Patton. His story was a modest rendering of events—having typed out Patton's famous speech to the Third Army just before the Battle of the Bulge. Nelson told me the movie Patton, which I'd seen at least twice by 1974, didn't tell half of the story. Even so, the movie Patton has always been special to me on several levels.

George S. Patton was a rugged, arrogant, egocentric individual. He was also a superb military commander and strategist. George C. Scott's inimitable portrayal of Patton was perhaps the role of a lifetime for the actor. In the movie, Patton admits he was a **prima donna** to General Omar Bradley (played by Karl Malden). This word, *prima donna*, is more of an expression, yet it is apt in description.

prē´mə ˈdɑnə

Prima donna is a noun that classifies the main female singer in an opera. In an idiomatic use, which is its

AN OLD-FASHIONED DRAMA QUEEN

second definition, this word is indicative of a drama queen. This is one who finds it impossible to work within a defined structure: one who has a high opinion of themselves. This term is derived from the Italian meaning "first lady."

The context of Patton's admission was that he had showboated so badly and exacted such extreme discipline on a soldier that it both clouded any good he might have been seen for doing. He became a black eye to General Eisenhower's administration. In admitting his tendency of being a *prima donna*, Patton was trying to wheedle his way back into favor in order to obtain a command in Europe following the Normandy Invasion.

Today, culture is loaded with divas and people who are bent on recognition for their extreme individualistic demonstrations of existence and personhood. *Prima donna* is a way of creatively referencing this detail. I have used this term many times over the years. It isn't cheeky nor demeaning. Yet, it is an exact classification.

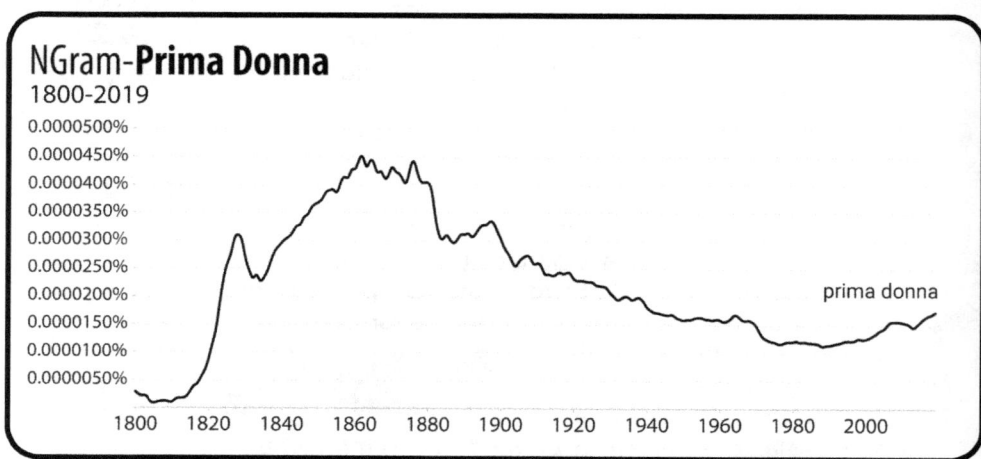

A BOOK CORNER IN THE EYE
1975

`Gunning-Fog Index: 11.51`

It is incredible that one can attend school for 13 years only to remember a few tidbits 40 years later that linger above the comedy, personalities, and oppressiveness of educational institutionalism, as well as all else that makes school the collective experience that it is.

My teachers would perhaps be dismayed to consider what has stuck out in my mind looking back from today. With my family background having a penchant for word craft and their use as sharp objects, it is no wonder that words impacted me over the years more than virtually anything else.

I was a poor student, perhaps because I didn't care about the monotonous nature of school. I didn't have the perspective back then to realize my interest in the details, which the educational process attempted to bestow on me could have taken me much further than it did. I was a subscriber to the mindset that you-pull-yourself-up-by-your-bootstraps. Even in elementary school, I'd already started taking classes at the University of Hard Knocks.

In any case, it is a wonder that a one of the first words to impact me was in Fourth grade. This grade is hardly the arena of intellectual development. 1975 was the year I clobbered Chris Clark, one of my school cronies, in the eye with the corner of a textbook over some disagreement. It was also the same year Tina Roll, the girl who had to sit next to me, got in trouble for even listening to me: I was a talker...

My teacher, Ms. Mazzara, taught most of our classes, as was the approach back then. The class that served up the first big words, which grabbed my mind was what we knew as social studies. We were learning about the big world we live in.

A BOOK CORNER IN THE EYE

The word was **ethnocentrism**. This noun is a sociological term coined in the early 1900s by William Graham Sumner. I don't remember exactly how the concept of this word was presented. But I got the picture instantly. It is the arrogance of pushing off one's beliefs on others from a sense of superiority, whether cultural or idealistic. This noun expresses an imperialism often accompanied by religious beliefs.

ĕth´nō-sĕn´trĭz´əm

Since that time, this word has been forever affixed in my mind. *Ethnocentrism* isn't exactly a practical word one can use all the time. But it is one that can guard the mind. I think the word is a descriptive pathology and a reaction of secular intellectualism against religious exuberance. Yet, there is a solid point. I feel that this word is a warning: let my actions and practices tell others what it is I think I understand to be true.

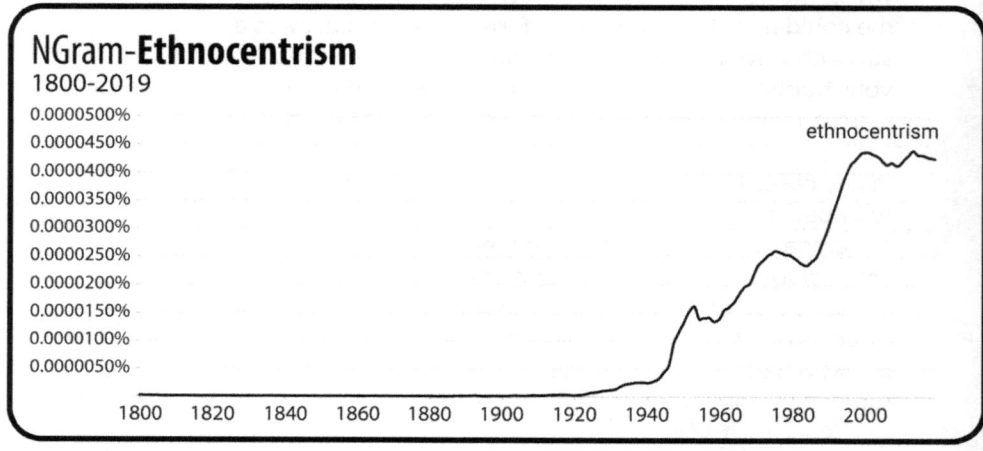

A LACERATING TONGUE

`Gunning-Fog Index: 11.58`

Some of my earliest memories are of my maternal grandfather, whom we affectionately called Uncle Geary. My sister, Jamie (Price) White—the first of his grandchildren—dubbed him *Uncle Geary* because all the men she knew in the family prior were "uncle" to her. It quickly stuck for all the younger grandkids: my brothers and all the cousins.

Philip Alfred Geary was a man of extraordinary talent and craft. He was a farmer, plumber, electrician, and water-well driller. He was also a horticulturist and a carpenter. He loved poetry and could recite verse prolifically on cue. He told more crass but funny jokes than any other 10 people I'd ever met. He was endowed with a lacerating tongue and was every bit the equal with pen on paper. The emotional toll he could exact with words was unequaled in my experience. I spent a good bit of time around him over the years.

Between 1976 and 1983, Uncle Geary regularly came to the house to help around the place. He'd get on regaling us about his past. I remember him employing the word **prig** to describe several people he viewed as exceedingly distasteful. He used this word with the greatest of disdain depicted in his tone and percussive enunciation. In his world, one could hardly be lower than a prig.

`prĭg`

The word prig has unknown origins. The oldest use of this word tells us it was descriptive of a thief. However, modern uses tend more toward slang applications. Today, this noun has practically been relegated to an entry in dictionaries, though it is hardly archaic. Prig typifies a person's arrogant preciseness that continuously looms to make him or her appear above their actual ability

A LACERATING TONGUE

or accomplishment. The tedious smugness of a person's exactitude is offensive to others, perhaps comparable to how ammonia fumes attack our nose.

In today's culture, experiencing such a person is not beyond regular occurrence. The human animal hasn't changed his spots. However, the evolution of cultural mores seems to affect the use and perhaps the understanding of this word. To castigate someone today as a prig directly or even generalize about the priggish nature of their behavior is maybe an offensiveness unto itself.

Modern cultural pressures aside, I like the word prig and its other forms because of its exactness. It is hardly a word I would throw around in everyday conversation. Yet, its specific descriptiveness is without comparison. I wouldn't hesitate to employ its adjective or adverbial forms in written copy or speech. The judicious use of the word prig is sure to garner attention for its sharpness and irregularity. In 2006, I heard the word prig used by Judi Dench in the movie *Casino Royale*.

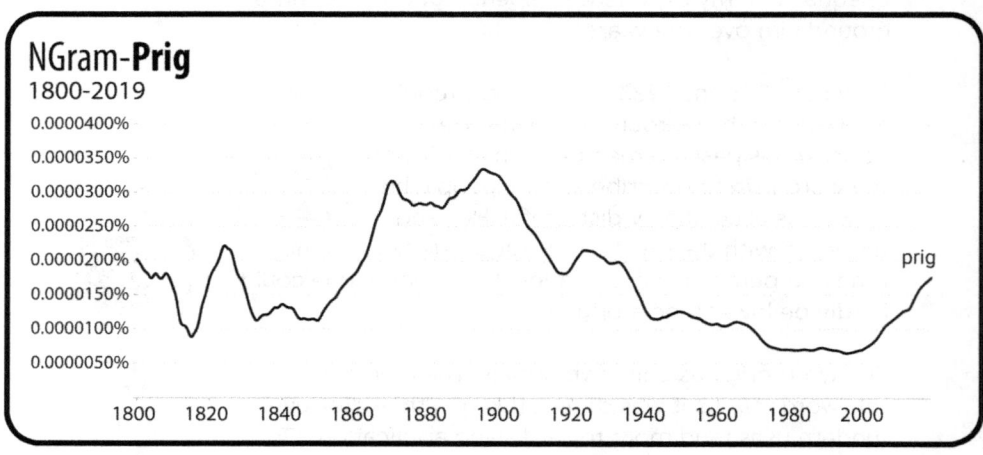

THE SOUND OF COMPLAINING
1978

`Gunning-Fog Index: 11.08`

One of my favorite actors of all time is Peter O'Toole, who died in 2013 after a 60-year career in theater, movies, and television. I bet I own at least seven of his movies. He was a class act par excellence, with few equals.

My father, Gail Price, was a fan of O'Toole as well. I remember watching *Becket* (a film I now own) on TV with my father, likely around 1978. Originally filmed in 1964 with several A-list actors, the movie is about the historical story of King Henry II, played by O'Toole, and Thomas Becket—a Saxon protégé and handler of the carousing King. Becket, played by Richard Burton, is appointed Lord Chancellor, which requires him to run Henry's court. He is adept and eventually promoted. The one-time confidant, Becket, eventually becomes an adversary in his new role of Archbishop of Canterbury. Becket, a man of impeccable compartmentalization, went from being the pragmatic lead man of a king's entourage to a consummate and uncompromising church leader. It's a tragic story that has been repeated many times historically.

This film was a smash success, with triple the box-office receipts compared to its production costs. Becket is rich on every level of production and appearance for the period. It is no less garnished in scripting. Aside from learning a bit of medieval history, I picked up the word **caterwauling** in this film.

kăt´ər-wôl´ĭng

Caterwauling is a noun expressing the loud wailing yowl of a feline in rutting season. The word could be generalized to mean a shrill sound. However, this term is often used metaphorically to describe the noisy protests of a complainer. The first two definitions are examples of

THE SOUND OF COMPLAINING

onomatopoeia—a word representing a sound. The metaphorical use is a stark correlative.

Most words featured in this book have direct antecedents other than English. However, this term came abruptly from the Middle English word *cater*, meaning "tomcat," and *wawen*, meaning the sound of a howl. The word came into existence in the 14th century. This word is still in ascension, denoting that it is nearly in as much use today as it was at its highest point in the 1930s.

I like this term because it is eminently descriptive. It could be taken as an insult or as condescension in modern culture. However, if it is employed indirectly, no adverse inference will be taken by its use. This word could entertain, such as in the movie, or be comedically applied for effect.

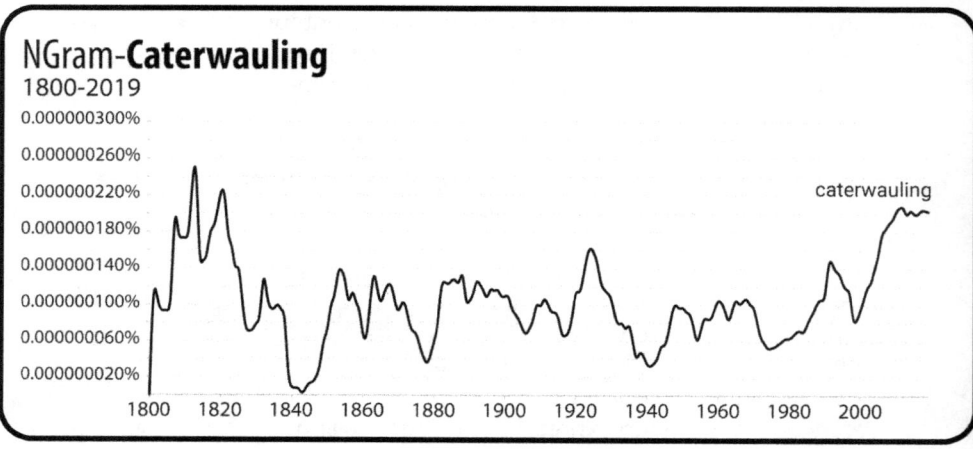

WHAT THE LEAVES TELL YOU
— 1978-80 —

`Gunning-Fog Index: 11.34`

I was able to spend significant time with three of my grandparents. Each had their specialty, which I look back upon with tremendous appreciation and admiration. My father's mother, Margaret Price, and my mother's father, Phillip A. Geary, were both flower enthusiasts—an involvement that in turn rubbed off on me.

Folks came from miles around to see Uncle Geary's gardens in Gibbon, Nebraska. He had irises, peonies, and roses everyone envied. Margaret Price's horticultural forays dealt with potted plants, exotics, tropicals, and succulents. More of her yard was under shade, encompassing an entirely different group of plants than the plants my maternal grandfather kept.

In the summers of 1979 and 1980, I worked for Grandma Price. I supplied the elbow grease for her many projects as well as regular upkeep. She had a hedgerow of barberry bushes, which I grew to hate. There is no way to work with them without getting impaled.

In the fall at Grandma Price's, everything sprawled all over the yard had to be brought in. Tropicals and succulents have no appreciation for the blistering-cold of Nebraska winters. So, over a couple weekends, I'd be dragging everything into the sun porch where the environment could be controlled in order to maintain these dainty plants, which were Grandma's pride and joy.

In spring, I'd have to dig up various plants and split them to keep from overcrowding their pottings. The dirt was usually cold and damp, which made for less fun for the finicky teen that I was.

WHAT THE LEAVES TELL YOU

In this context, I learned many things about plants, including some that can apply to real life outside horticulture. Take the word **variegated**, for instance. Grandma had variegated hosta plants. This is a shade-loving plant that has a common oddity. Some cultivars have a bi-colored leaf, commonly green and yellow or green and cream.

vâr´ē-ĭ-gā´tĭd

The adjective variegated comes from the Latin. It describes the condition of exhibiting more than one color. Such is usually a mutation cultivated to develop a stable, repeatable variance. Most times, variegated references botanical realities. With animals, variance in appearance and coloration is frowned upon, if not ruthlessly prevented. Yet, with plants, variation can afford growers, enthusiasts, and gardeners a look they want that no one else has.

Since *variegated* describes variation, many things are differentiated strictly for their variegation. Marble can be variegated. Black-tipped sharks are a species because of their variegated dorsal fin. Yarn can be variegated. Thus, the term *variegated* gives a person more creativity to differentiate when communicating.

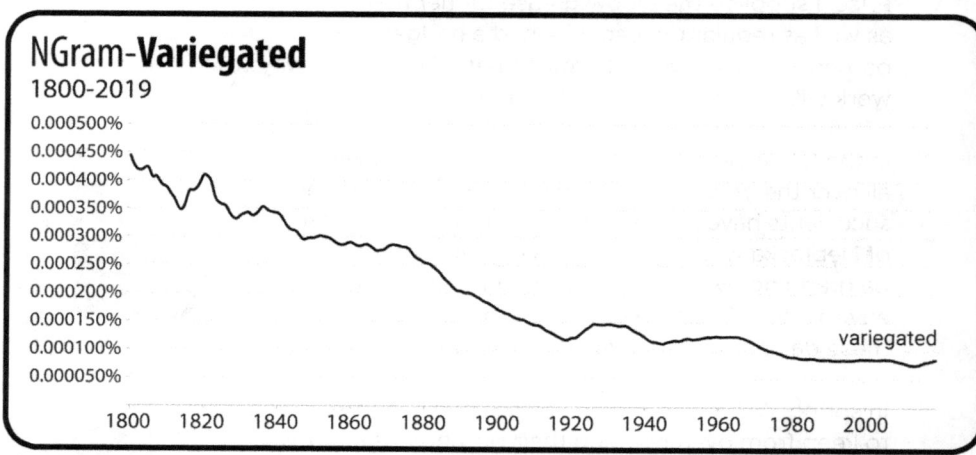

THE STUFF YOU LEARN AT CHURCH
—1979-83—

Gunning-Fog Index: 10.54

Church proved to be a source of education beyond religious thought. I've often wondered if pastors realize their influence beyond the message they seek to communicate. I am sure, in my case, people of those capacities would cringe at the other things I learned.

Elmer H. Murdoch was an interesting person. His delivery was rousing with rare exception. I remember a friend bringing his parents to services. His folks were "common folk" in that the father regularly expressed himself in unvarnished ways. As the service carried on, Murdoch took the podium to lead music, which I think Murdoch enjoyed the singing more than the leading... In any case, my friend's father was floored by Murdoch and blurted out, "He's a hell of a singer." My friend nearly crawled under the seating because everyone in two rows on either side of them heard it. Church folks are a wee bit narrow about such things. You get the stink eye for this sort of thing. It's a regular "ministry" of the religious crowd.

Somewhere along the line between 1979 and 1983, I remember Murdoch using the word **huckster** to describe how some push an agenda or a foreign teaching to what we find in the New Testament. *Huckster* best describes the approach of some or the fact that their content is suspect.

hŭk´stər

From 13th century English the word has always been spelled *huckster*. However, this noun came from the Dutch word *hokester*, which meant "peddler." In today's English, this word has several meanings, from someone who produces promotional media, to someone who is mercenary in efforts to profiteer, to a person who markets questionable materials

THE STUFF YOU LEARN AT CHURCH

Today, this word is used chiefly in the negative sense, depicting either the nefarious or ridiculously pushy. This word is just as in use as it was in 1800. Yet, it is a word few know. Context will tell most people what you mean if you use it.

Creative description is a worthy pursuit in print or speech. If we are less concerned with being politically correct, we can be wildly funny and particular without intending to be offensive. This word can be used as Murdoch did to build consensus around an idea or identity over and against the distractive proposition of other notions or ideals.

I've used this word quite commonly in a non-pejorative sense. I would be more inclined to stick to descriptiveness of approach than judgment. I would not label or call someone a "huckster" in the direct sense. If one used this word to differentiate the approach someone used, such would be a good employment of the word.

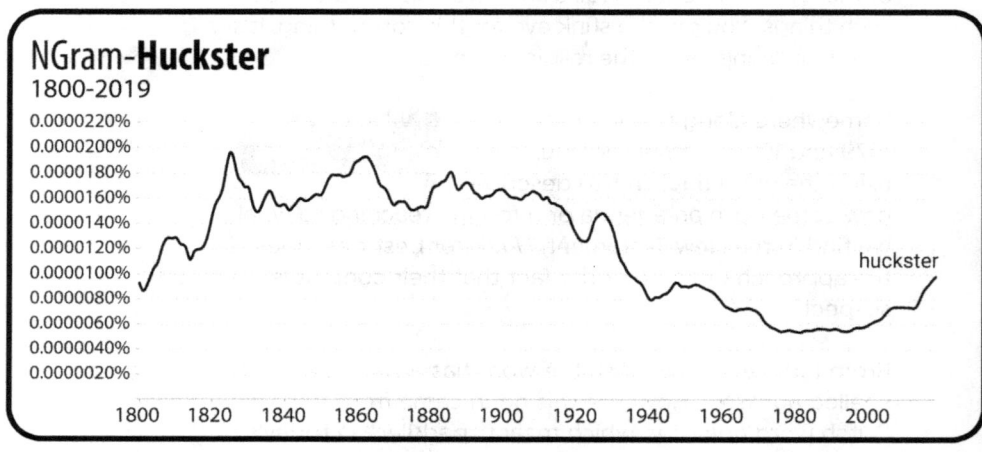

LONG-TERM TRAINING THAT STICKS
—1979-83—

Gunning-Fog Index: 11.01

For 12 years, my wife, Pam, and I worked on English proficiency with Japanese foreign students at the college level. One of the critical aspects of their learning was learning to listen. For natural-born speakers of any language, listening is less of a discipline, but it shouldn't be. Everything that is said must be thoroughly mulled over because there are things we will miss if we don't.

I never realized how much I "listened" until writing this book. It seems as though my primary means of learning has been close listening, followed by rigorously chasing details. Sometime between 1979 and 1983, Focus on the Family broadcast had an unlikely speaker during one of its segments. The unlikeliness of this speaker is that he was clearly liberal in every sense of the word, but Dr. James Dobson and Focus on the Family were ultra-right-wing conservatives.

In any case, this speaker, Tony Campolo, shared thoughts that were attractive to Dobson and his audience. I remember several things from that presentation, not the least of which was a new word: **inculcate**. It was the first time I heard that word.

ĭn-kŭl´kāt´

The verb *inculcate* is an interesting term. It describes something that everyone does to some degree throughout their lives. It comes from the Latin *inculcatus*, the past participle of *inculcare*, which literally means "to tread on." In English, this word means to cause learning to happen through repeated impressing and admonishment. The repetitious nature of this type of teaching is like walking over the same ground time after time so the subject becomes second nature.

29

LONG-TERM TRAINING THAT STICKS

We inculcate our children or people in our employ. We are caused to learn ourselves by the repeating of a process or admonitions to toe the line in various concerns. Knowing what something is called is essential because it gives impetus and importance to it.

Inculcate is not a word most are going to use frequently, even in speaking and writing. However, if we know such a word, using it in the right spots will slow people down and grab their attention. Communicating isn't just about elocution and enthusiastic connection with people. It's about the words, what they mean, and getting people to understand before they drift off on an unimportant tangent. Engaging listeners and everyday people with our word choice means having words to choose from. A vocabulary isn't about impressing people. It's about using the words available to us to make a point and influence. Inculcate is an important word because it describes what we should be doing every day.

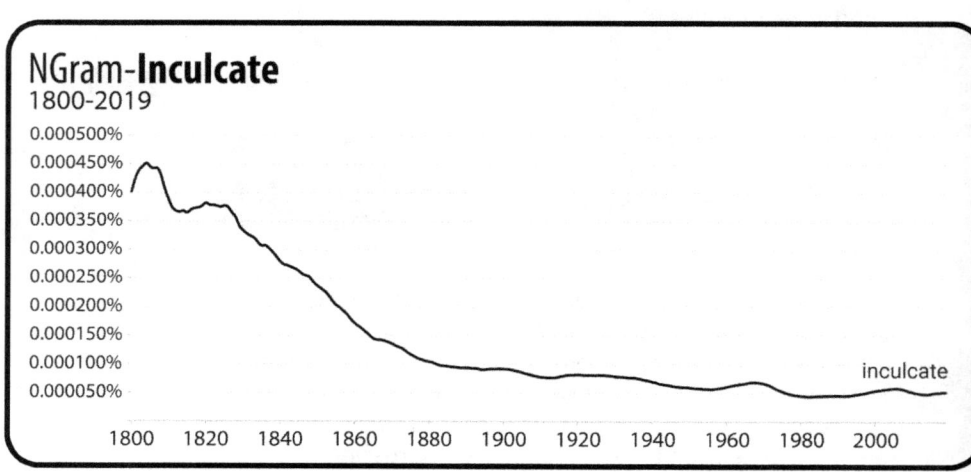

CLOUDS THAT SPREAD DISEASE
—1979-83—

Gunning-Fog Index: 11.74

As mentioned previously, I was "in" what calls itself church from when I was three weeks old until I knew better, which was about 43 years. In some ways, I have a lot to be thankful for in this connection, even though I now have many justifiable misgivings about the modern concept of church in any version. I guess the old saying ought to apply: chew the meat and spit out the bones.

Elmer H. Murdoch was a preacher of extraordinary personality, conviction, and delivery. Many who knew him back in the day would agree heartily and without reservation. He was a man of music, endowed with a good education, had a sharp intellect, and was charming by all considerations. He preached with passion but was not theatrical for effect. What he presented was from the most profound conviction and was eminently sound.

He used to lead hymn singing during services and special occasions. These storied songs moved him significantly because of the message and the music in which they were encased. Everyone was vicariously moved and enthralled after his turn at bat. When you attended one of his services, you were energized and challenged. I don't remember having difficulty recalling his subjects or content minutes—even weeks—after he delivered it. His teaching wasn't mealymouthed blathering or stodgy intellectualism; it was practical and encouraging.

I remember a particular service between 1979 and 1983 where Murdoch spoke about the spread of spurious teaching and secularized idealism, infecting what was thought of as church in those days. He used the word **miasma** to describe this degenerative infiltration, which was an apt word.

mī-ăz´mə

Miasma is a noun originated from the Greek word *miainein*, meaning "to pollute." In modern English, this

CLOUDS THAT SPREAD DISEASE

word means a thick cloud containing an unhealthy or unpleasant element. It could mean an atmosphere or environment that depletes or corrupts. The range of meanings is foreboding. Historically, a miasma was thought to be a natural phenomenon that carried diseases such as Black Death or cholera. Murdoch's use was then a figurative application of this notion.

English is fantastic for the figurative applications. A novelist can use a word like miasma to paint a dark scene. A journalist can use it to concern readers by emphasis. Miasma is a wonderful word because it can be used in word pictures to powerfully drive the point of vulnerability, danger, or the presumptive mystery of what might happen if miasma does what it is thought to do. This word is a bit theatric because it describes an alleged reality that has not been proven.

Note: *I recently heard miasma used by the character Dr. Sheldon Cooper on The Big Bang Theory, "The Apology Insufficiency," Season 4, Episode 7.*

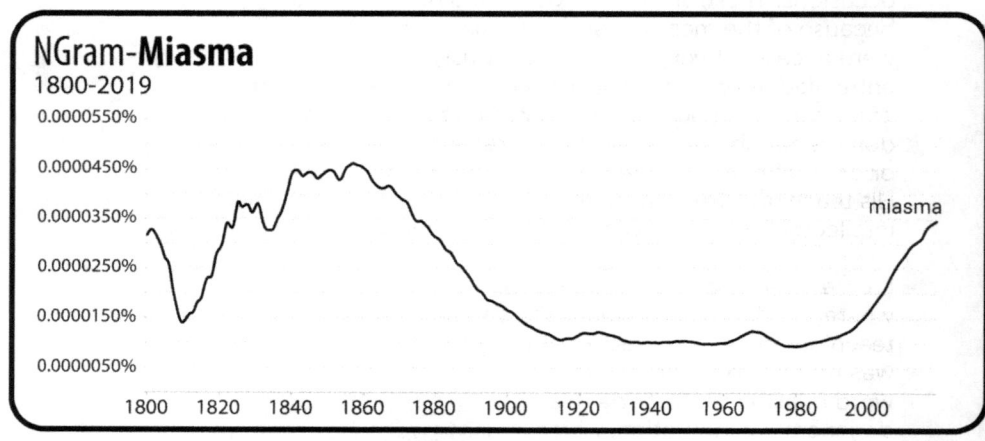

SKIN-TONE TALK WITHOUT RACISM
—1979-83—

Gunning-Fog Index: 8.86

I grew up in "church." The place I went to regularly featured speakers from all over the world. The regular pastor would go on vacation in the summer months, and one particular speaker came in to pinch-hit fairly often between 1979 and 1983. This fellow was large in more ways than one.

Back in the day, he was a football player. Even though he'd gone into preaching, he maintained a rough-and-tumble persona. For instance, he threatened to take some of the "sleeping" leadership at our church to his gospel ranch camp and put them all on some brahma bulls to wake them up. At another point, he noted teaching his sons to box, which was looked down upon by folks in his church. When asked why he would do such a thing, he responded, "Because my kids play with church people's kids."

In any case, this speaker had an effect on people wherever he went. The response was regularly a groundswell. He was a storyteller rather than a typical "preacher." I think this is why he connected with people. His name was Gordon Peterson.

Few who ever spoke at my church had more impact on me than this man. Years later, I can still quote verbatim passages and lines he gave in context to his presentation. I would say that after 40 years, that's a hell of an impact.

Peterson related a story at one point about a celebrity in Minneapolis, MN. He spoke to this man as they passed one another between television shows. He went on about the man describing him as **swarthy**: a word I'd never heard before.

swôr´thē

This adjective is interesting, given today's cultural sensitivities. You can hardly refer to something about a person without being perceived as offensive; don't even start with skin color. Yet, the term

SKIN-TONE TALK WITHOUT RACISM

swarthy refers to dark complexion, but not in the sense of ethnic or racial identification. Swarthy is a safe term.

This word shares a background in Dutch, High German, and Latin. Old High German had a word *swarm*, meaning "black." The Latin word *sordes* meant "dirty (grungy)." A Dutch term, *swart rutter*, referred to marauding bands that camouflaged their faces in dark colors.

Thus, swarthy is colorful. It could mean anything from a sinister person in a metaphoric usage to a dusky complexion in specific meaning. Often, I hear character descriptions on TV or read such in books. Most are so nondescript they might fit any of a hundred people. Words like swarthy are more specific and can be used contextually for various applications.

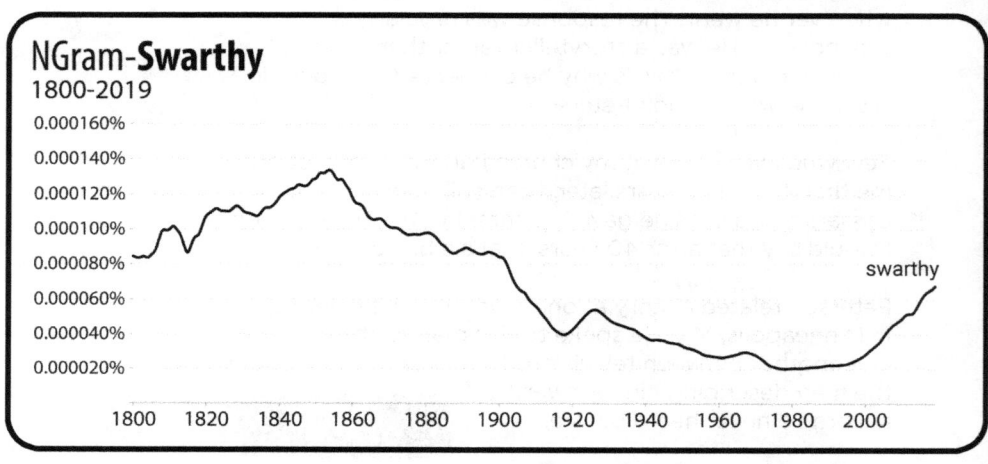

CHECKED OUT
BEFORE GRADUATION

Gunning-Fog Index: 11.79

At the end of this era, yet still in formal school, came another word that caught my awareness. For the first 12 years of school, I attended Millard Public Schools in what is now a suburb of Omaha, Nebraska. However, in my last year of school, our family picked up roots and moved out to the sticks. In some ways, I enjoyed it. At Millard, I was just a number. In Oakland, Nebraska, I felt I had some notoriety as "the city kid" for whatever advantage that afforded me.

I was in one of those courses where it was easy to bounce one's head off the desk if you weren't careful. Mid-afternoon, second semester, in the last year of high school... Who was really paying attention, right?

One of the enjoyments of my life has been history. I continue to be fascinated with both the stories of history makers as well as those of the forgotten. I prefer a historical account to virtually any other type of reading. The things we as a species haven't learned from history have become a monument of colossal obliviousness. I digress...

I was in American Government class. Mr. Clayton Steele was the teacher. I remember his style was similar to Ben Stein's character in *Ferris Bueller's Day Off*. In a similar fashion, Mr. Steele recited a question in the hope of engendering the correct answer from a listening student. But the class was half checked out. The teacher was okay, but the subject, or perhaps the curriculum, was just short of torture.

The word that caught my attention was **usurpations**. This noun

yo´o-sûr'pă-shen

isn't exactly a $500 word, but it is practical. I believe the context of its appearance to me was in regard to the intellectual presuppositions upon which American

CHECKED OUT BEFORE GRADUATION

independence was couched. The root word is *usurp*: to take over without legal or legitimate right, perhaps assuming control through deceit. Anyway, America's self-governance was primarily motivated by the encroachment and manipulation of the English crown in the daily affairs of business, life, and political administration in the 13 colonies.

Usurpation is quite descriptive, though not widely used. You could read 200 books and not see this word appear once. However, no day goes by when you won't observe its reality in management, politics, society, and family interactions. It seems second nature to cut into someone else's territory and take over, not realizing the caprice of usurpation.

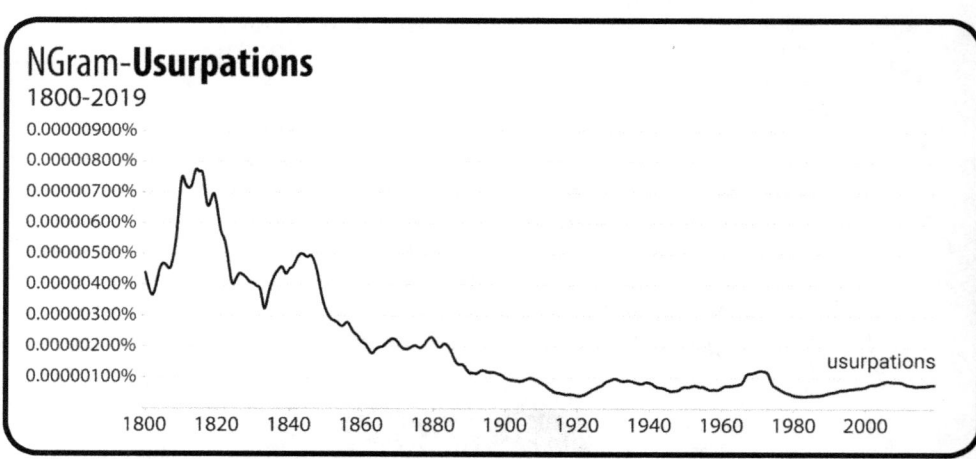

WHAT MUSICAL APPRECIATION CAN TEACH YOU

> Gunning-Fog Index: 10.52

I have always appreciated music. I'm told my tastes are extensive. I suppose, according to some, it is true. A perusal through my iTunes library reveals a treasury of everything from Mariachi to Rock to Dixieland Jazz, from Pete Seeger to Green Day, and Floyd Cramer to Bruno Mars...

The music itself is just part of my appreciations. Stories involved in the music and its makers heighten my treasurement. Take Mozart, for instance. Few realize his accomplishments, as he is one of the most prolific classical composers. In 30-odd years, he composed 626 pieces of music, something Paul McCartney hasn't achieved in 75+ years. In addition, Mozart's work was far more an achievement than a collection of four-minute tunes. Sorry, Sir Paul.

In 1984, I graduated high school and entered the military. That same year, a foreign film company created the movie Amadeus—a fictionalized account of Mozart's storied life and music. The film, rich with scripting and costuming, is more characteristic of a high-cost Hollywood epic.

The movie depicts Antonio Salieri (played by F. Murray Abraham), a contemporary of Mozart, who succeeded in life through hard-fought personal development, complicated further by the connivings of court life. Yet, when Mozart (played by Tom Hulce) arrives in Salzburg, Salieri is overshadowed by charisma, genius, and intrigue. Salieri, though accomplished, quickly realizes what the contrast between the two could mean. He blames God for "blessing" Mozart so exquisitely. Then Salieri vows to fight God and secretly drive Mozart beyond human capacity, and in a way, killing him.

The story begins with Salieri, years after Mozart's untimely death and still haunted by his actions, ranting

WHAT MUSICAL APPRECIATION CAN TEACH YOU

in delirium about **absolving** everyone in the house of bedlam where he convalesced. The word absolve does not find a lot of eyes or ears these days.

Absolve is a verb of Latin descent. This religious term means to declare an offender has been released from guilt. The prefix "ab" means "not." The root word solve needs no explanation. The two meanings seem counterintuitive, i.e., "not solve." Perhaps the correlation means not to find the usual solution but rather another way: as in amnesty. This last bit is conjecture on my part.

A word like *absolve* gives the feeling of superiority—if we are going to exonerate someone, we hold a strong position over the erring person. I like this word in the form of a joke, as in teasing folks. The word could be used in condescension as well.

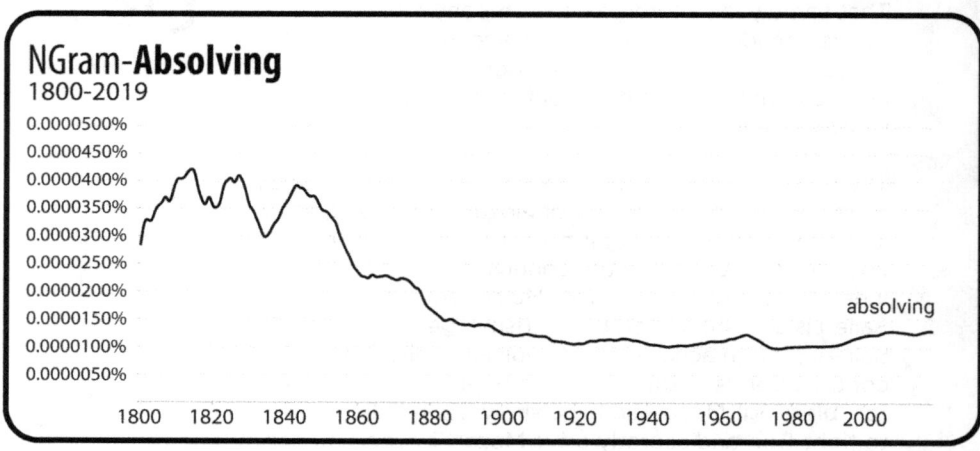

YOU'RE IN THE ARMY NOW
—1984-87—

`Gunning-Fog Index: 11.05`

Military service was another world for me. It provided the means to "grow up" in more ways than one. It was also an arena where many new terms entered my understanding, and I'm not talking colorful metaphors or acronyms. I served Uncle Sam in the Army from 1984 to 1987.

Early in my military stint, I sustained a debilitating injury as a tank mechanic. A 1,500-pound tank transmission fell off a forklift on my foot from about three feet in the air. Due to ongoing treatments and surgery, I was assigned light duty for the remainder of my service. In any case, my colonel sought to resource me into another work slot where I could be useful. I became a Public Relations Officer for my battalion: the newly reactivated 2nd of the 6th Cavalry.

One of the opportunities afforded me in this role was going to Washington, D.C., an honorary convention for select soldiers. Fort Knox had its group, of which I was a part. The convention had the typical muckety-mucks, seminars, and tours of the capital. But the most exciting thing for me was an exhibition of military hardware. On display was everything from tanks and field gear all the way to small arms: pistols and machine guns.

As a tank mechanic, I was drawn to a pair of tracked vehicles. One was a Bradley M3 fighting vehicle; the other was the newest M1 Abrams tank. However, these two appeared much different than any at Fort Knox I'd seen. They had rows of 12-by-12-inch square panels running back and forth across the front and sides of the turret. The front slope and side skirts were similarly covered. I asked the attendant, "What's the deal with the square pads?"

The representative explained that these "squares" were loaded with shaped explosives. They were designed to explode when impacted by incoming munitions. The net effect was that inbound projectiles would be deflected.

YOU'RE IN THE ARMY NOW

These "squares" were mounted on little posts raised off the tank's surface. Thus, they were called "**appliqué** armor." Israelis adapted this armoring idea from earlier in the century.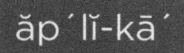

Appliqué is a French noun meaning "to add on to the exterior." I've found this term valuable in writing as it can express a perception of superficiality: the putting on of appearances or even affectation. I used *appliqué* in my first book, *The Diluted Church*. Interestingly, early uses of this term described ostentation, jewelling, or plating affixed to armor for victory marches and official celebrations; thus, *appliqué* is quite befitting of my usage.

Note: In the movie *Star Trek 4 : The Voyage Home*, Spock uses this terminology "colorful metaphor."

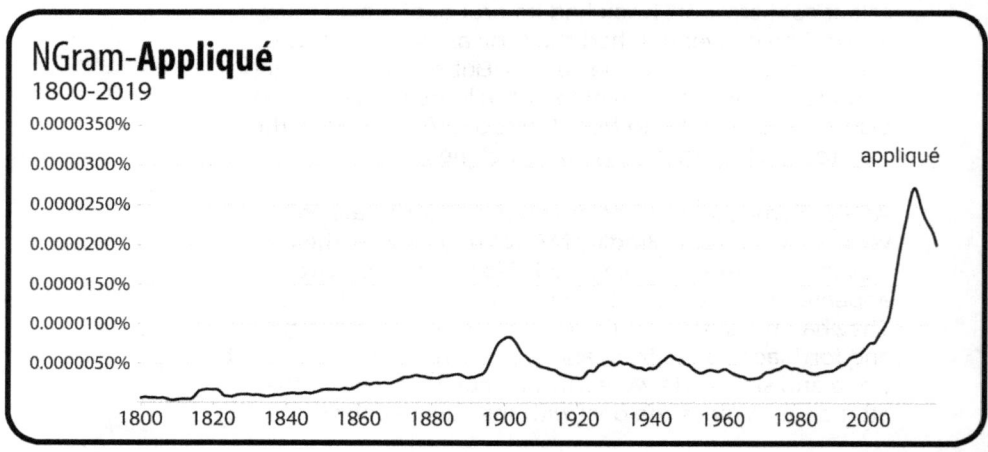

A DRILL SGT. TAUGHT MORE THAN PUSH-UPS
1984-87

Gunning-Fog Index: 10.96

As I mentioned before, my military experience 1984 to 1987 served me well. I grew up, got out of the house, and learned about myself and the world outside of parental involvement. I joined as a punk and came out a man... Even so, the Army was suitable for much more than growing up.

There was an incalculable growth of vocabulary going into the military. In the first nine weeks, I learned everything from acronyms for all the essential places and involvements to actual words conveying significant meaning in my new context at a prodigious rate.

I remember my drill sergeant, Sgt. First-Class Darden. Wow, after 35 years, I remember his name without having to think about it. That is what you call impact, right? He was a short, light-skinned black man who could run like the wind. He was excessively compartmentalized. None of us knew anything about him besides what stood before, or over us, throughout Basic Training.

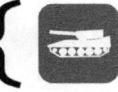

One term he used continually was **esprit de corps**. We, as new inductees, were accustomed to many drill sergeants during Basic Training, but only one said anything about the esprit de corps. Thus, I think this word spoke out his personal ideals. This is conjecture because I cannot verify his philosophical disposition—it merely occurs to me this way, looking back.

ĕ-sprē´ də kôr´

Esprit de corps is of French extraction, literally meaning the "spirit of a group." This noun relates to morale. To be more exact, this term is a positive application as in devotion, loyalty, and enthusiasm, which inspires the group to "be all you can be," as was the Army adage of that era.

A DRILL SGT. TAUGHT MORE THAN PUSH-UPS

It is preeminent that a group has high morale, which informs their drive to accomplish. Esprit de corps has as much to do with corporate and industrial concerns as that of the military's. Wherever groups of people accomplish something, what the group feels about itself and the collective contribution of the ensemble is paramount.

The Japanese business mindset is dependent on this same approach. In Japan, everything is about "the group" as a group rather than an assemblage of individuals. In America, everything is about the individual, and the team is a close second when it is necessary. In either case, the essence of esprit de corps is valuable to success.

Using this word educates. I've used this word a number of times over the years. It's a high-impact, minor-application word with which we can teach and inspire, whether it is a little league team or a group in an engineering competition.

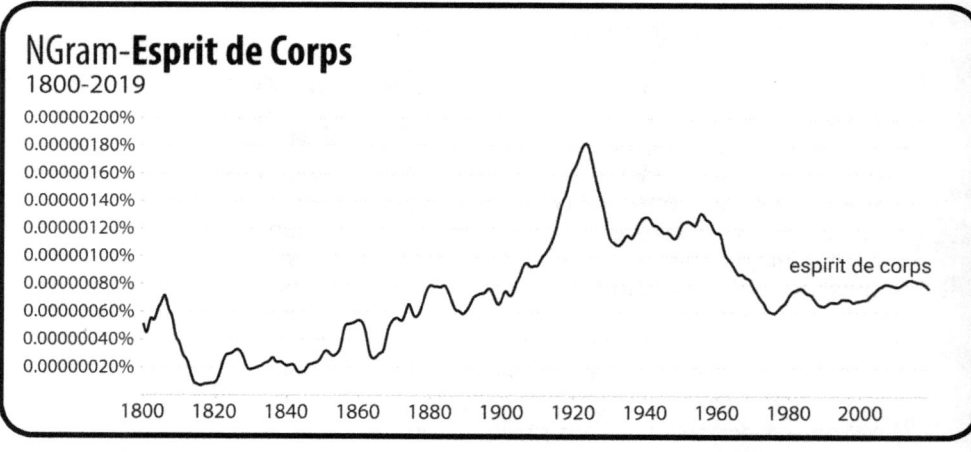

WORDS WE REDUCE THE INFINITE BY
— 1987-89 —

Gunning-Fog Index: 11.41

After serving in the military, I returned to Omaha, Nebraska, to attend Omaha Bible School from 1987 to 1989. These were good years of learning and readjustment to civilian life. As it was called, OBS was a school of exegetic study through the Bible, meaning studying through texts, which interpret themselves by context and interior information. This school was also the environment in which I learned several words that continue to enrich my life and understanding.

I don't remember the exact situation in which

ăn´thrə-pə-môr´fĭz´əm

the word **anthropomorphism** came into my understanding. But it is a fascinating word that describes something we see in application regularly. Anthropomorphism isn't a word found in the Bible, but it truthfully describes an observability in some stories in the Bible, as well as in our day. This word is somewhat common in the context of modern sociology classes.

Anthropomorphism originates from the Greek word *anthrōpomorphos*, meaning "in the manner of a human being." This noun is a puzzle of many parts. The prefix "*anthropo*" relates to humankind, being human… The word anthropology has the same beginning. The defining root is *morph*, which, standing alone, means "to change." Yet, in this construct, it refers to structure or form.

The suffix "*ic*" changes a word to the adjective form. In literal application, anthropomorphism means applying human traits, emotions, or acumen to inanimate objects or animals. The context in which I learned this word concerned doing the same thing to God, holding Him to all that motivates or describes mankind.

Movies and specific allegorical stories are where we might observe anthropomorphism. How many animated stories

WORDS WE REDUCE THE INFINITE BY

from *The Jungle Book* to *Antz* depict animals with human traits? How about C.S. Lewis's *Chronicles of Narnia*, where beavers and other animals talk, think, and respond in human ways.

I don't see a problem of allegorically using animals or even inanimate objects this way. But anthropomorphizing God's emotions, values, and ideals has killed more people than perhaps any other mindset. Exegetic study in the Bible helped me see how the religious community is guilty in this regard. They put the notion of hate in God's mouth for things people in institutional religion hate. This is done to "authorize" their own ideals and agenda—never mind what God clearly said or revealed about Himself.

In relationship to God, anthropomorphism is dangerous whether you believe in Him or not. All it takes is some nut job to attribute various human traits to God and use that as an authorization to do something dastardly.

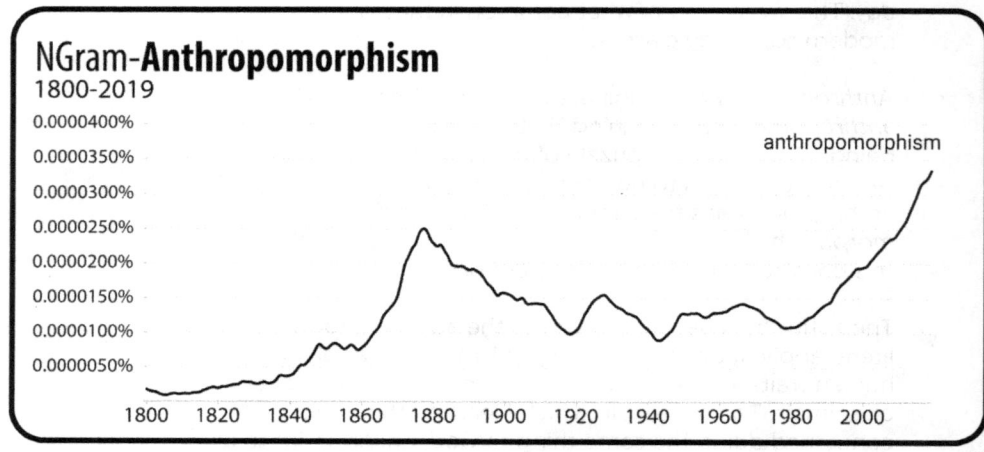

TAKE RELIGION OUT OF ITS' CONTEXT
1987-89

`Gunning-Fog Index: 13.76`

Still, during my Omaha Bible School days, I learned other words of practical value. One would think that only religious words would be the likely imprinting of a Bible school setting. While I learned a lot about that, remarkably, most of the words we've looked at from that setting have been philosophical. The one we are about to look at is religious—partly.

In looking at lists of words from Verbal Advantage, Quizlet, and Majors SAT preparatory material, and two other vocabulary lists, I've noticed many words don't make these lists. I've often wondered if there's a reason for this fact in specific cases. Is there an effort to deemphasize certain things?

Part of Bible school was learning how texts in the Bible have been understood or used. The same is true of religious concepts and theological ideas, which have been used for centuries, concerning which significant disagreements exist. Church discipline is just such an area of contention.

Initially, authority in church was thought to be for maintaining order and strict adherence to "the correct" teaching. However, upon study of the Bible, we'll find that concept to be ridiculous and abusive, which history abounds with examples at the hands of the institutional religious community of virtually every sect. Even so, religious and philosophical ideas, articulated in words, still afford us practical use irrespective of their original purpose. The obstacle will be disconnecting the religious connection people assume with this word. I don't recall the exact details of learning the word **anathema**, but it was during discussions of "church history" at Bible school.

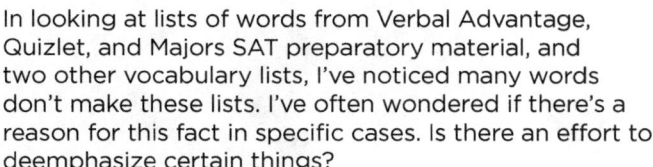
ə-năth´ə-mə

TAKE RELIGION OUT OF ITS' CONTEXT

Anathema is a noun. It means a formal denunciation that involves excommunication from a community or group, usually a church organization. Anathema has several other meanings, such as use in a self-perceptive role where someone becomes detestable in your view. The word originated from the Greek word *anatithenai*, meaning "to dedicate."

Anathema is a sticky word because of its religious implications. However, you could use the word this way: to impugn a homosexual is a social anathema these days. Or you could use anathema this way: his joining ISIS was an anathema to his family and country. In both cases, religion has got nothing to do with "the anathema" being understood. Practical use will depend on context and associations to be precise. Perhaps one of the best things religion gave us (past tense) is vocabulary and communication clarity.

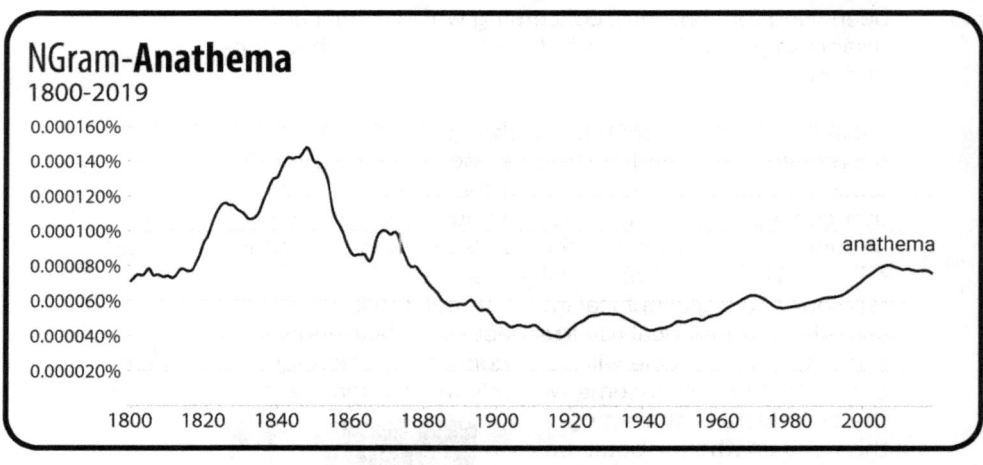

ELIXIR SALESMAN IN ANOTHER WORD
— 1987-89 —

Gunning-Fog Index: 14.26

Still at Omaha Bible School I caught onto another colorful and practical word. This word could be used as an insult. But the more exact usage describes a particular type of fraud or misrepresentation that we should not be afraid to point out. I don't recall the precise context during Bible school wherein this word came to light, but it is a word I remember and use because of its specificity.

This noun represents a shameless pusher of goods and items to the unwary. The frontier and throughout modern history have been the stage upon which flamboyant, fast-talkers have something you might think you need, or they make something you don't need sound like something you do. Such was represented in the movie The Outlaw Josey Wales. An "elixir" salesman accosts Josey Wales, touting his potion as having the ability to do almost anything. Josey properly treats this **charlatan**; he spits chew on the guy's suit and asks how solution works on stains.

shär´lə-tən

The word charlatan dates from the late-16th century, Italian *ciarlatano* meaning "fast talker." It is a derivative of the word *cerretano*, which describes an inhabitant of Cerreto, Italy—noted to be a hotbed of hucksters and tricksters. Part of the meaning associated with this word is one who is overconfident, a braggart, or a showman. The practical meaning of charlatan is a shameless pusher of goods and items to the unwary.

The word has been used in conjunction with faith healers, doctors—or so-called doctors, lawyers, or any profession where opinion or an educated pronouncement assures money changing hands. Charlatanism is a charge leveled when such the pronouncement or the bona fides of the person making them are found to be false, which causes loss or damage.

ELIXIR SALESMAN IN ANOTHER WORD

Today, we are not so advanced as human society to where we no longer have charlatans among us. Late-night commercials, real estate deals, and even news media are common areas where we can find hoodwinking and charlatanism. Many politicians are charlatans of the highest order.

We should give expression to this type of reality even though it is negative. Charlatanism is a personal type of fraud where people attempt to draw us into a disadvantaged situation through our own approval and interaction. I do not have a problem identifying a person as a charlatan if, in fact, their purposes are proven to be premeditatively dishonest or harmful.

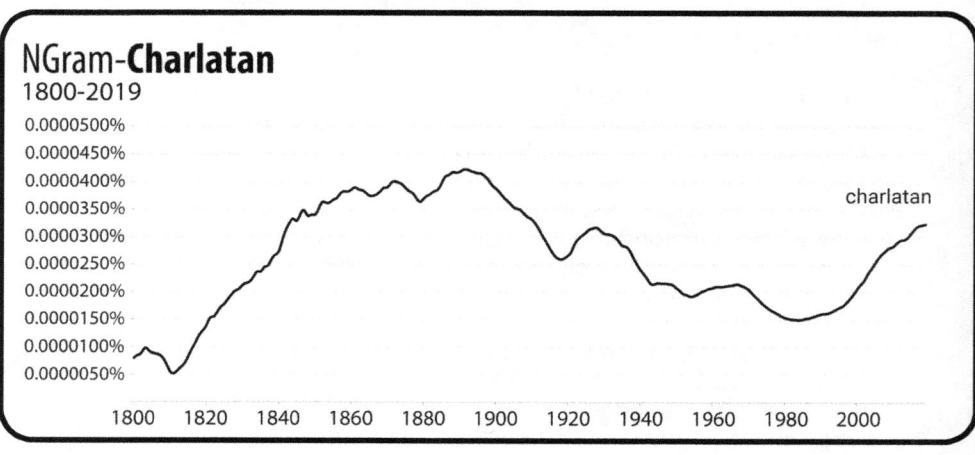

BEWARE OF MIXTURES
— 1987-89 —

`Gunning-Fog Index: 11.88`

While at Omaha Bible School, I learned a good bit more than strictly the Bible. The director, Ollie Olson, was a well-read teacher. His vocabulary enriched mine on an everyday level, as well as toward philosophical understandings.

I remember a lot about Bible school. But I don't recall the exact situation of learning specific words. For me, philosophical aspects remain essential because many terms in which concepts are couched represent actual realities. Take, for instance, the word **syncretism**. You'll not hear this word from 1 in 500 people. Even so, the word represents an all-too-common reality that is worth rethinking. And after we realize what it is, we'll notice its occurrence.

sĭng´krĭ-tĭz´əm

Right away, the first four letters present an air of familiarity. Anyone who has a Ford these days will recognize SYNC on their dash. Maybe the letters *cret* elicit a notion of secrecy. And *ism*, in the words of Ferris Bueller, "It's not that I condone...any 'ism' for that matter. Ism's, in my opinion, are not good."

The noun *syncretism* describes a fusion of conflicting ideas, perhaps even an undisclosed agenda to bring about this fusion. The word has Greek origins.

Ollie Olson used the word *syncretism* somewhat frequently to describe the combination of ideas, which usually leads to confusion. Interfaithism, the attempt to homogenize major religions, is a fine example of syncretism. Combining times of remembrance with pagan ritual days is another example, e.g., winter solstice and Christ's birth.

Syncretism doesn't always have to relate to religious things. Mexico is a cultural syncretism between native

BEWARE OF MIXTURES

cultures and Spanish influences from 15th century conquistadors. Today, there is nothing absolutely Mayan, Aztecan, or Spanish in Mexico; the culture is almost wholly a homogeneous amalgamation.

Getting back to religious things, when ideological synthesis occurs, what once was on either side fails to be distinct, or identification becomes meaningless. This is the danger of syncretism. The underlying idea of syncretism is that nothing matters except for the motive. World peace and a reduction in violence are two common motives based on syncretism. However, there is no proof changing words and meanings to foster "unity" will reduce mankind's fundamental weakness toward violence. That equation has never worked.

1950s Evangelicalism once meant something. But because of a blend of various dissimilar notions, today, Evangelicalism is indistinct and virtually meaningless. This syncretic process can happen to something absolutely true, as well as within an ideology.

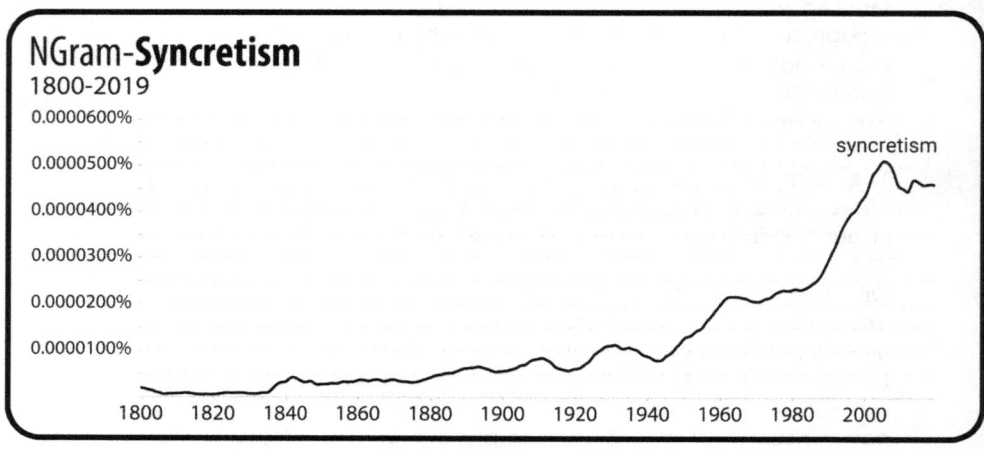

A STINKY WORD THAT IS FUNNY

Gunning-Fog Index: 12.43

Sometimes, a word can present itself to us in the most unlikely sources. I worked as a Pattern Maker at Omaha Steel Castings Co. between 1989 and 1992. The job was fascinating, and the people who worked there certainly provided a level of entertainment and education.

One fellow, Miguel Martinez, was a pattern runner. He stored patterns and retrieved them for production, either running them out to the pour floor or into the pattern shop, where I worked, for repair. As shop guys tend to do, we regularly shot the bull—trading stories or trying to impress one another.

Miguel liked to read. He went to many Broadway productions and traveled the world before he got stuck in Omaha. He was what I would consider "cultured." He was mildly philosophical, conversant on a wide variety of subjects, as well as funny.

I remember one of his reminiscings where he used a word I'd not heard before: **flatulent**. As I remember, his tale related to an off-Broadway play he recalled as *The Flatulent Lady*. I've not been able to verify this title since. However, the word was odd enough that it stuck with me instantly. Years later, while watching *Patch Adams*, I caught the late Robin Williams, who played Adams, using the adjective form of this word in a scene where he is on trial.

flăch´ə-lənt

Flatulent is one of those "funny words" to me. Not so much because of what it means but more because of the effort to step around a crass subject.

This adjective came to English from French through the Latin word *flatus*, which means "to blow" or the effect of wind. Its noun form, flatulence, is descriptive of cramping or a bloated feeling one might experience in

A STINKY WORD THAT IS FUNNY

the digestive process. Perhaps it implies illness. Flatulent is, in one sense, more of a medical term.

In a more descriptive application, either noun or adjective, this word can be used metaphorically to describe someone who expends pontifications, gesticulation, or deceptive reaches beyond professional or experiential accomplishment. The evening talking heads could be broad-brushed regarding being flatulent or foisting the flatulence of their best guesses or even prejudice.

Flatulent is another word I really enjoy the use of. It's surefire to rivet an audience or person. It is powerful in its implications and secondary meaning. There is an increasing applicability in society for various types to talk in a flatulent way, whether it is polluting the air with chatter or idealistic postulation.

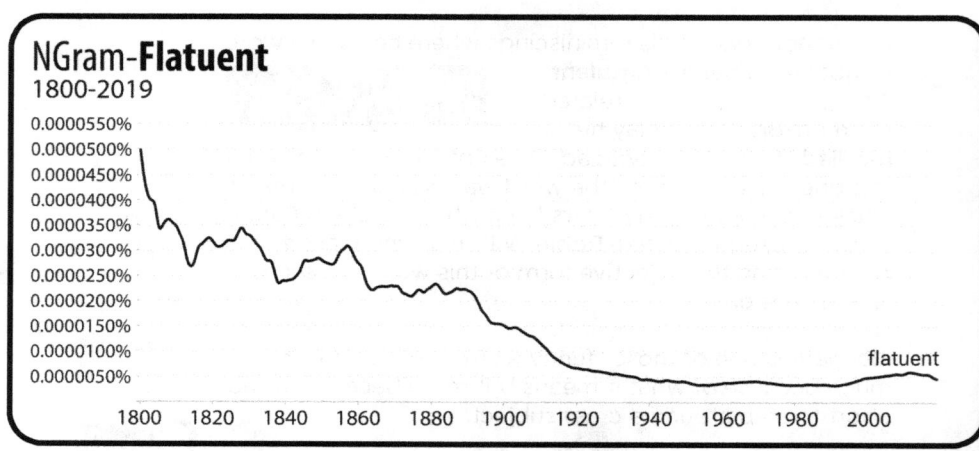

TRADITIONS OF RESPECT
—1989-92—

Gunning-Fog Index: 12.27

Religion is always a subject close to the mouths and hearts of men (gender neutral). I believe people are generally religious, aside from what naysayers and alleged atheists attempt to make us believe.

While religion seems to calm the souls of men, I believe it does funny things to people as well. Beliefs ofttimes accompany changes not only in behavior but also in practice. As such, rituals can be a big part of religion. And ritual is just one of the funny things religion can do to people.

Still at Omaha Steel Castings Co., I loved the work. It was all engaging from factoring thermal shrink into pattern dimensions, rigging the patterns with flow-gating, and eventually purchasing and running the blueprint filling.

As with any job, there was the usual parade of characters, notwithstanding the religious types. Being vocal about religious subjects drew interaction from any and all who had motives in this realm. One fellow in particular, Jay West, enthusiastically weighed in on this subject. He was not only a heavy dialogue contributor but also a rotund individual, to put it lightly.

Jay was extremely opinionated, which usually goes along with religious territory. He was semi-intellectual, using deep philosophical concepts couched in big words. One time, while taking a swipe at a particular religious group, Jay used the word **genuflect**. This verb's linguistic ancestry is Latin, noting a religious action towards a hallowed object or a god: *genu* refers to the knee, and *flect* relates to bending. However, *genuflecting* can just as well refer to crossing one's self, nodding solemnly, or any action that depicts the attempt to worship or show reverence. Saluting is genuflecting as well.

jĕn´yə-flĕkt´

TRADITIONS OF RESPECT

Genuflection can be a ritual or a genuine response. Recently, I attended a service where a woman curtseyed towards an altar before being seated. The resurgent folk artist Rodriguez, who was tossed aside by the music establishment of his day, authored incisive and pithy social criticism in lyrics equivalent to Dylan. He used the word *genuflect* in another way to illustrate empty cultural tradition in his ballad, *A Most Disgusting Song*.

Genuflection, whether religious or otherwise, is something many people do. I feel it is a relatively passive, cold involvement. Perhaps we can make folks aware by drawing attention to it by using this word. We might be reminded to develop and live in ways that encourage a more personal interaction between ourselves, people, and God.

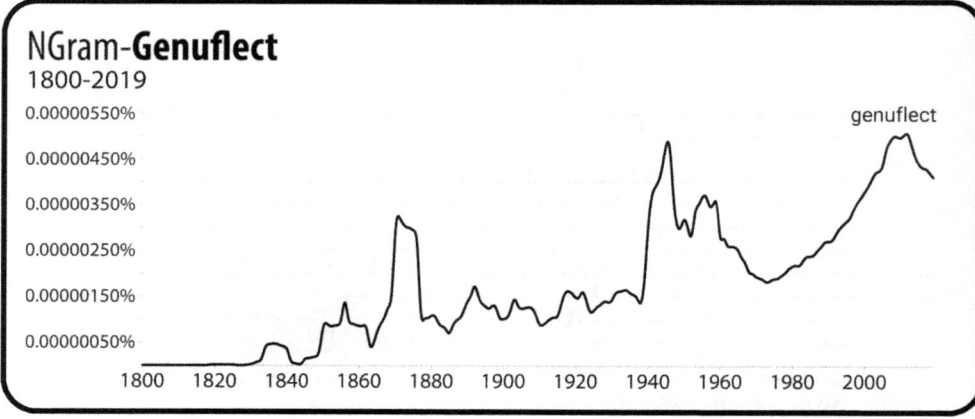

GETTING PUT IN SOMEONE ELSE'S PLACE
1992

Gunning-Fog Index: 11.07

In 1992, I was still involved with what calls itself church. Part of our outreach was short-term missions. This concept is where small groups of people go overseas to visit missionaries and undertake a few projects. The purpose was to extend help while getting one's toes wet regarding missionary work.

As I prepared for one of these short-term outreaches to Mexico, our leader served up a dose of religious vaccination that metastasized into an immunity rejection toward institutional religion. It's not that my appreciation for God changed; however, my tolerance for religiousness has shrunk precipitously.

As part of our short-term mission's preparation, we had regular classes together in order to develop our minds outside of the cultural perspective we grew up with. The danger was that we could take our notions overseas, thinking we were "right" when, in reality, our view had been just one of many that were acceptable. This problem is an observation of ethnocentrism in practice.

As I mentioned earlier, I grew up in a family that used a wide palette of words. However, I've discovered that we didn't have a corner on all aspects of those words. In my recollection, my mother, Karel Ida (Geary) Price, used **lambaste** quite frequently. It's a word I understood and one I employed liberally—in quite the correct context when I used it.

lăm-bāst´

This verb has its origins within English. It means to assault violently in a verbal way. Censure is a similar word. I've always enjoyed this word, *lambaste*, for its flair. The only problem was I grew up mispronouncing it. I had no idea. This point was before I started consulting dictionaries to avoid embarrassment from self-righteous and arrogant people who want to put you in place.

GETTING PUT IN SOMEONE ELSE'S PLACE

During our short-term missions class, apparently, I used this word one too many times around this "leader," John Rice. At one point, he lit into me about my mispronunciations as if it were some great evil. I pronounced lambaste with a short "a" sound for the first two vowels. He sternly corrected me, lambasting me in a turn of irony in front of the group for my pronunciational faux pas. The word is correctly pronounced *lăm-bāst´*.

Twice in my life, others have negatively "set me straight" concerning pronunciations. Can you believe this? I don't know if their objective was to personally make me feel foolish or if they just had mean streaks. In either case, these situations have value. Such has never deterred me from using an ever-widening stable of words. But regular dictionary use has become a salvation from those who would crucify me over a word.

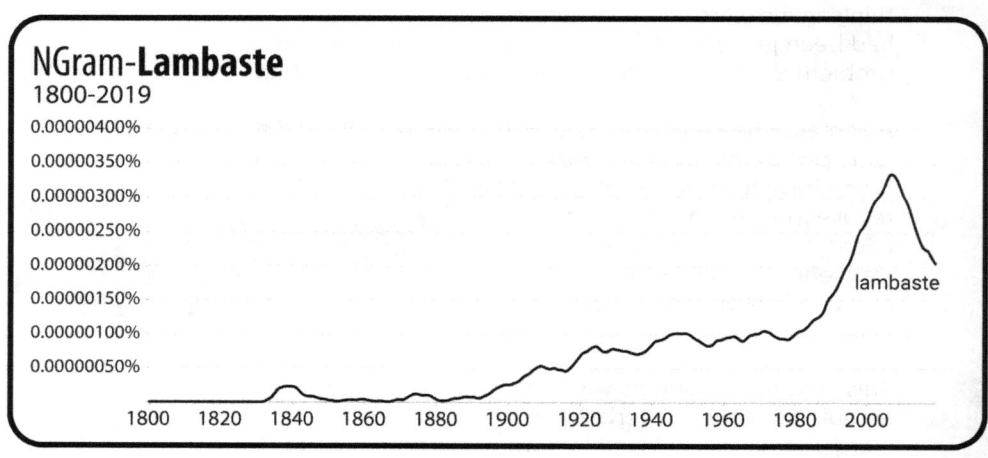

LEAVE IT TO AN INTERIOR DESIGNER

`Gunning-Fog Index: 12.42`

Between 1992 and 1994, I worked as a salesman for a lighting showroom in Omaha, Nebraska, called United Electric Supply. Designers, builders, and walk-in customers came to us to learn of new lighting technology, lighting techniques, or to order needed fixtures for their homes. Designers helped high-end customers pick out their lights so their selections would further accentuate all the other elements of the interior design already in place.

Designers are fairly interesting as a group of people. Many are flamboyant types, and some are goofier than pet coons. Some could be thunderclouds, still others arrogant and somehow transcendent over the rest of us ordinary folk. Some let their work speak for them. And some are very friendly—average people themselves. God bless the latter! There can only be so many flamboyant folks.

At United Electric, I remember two designers particularly. Alice Cizek was a red-headed fireball. When Alice walked into the showroom, everybody headed for cover like rats off a sinking ship. I became her salesman of choice and enjoyed no competition for her business. Another designer lady was the affable Ellen Hansen. She was a delight in all measures. She was laid-back and funny. She often worked on the designer showcase of homes in Omaha, called the Street of Dreams, which she kiddingly referred to as the Street of Nightmares.

In any case, I learned the adjective **eclectic** from this woman. This word came to English from the Greek *eklektikos*, which means "to select from or to gather." In English eclectic, the meaning is more distinct: to select from, or collect, unrelated items or from various sources that do not seem to have a connection.

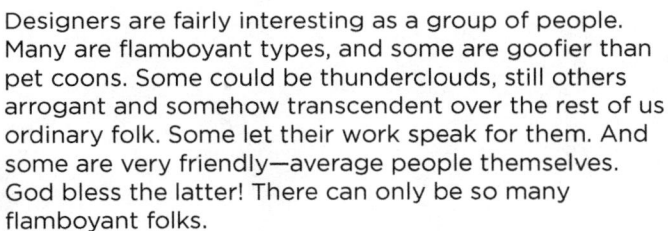

LEAVE IT TO AN INTERIOR DESIGNER

A house could be eclectic in decor. One room could be an early empire, another art deco, and still a third could be Nanyang design—in other words, a house of many different looks. An art collector could have a collection of some American folk art and some impressionism, which are utterly dissimilar. Eclectic can refer to art, philosophy, beliefs, design, or techniques. The outcome would be considered eclectic in any field where someone can combine totally unrelated aspects into a functional presentation or use. If a person had the habit of combining dissimilar items, which became their trademark, they themselves would be considered eclectic.

I like this term because it perhaps gives a pass to the unconventional in looks or approaches. This word recognizes flair and non-traditionalism as allowable, practical, workable, and even fashionable. The world would be a rather dull place without eclectic possibilities.

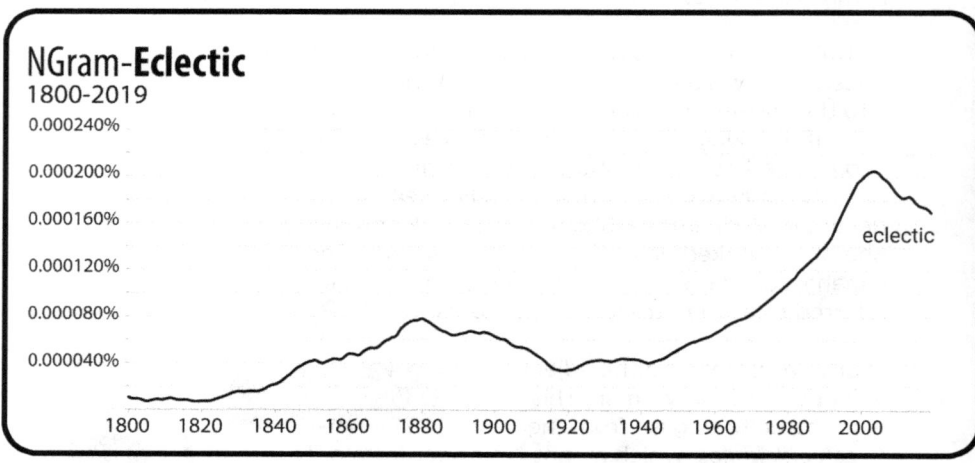

ANGER IS SOMETIMES HYSTERICAL
1993

Gunning-Fog Index: 12.65

As you will notice, I find some words hysterical in several places in this book. This perception may not be because of how they sound but because of what they represent. I believe I came across the next word in 1993 in conjunction with an event I will share.

Apoplexy is no laughing matter. This medical condition describes the sudden loss of feeling or body movement because too little blood is going to the brain. This condition happens because of profuse hemorrhaging in other parts of the body. In some cases, apoplexy can also be considered a type of stroke.

I have fallen in love with the adjectival derivative **apoplectic** for its metaphoric use. In this light, the word is known chiefly to represent

ăp´ə-plĕk´tĭk

extreme and explosive anger, the imagining of which is reminiscent of one of Yosemite Sam's fits of rage, which is partly why anger amuses me.

The word apoplectic came from the French word *apoplectique*, from Latin word *apoplecticus*, and the Greek *apoplēktikos*. This specific physical malady has been identifiable for centuries, hence the linguistic migrancy between languages down through the centuries.

In similar fashion, anger has been a longstanding human trait observable in degrees. One degree can relate to volume, or someone can be ballistic, resulting in physical actions. The attributes of this level of anger compare to a seizure associated with stroke or heart attack.

I find other people's anger funny because it is often contrived and unnecessary. From the outrage someone expresses following a prank to the gripping anger that

ANGER IS SOMETIMES HYSTERICAL

seizes someone to the degree of contortions—the entire spectrum is thoroughly amusing to me.

I remember one such apoplectic fit at work in the mid-1990s. Dennis Sullivan, a co-worker at Drake-Williams Steel, filled in as an interim boss while the superintendent took a vacation. Sullivan hated me with a virulent passion of biblical proportion. He was a known rage-a-maniac, so his feelings toward me were of no concern. One day, he tried to embarrass me in front of a number of people. Without thinking, I retorted, "What is the matter with you, Dennis—were you potty trained at gunpoint?" Euphemistically, I was suggesting early-childhood trauma as the reason for his behavior. Sullivan apoplectically exploded into a profanity-laced tirade, slamming an armload of shop drawings on the floor, then hastily conducting himself through the shop, still aburst in continuing obscenities.

The word apoplectic is tremendously expressive. Anger of this level is not uncommon. Using this word powerfully communicates the extremeness of some behavior. Apoplectic could also be used comedically or even to defuse escalating situations.

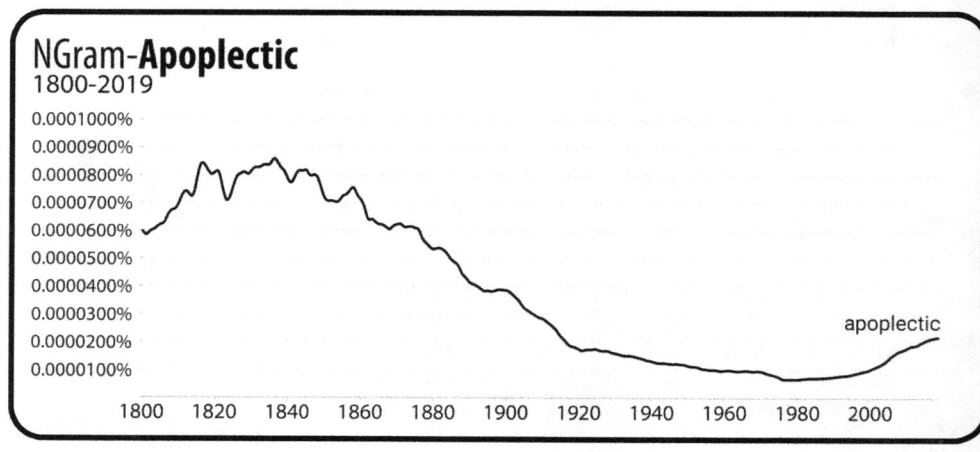

ANY WHICH WAY YOU CAN
— 1994-01 —

`Gunning-Fog Index: 11.34`

As a Purchasing Agent, one meets a lot of people. Everyone in the company is your customer. Salespeople and factory reps also vie for your time in this profession. This job is a tremendous whirl of activity: researching and making products appear just in time… From 1994 to 2001, I worked for Drake-Williams Steel, a structural steel company. This job I recall with many fond memories.

I got to know some of the salespeople who called upon me year in and year out. Some I got to know reasonably well. One of the welding salesmen was from a company called Praxair, one of the largest welding distributors in the world. Michael Mennem caught on to my affection for wordplay during our interactions.

Every now and again, sales reps would take me to lunch to discuss business opportunities. Mike took me to one of these luncheons and on the way played up on my penchant for wordplay. He mentioned taking a "**circuitous** route" to a restaurant. He emphasized circuitous as if it were a cue.

`sər-kyōoˈĭ-təs`

Well, I caught it all right—that was the word of the day. It was one I'd never heard before, but context and the word explained itself.

This word is another contribution of Latin. The adjective is descriptive of an indirect or a roundabout path. The first syllable *circ*, is the basis for the word circle; however, it isn't the root word. *Circuit*, the root word, is a stand-alone word, meaning "a path, an itinerary of venues or events, an administrative area, or an electrical term, meaning wires forming a path for electricity to follow." The "*ous*" suffix is a French-Norman inclusion denoting "the nature of."

Circuitous can be a practical word in many ways. A person's insight can be circuitous, meaning it doesn't

ANY WHICH WAY YOU CAN

have a conclusion or is not lineally complete. Circuitous could be used as Michael Mennem did; that is to say, we are not going the most direct way to an objective. Figuratively, it could mean that you are going on an adventure.

In any case, circuitous is distinctively practical. One can have fun with it, or one can be severe. It's a word that takes the place of four or five others to say the same thing. Circuitous is a word that will stand out in what you say and make you stand out for having used it.

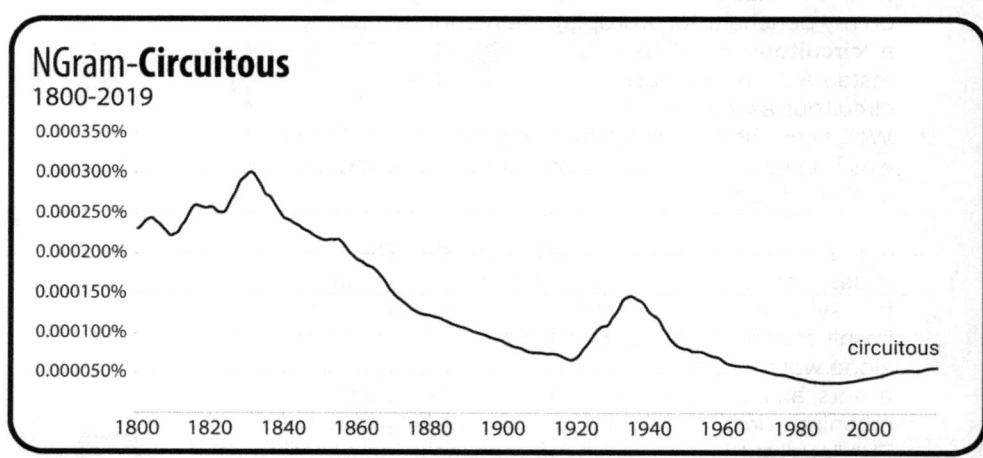

A STORE BY ANOTHER DESCRIPTION
—1994-01—

`Gunning-Fog Index: 11.62`

Another person I met as a Purchasing Agent for Drake-Williams Steel (1994 to 2001) was a peach of a guy and a hell of a salesman. In three years, he took his company's business with mine from $5,000 yearly to more than $100,000. It wasn't that I wholesale gave business away to him. He earned it, and it made good business sense on my end, or it wouldn't have happened.

Jason Smith is a guy I really hit it off with; we still talk every now and again, even though he's been halfway around the world in Denmark and Australia over the past decade. He, too, is an ideating person like myself. Back then, we'd sit over lunch and talk about doing all sorts of different schemes. He had a colorful vocabulary as well.

I remember him talking at one point about a clothing store for men in Omaha, which no longer exists. He was a good dresser and mentioned this store at one point, describing it with the word **menagerie**. I believe that I was aware of this word prior.

mé-na-je-rie

If I remember right, my paternal grandmother used this word as well. However, the word never "registered" as when Jason dropped it one day in the context of this clothing store.

This noun comes to English from the same word in French: *ménagerie*, which refers to the management of a household or farm. In English, this term could mean a location where animals are trained or an exotic collection of animals, like a zoo. Or it could carry a metaphorical meaning, such as in Jason's use: a collection or mixture.

The word menagerie is creative. There are twenty other words one might use to communicate a wide variety or to be specific about what type of animal reserve one is referring to without using the word menagerie. In most cases, I've highlighted words because of their

A STORE BY ANOTHER DESCRIPTION

unusualness or their exclusivity. However, even a general word can draw attention because it is not common.

One could use menagerie metaphorically in as many ways as it might be in its straight, first-definition sense. The point is that this word is flexible, and its use shows creativity while drawing attention to what is being talked about. Creativity is vital for a speaker or a person who wants to be distinct from the hordes who speak all the time but are not as noticed for what they say or why they say it.

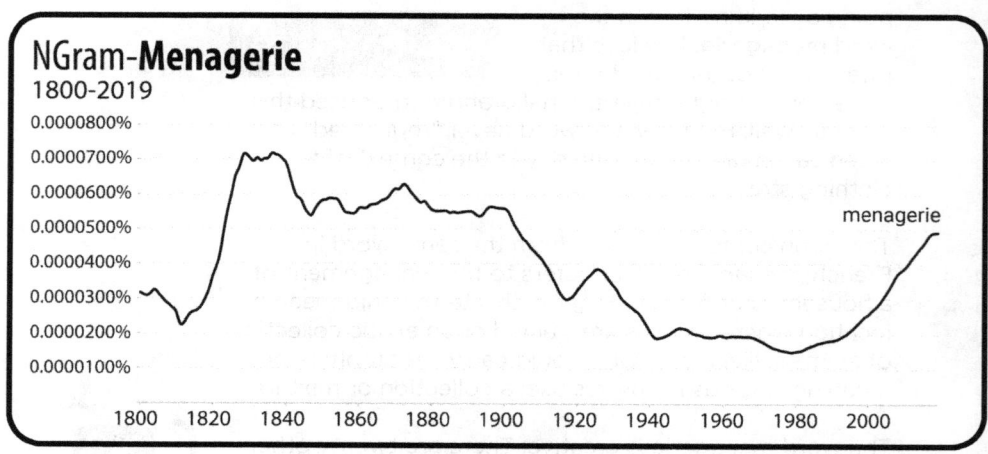

FROM THE MOUTHS OF FOREIGN SPEAKERS
1995-98

`Gunning-Fog Index: 11.13`

Over the years, my wife, Pam, and I have befriended many foreigners. We were involved in helping people learn English (pronunciation, listening, and confidence) as well as in practical matters of navigating traditions, cultural obstacles, and how things work in this country. The life of a foreign student or immigrant is a tough involvement. I've thought many times about what it would be like to move to another country and attempt to survive on as little as many come to this country with.

One thing I learned in this activity was that foreigners can have shocking vocabulary beyond that of many native-speaking Americans. This seems counterintuitive. One such example involved a family of Bosnians who immigrated after the Bosnian War. We met them between 1995 and 1998. Esad and Dijana Taslidzic were semi, high-society people in their former country. Esad was a successful modern-style architect. They fled the country at the height of the war. Their story was harrowing.

We'd gotten to know them reasonably well. We took them out to places, invited them to our house for social occasions, and went to their home for cultural exchange. We learned that Bosnians love to party and dance! In this context, Esad and Dijana got to know us.

One day, Esad mentioned that he thought I was a **polyglot**. Taken aback, I had to act as though I understood because I'd never heard the word prior. In working with all the foreigners, I always picked up a few words for fun, like *mangekyō*, the Japanese word for kaleidoscope. Who learns such atypical words in another language? I guess this penchant did not escape Esad's attention. What is impressive is his understanding of this type of pathology. Out of 1,000 college students, how many would know the word polyglot in a practical sense?

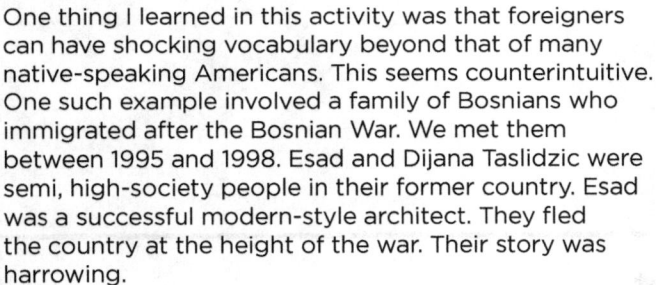

pŏl´ē-glŏt´

FROM THE MOUTHS OF FOREIGN SPEAKERS

This noun, *polyglot*, comes from the Greek *polyglōttos*, from *poly-* and *glōtta*. The prefix *"poly"* means "many or varied." The root word, *glot*, refers to the tongue or speech as it pertains to language. Polyglot can mean "multilingual" or just a diversity of elements from various languages, such as describes me.

This word can be used to describe anything from cuisine to the collective inhabitants of a place, which contains a variety of heritage or extractions. In our increasingly multicultural society, polyglot is a word that quickly notes diversity without using the very tired word *diversity*. I grow weary of using politically-correct buzzwords when it could be just as well said as polyglot.

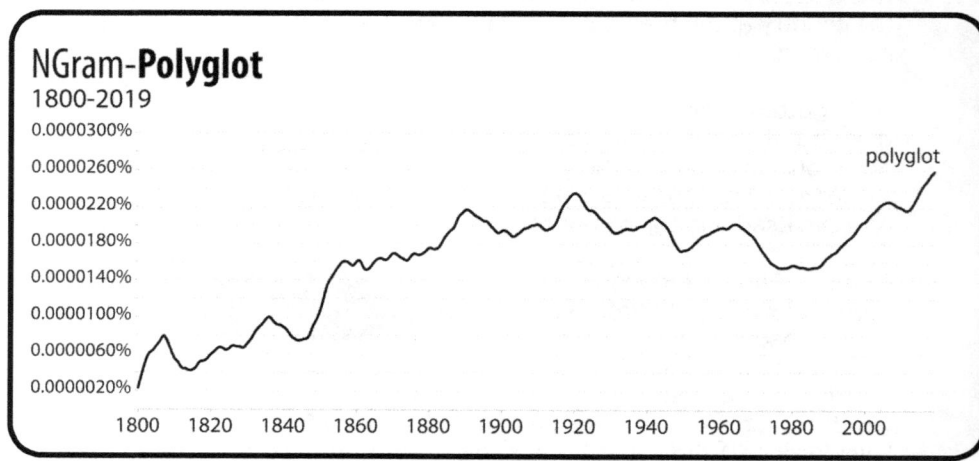

A TUNE WORTHY OF A WORD

Gunning-Fog Index: 11.96

Once, we lived in the historic neighborhood of Benson, a town swallowed up by a sprawling Omaha metroplex. Our house was built by one of its earliest mayors and featured a wrap-around veranda porch, Corinthian pillars, and 4,400 square feet of living space. The home was beautiful.

In those years, from 1995 to 1999, we were going to an Evangelical Free Church. One family from the congregation lived just down the street from us. The Hillmers, Steve and Gayle, along with their four children, were friendly folk. We spent a little time at their home, and they at ours. Living close to folks who went to the same religious building we attended was odd in that such had never been my experience.

From all our conversations, I don't remember the context, but I do remember a word Steve used at one juncture: **reverie**.

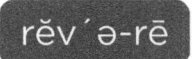

Having grown up steeped in classical music, I immediately harkened back to a piano piece by impressionistic composer Claude Debussy: "Reverie." In my younger years, I never took note—please excuse the pun—that reverie was something beyond just the name of a piano piece. I thought it akin to a title like *Bolero* or *Peer Gynt*. However, after Steve Hillmer used the word reverie in conversation, I got the memo: it was indeed a practical term.

This noun is not commonly used today, even though it is in no way archaic. The word comes from Middle French, *rever* meaning "delirium, to meander, to be delirious." The, "*i.e.*" was added in the French word *rêverie* to mean "revelry." In modern English, this noun means being pleasantly lost in a daydream or musings. Poetically, the

A TUNE WORTHY OF A WORD

composer Debussy was French, thus making sense for his use of Reverie to name his dreamy piano composition.

Reverie, a foreign concept in the modern technological society, is not an unneeded or antiquated notion. The contemporary soul languishes in the speed of busied passivity in the digital age. Rarely do we see anyone without the appendage of a gadget entertaining, preoccupied, and distracting them. It seems almost foreign not to broadcast or tweet our modern frivolity.

Reverie still exists, though it may seem more childlike, predating technologic fixation and harried busyments. If we are not running for work or the kids or to catch up from digital preoccupancy, we don't exist, or we are sleeping. A simple daydream, relaxed reverie, or unfettered imagining is a luxury few have and even fewer know.

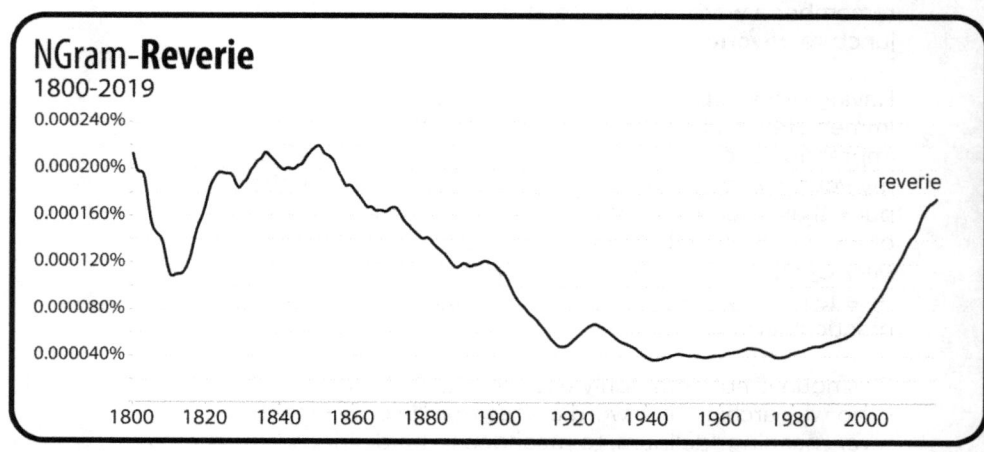

NOW NEGATIVE ISN'T NEGATIVE
1997

`Gunning-Fog Index: 13.16`

To my age group, John Wayne perhaps informs much of our way of thinking about life, what's right, and how to carry oneself as a man. This is not to say Wayne's approach or perspective were impeccable. Far from it! It is to say we just grew up propagandized by the silver-screen portrayal of "manliness."

Among Westerns and war flicks, or the stereotypic acting in most of Wayne's roles, you would not think about his films from the perspective of vocabulary. Yet, in reality, if one were to watch his films from this viewpoint, they'd find an extraordinary conglomeration of unusual words bandied about amongst all the overheated *machoism*.

Another word I caught in Wayne's films in 1997 was **petulant**. The specific movie was *McLintock!*. It is not my favorite Wayne film, but it's entertaining. It's a cheesy attempt at comedy, complete with slapstick buffoonery and a great cast. It is an enjoyable picture.

pĕch´ə-lənt

Petulant is an adjective that came from a word spelled the same in Latin, which meant "immodest." Migrating into French, the pronunciation changed (*pétulant*), yet the word came to be understood as "imprudent." Coming into the English added the impressions of pettishness: constantly whimpering.

Petulance describes an increasing constituency in modern population. Pop culture is all-pervasive, and society seems to measure everything from a pop-culture perspective. Petulance is very much intrinsic to this point of view because it is an act. An increasing litany of actors (gender neutral) are portrayed or portray themselves in the characteristic of petulance.

While petulance once may have been a pejorative most often associated with the wiles of the feminine

NOW NEGATIVE ISN'T NEGATIVE

gender; now, this term is equally descriptive of many men: moodiness, sulky, insolence, petty rudeness, easily annoyed, peevish, and even capriciousness. Petulance is a cultivated attitude and response. Actors like Russell Brand and the character Sheldon Cooper on *The Big Bang Theory* made book in variations of petulance. Russell Crowe was once described this way in a UK piece by Andrew M. Brown.

Petulance is something to identify that which could not be characterized entirely in other terms or even a string of them. It is perhaps the attitude of the age in which we live, one of entitlement, of self-aggrandizement, and one which, if you interrupt or withhold what is thought due, will result in petulance.

In the heyday of John Wayne, petulance was thought of as negative and childish, as portrayed in *McLintock!*. Now, it is a pandemic reality in a generation and culture that has no anchor.

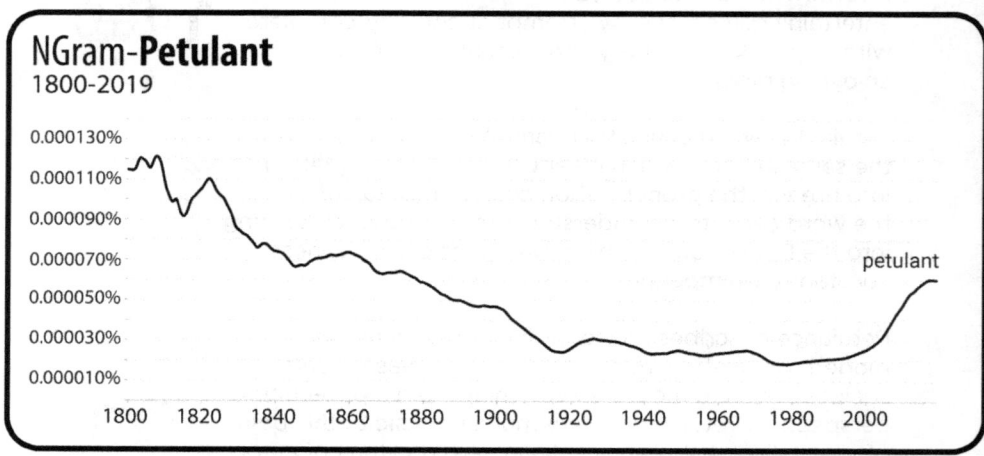

A PRECIPITOUSLY INCREASING IDENTIFIABILITY

Gunning-Fog Index: 15.66

Chance happenings and steady introductions in life serve us more in interactions with people than employment or designated social events. I've enjoyed a significant number of people over the years from either pool of interaction. Some folks are lifelong connections, others are flashes-in-the-pan. For me, people have been the proverbial life is like a box of chocolates—you never know what you're going to get.

When our kids were young, we developed an acquaintance with a couple and their gaggle of children: a yours-and-our arrangement. After drifting from them over a couple years they regained prominence in our involvements because of their plague of martial vexations and general incongruity.

We've discovered a particular and precipitously increasing identifiability among those we know amid this relational involvement and in years since. This discovery is **histrionics**, or what we now know as histrionic personality disorder. As of the writing of this book, our family knows six specific people who live life as certifiable histrionic types.

hĭs´trē-ŏn´ĭk

Histrionic is an adjective derived from the Latin word *histrio*, which means "actor." It morphed into *histrionicus*; meaning "pertaining to acting or actors." It is unclear when *histrionic(s)* broadened to infer a psychological condition and acute interpersonal conduct. Today, however, *histrionic* is not widely used outside its second definition as a mental evaluative.

Histrionics describes a person of incessant outrageousness and erraticism. Such people have a hyper-obsession with their appearance. They are driven to be the center of attention and employ all sorts of contortions to accomplish what has become

A PRECIPITOUSLY INCREASING IDENTIFIABILITY

a subconscious objective. They relate to everyone in impressionistic, non-detail details: chatty but often in rapidly changing fervency. These people are highly suggestible and easily influenced. They commonly communicate in inappropriate ways, at malapropos moments, or about the most lurid and absurd subjects.

With more than six people we know personally who are mired in this behavior, and with American culture becoming increasingly narcissistic—understanding not only this word but also how to deal with the reality it represents will be enlightening. America has become a land of extremes, and mental conditions or the decomposition of social comportment are no reservations from this decline. Expanding our perception being able to articulate the meaning, weightiness, and consequence of histrionics—especially as it develops into disorder—is of great value.

Not to be negative and unrealistic—histrionic also has good meaning; its first definition means "theatrical." However, the second definition quickly outstrips any other use of the word.

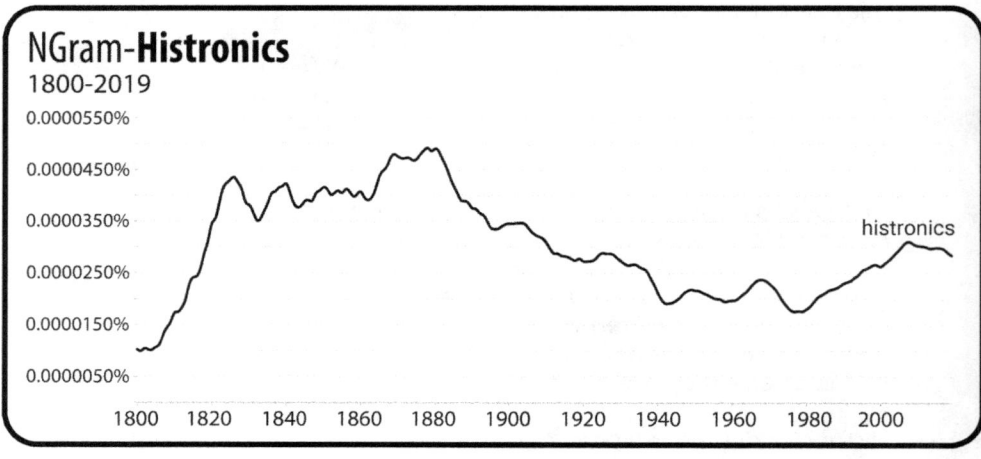

CAT AND MOUSE CHARACTERS
1998

`Gunning-Fog Index: 11.13`

For years, I grew up using a particular number of words. I cannot remember how, where, or from whom I got these words, but they are significant to me and the way I communicate. Idiomatic phrases and colloquialisms are also a big part of the way I interact verbally. It's all part of creative dialogue and well-seasoned conversation. I will find some of these words in media or entertainment in a few cases. To me, these mentions are confirmations of creativity.

In the mid-1990s, we as a family used to rent VHS movies—remember those? We'd go to the local Blockbuster and select a few movies every few weeks for cheap entertainment. In 1998, I finally watched *In the Line of Fire*. The thematic content was a little more adjusted to all the adults (foreign students) living in our home at that time. This movie was gritty and high-tension.

John Malkovich (who played Mitch Leary) is one of Hollywood's ultimate bad guys. In this film, he rocked his character's role as a former CIA assassin who went rogue and became a threat to the current president. Leary is eloquently cerebral. Thus, the interaction between him and Clint Eastwood's character (Frank Horrigan) is a cat-and-mouse game of touché comments and fatalistically provocative dialogue.

Leary stays incognito for most of the movie but is dubbed as Booth because he identifies with Horrigan in this manner in an early phone conversation. Leary also seems to personally identify with Booth because Leary notes Booth "had **panache**." This was the first time I could remember a source using this word, even though I'd used the word for years.

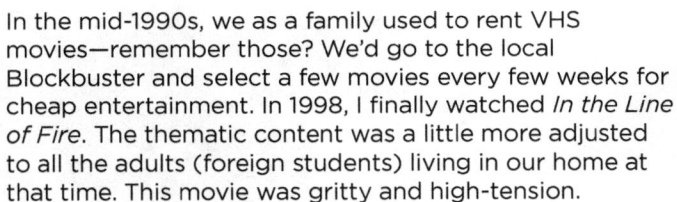

Panache is a noun from the Middle French pennache, which means "plume." In English, this word means

CAT AND MOUSE CHARACTERS

flamboyance in style or action, or flair, or verve. This word could mean "decorative armor or helmet." In most cases, this working definition is the usual application for most people. Panache is a decoration to the conversation. It is a word in ascension in occurrence.

I like this word because using it is a form of panache. However, in today's culture, flamboyance is almost a tenet of being anyone of note or noticeable from the mere masses. In such an environment, saying someone has a panache is like saying they are off-the-charts flamboyant. We could use panache in the adjectival sense to broaden our description or emphasis. Even though this word is on the upsurge, it still has tremendous impact and application.

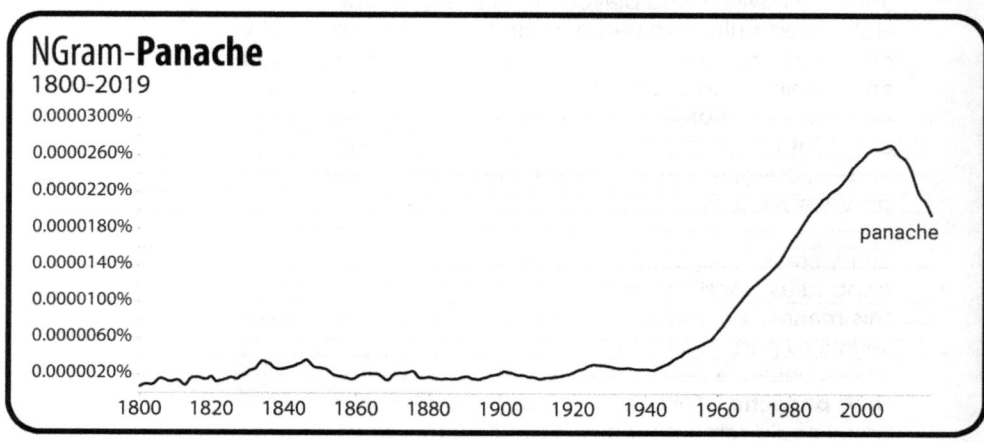

POP-CULTURE EDUCATION

Gunning-Fog Index: 11.97

I remember my aunt, Ruth (Geary) Mohar, my mom's youngest sibling, taking my sister and me to the Indian Hills Theater in Omaha, Nebraska. The screen was elliptic to provide for old Cinerama/Cinescope films, which were shot and shown through three devices. The movie we saw at this particular time was Star Wars, which was best seen on such screens.

Twenty-two years later (1999), my wife, Pam, and I took our kids to the next installment of the Star Wars saga, *Episode I*. This series of films were prequels, which, to this day, I don't understand why George Lucas went this way with the next set of films. The special effects and equipment depicted were superior to what was in the prior trilogy.

One detail in *Episode I* stuck out to me above all else. Ewan McGregor's character, a younger Obi-Wan Kenobi, speaks with the Gungan leader, Boss Nass, about the inherent connection between his society and the Naboo—a surface-dwelling culture. He uses the word symbiont to summate this connection.

Symbiosis took on the meaning of "mutualism" in Latin, referring to "two things benefiting from an interaction together." According to Merriam-Webster's dictionary, this word originated from German *symbiose* and Greek *symbiōsis*, which started out to mean "living together."

sĭm´bē-ō´sĭs

In practical terms, this word speaks to interdependent relationships that are required to exist. An example of a symbiotic relationship can be seen with clownfish and sea anemones. A clownfish's bright colors attract predatory animals, but the Anemones provide protection. Clownfish are unphased by the sting of anemones; however, most predators do not share this ace in the hole.

POP CULTURE EDUCATION

Pop culture does us a few favors in using uncommon words. I can't recall ever hearing this word in either form before or since *Star Wars, Episode I*. Yet, the word remains etched in my mind as a significant term that can be used occasionally without sounding pretentious. We might even look at the Ngram's chart below and see that since the year 2000, this term has maintained a high usage. Is not interesting that potentially a movie could have this effect?

Symbiotic/symbiosis can be an endearing term when discussing a mutually rewarding relationship in business dealings or negotiations. Our word choice provides flair and focus. If you use an uncommon word, the best kind of people will focus and take note. Frequently, context will key others into the meaning of your usage. A well-placed word speaks well for you and draws attention to the importance of what you are talking about.

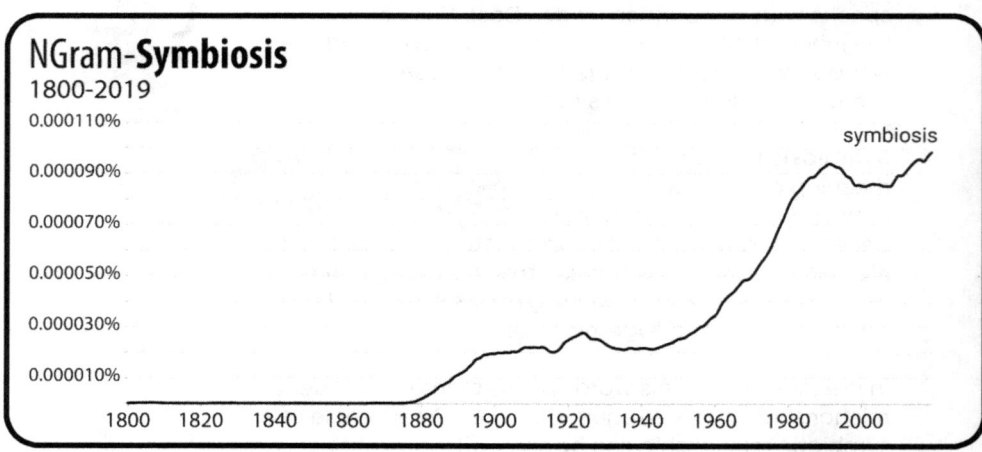

THE GREAT DIVERGENCE
1999

> Gunning-Fog Index: 11.41

From 1999–2000, our family took a giant divergent turn from the usual 2.1 kids, three-car garage, and job changes every seven years. We got it into our heads to migrate into missionary work. We'd been working here in the U.S. with international students on English proficiency through social interactions and offering a live-in situation to them.

The thought was to go overseas and use English competency as a means of interaction and friendship to eventually talk about God for those interested. My thought of missionary work was to do real-life interactions instead of "Here, listen to me recite my favorite gospel tract."

In order to go into this kind of work, it is traditionally thought that a person needs an organization to help support them in practical terms. We learned that this proposition is, in most cases, far afield from what it seems.

Part of the approach to mission work is informing those who support you financially. This apprising is dubiously called a "prayer letter" because it is more about getting people to give than telling people how to pray. Sending agencies encourage this approach because they get a cut of the money sent to missionaries.

Often, these *prayer letters* are like miniature newspapers. Missionaries try to be catchy in their efforts, playing up on this caricaturization of newspapers. We were no different. Our title was "The Price Promulgator." I don't know where I came across this word, **promulgate**. But this adage had a ring to it.

prŏm´ əl-gāt´,

The verb promulgate is not commonly used. I've only seen it in print four or five times since our missionary

THE GREAT DIVERGENCE

debacle. Promulgate has several meanings: "to declare as doctrine or fact, to make known, to press into action." Promulgate is another endowment from Latin. The Latin *promulgare* means "pro-forward and extract," as in an emulsion, which is where our English expression comes from. The purpose of an extract is to affect that into which it is poured.

We effectively promulgated our involvements through our newsletter. The only problem was the organization we worked with, YWAM (Youth With A Mission), was, as we found out, an industrial complex of missionary representation. It turned out to be more of a controlling and fleecing operation than anything else.

We discovered missionary work could be far more straightforward and effective without leach organizations. It was a harsh lesson; we invested in ourselves and lost that investment with the organization because we found their approach intolerable, if not cultic.

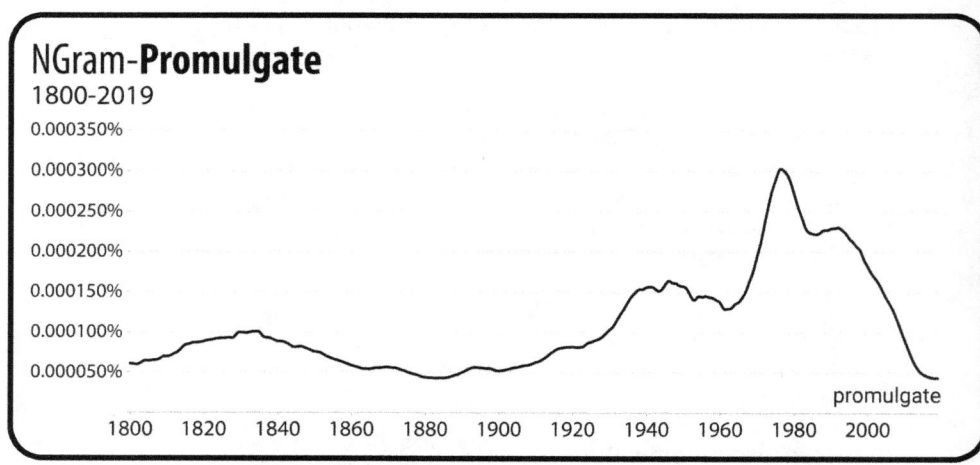

MANAGEMENT SHENANIGANS
2001

`Gunning-Fog Index: 12.53`

Virtually everywhere I've worked, I learned something other than the company's *modus operandi*, its policies, or computer and software systems. Going to work for an MRO company (**M**aintenance, **R**epair, and **O**perations) in 2001, Fastenal was no different. In a former association as a Purchasing Agent, and being Fastenal's former customer, I was a prime candidate to be this distributor's Asset Manager.

In principle, I was to access store operations pertaining to inventory. I'd check their records to see if any "funny business" was happening. Reports were submitted to a different management group instead of the divisional managers. However, I was the division manager's eyes and ears in the field.

My division manager, Scott Souter, was a character. Eventually, we traveled together through the division's 17 stores, where we glad-handed, congratulated, or he "lowered the boom." The division manager was a typical manager, tight on numbers and pragmatic in practice. He loved to laugh but had an edgy side.

We'd stay in the same hotel room as a part of his tight-fisted practices. He'd get bored before lights out. Sometimes, he'd pick up the phone and crank-call someone in the local town that night. Through general information and people's common emotional triggers, he'd whip up a heated exchange about "their" alleged "lousy cat" being in "his yard." This approach was a surefire equation to hilarious live entertainment, the likes of what you commonly find on YouTube these days.

One of this manager's favorite words related to when things were coming to an end in one store or another. I knew a critical moment was about to occur when he uttered, "That's the **coups de grâce**." This expression is another French contribution

kōo´ də gräs´

MANAGEMENT SHENANIGANS

to English. This noun means "the concluding blow," or more literally, "a stroke of grace," as in, to put something out of its misery. Its use is similar to a common colloquial expression: the final straw. As in almost all other interactions, this manager said, "coups de grâce" with a certain theatric flair—a deep, gravelly voice accompanied by an accent.

Modern English is quickly evolving into a language of expressions and colloquialisms. I feel there are good and bad sides to this trend. The good side is creative communication. The bad side is cliché and low-culture epiphenomena: a type of esoterica, if you will.

Why say a common, overused, and perhaps hickish expression like "the final straw" when you could use a more melodramatic descriptor? We are judged by our words. Why not make them engaging?

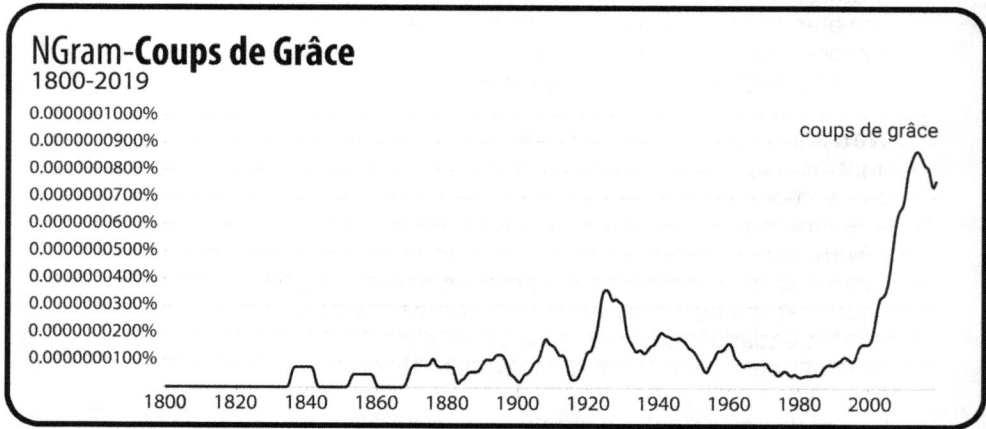

HOLLYWOOD'S ANTHROPOMORPHISM
2001

`Gunning-Fog Index: 10.59`

In 2001, my wife, Pam, and I took our kids to see the animated film, *Antz*. It was reasonably entertaining. It was one of those movies with several strata of content. It was as good a film on straight appearance as well as its allegorical import. As per usual, I never look at just the surface of anything.

It has been years since I wrote a review of this movie. I'd written it because the movie was more than it purported itself to be. Craftily woven between the lines, the themes, and obscure messages, its purpose blew my mind. I posted the review on my former blog. This post achieved the highest number of unique hits, over and against any other content on the entire blog site. The hits came from all over the world but mainly from .edu-type URLs. I want to think my work was convincing. However, the groundswell was more likely that the topic of this movie and classroom discussion spurred interest. My content merely provoked continuing dialogue.

Ostensibly, the film is an animated story of bugs who carry out an anthropomorphic life to illustrate injustice. This injustice plainly points at a society that keeps people in dead-end work while the rich rule over everyone with caprice, distance, and a sense of divine right, and, by the way, all this at the loss of the blue-collar types. The story paints anarchism as pure as the driven snow.

The film features an all-star cast of voices a mile long. The main character is an ant named Z, played by Woody Allen. While escaping from the oppressive ant colony, he goes on a walkabout in a park towards "the **monolith**," which is supposed to be a landmark towards freedom.

mŏn´ə-lĭth´

Monolith was still a new term to me in 2001. This word is partly understandable. I knew the prefix *"mono"* means

HOLLYWOOD'S ANTHROPOMORPHISM

"one." The *lith* part was a stumper. The direct forerunner of this word is found in French with merely an alternate spelling: *monolithe*. Initially, this word developed from the Greek word *monoliths*, meaning "a single stone." In English, not much has changed. This word could also mean a featureless building; figuratively, it could be an impersonal group, intractably singular, uniform, and immovable form.

This word is on the upswing in use. I like the symbolic use of this word: church is a monolith, politics is the same, and the kabbalah of educational and scientific establishment could be described as a monoliths. Anything institutional is a monolith that seeks to continue existing because it has for so long, not because it is necessary, productive, or correct.

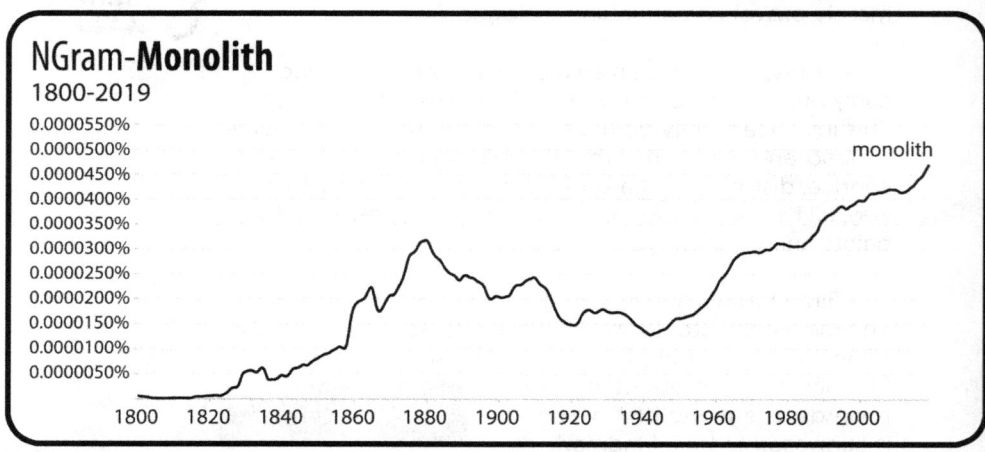

VERBAL BOMBAST AND PIANO LESSONS

— 2001-06 —

`Gunning-Fog Index: 10.77`

Over the years, our children became interested in some of our interests. From 2001 to 2006, our children, Genesis and Roman, did piano lessons. For a good bit of that time, we traveled to Lincoln from Omaha to maintain the same piano teacher. This provided a fair bit of windshield time.

I am interested in what people talk about politically. It's not that I take either side of the argument. Frankly, I find either side to be deceptions of false dichotomies. If you follow either party's thinking, both only lead to stalemate, collapse, and, finally, tyranny.

To stay informed, I listen to various talking heads from NPR liberals, to conservatives, and libertarian shows. On our way to and from piano lessons, I tuned into Dr. Michael Savage to get a shot of some political rage-a-mania. Savage is entertaining with his pompacious and guttural denunciations of everyone from Rush Limbaugh to President Bush. Here is a host, misconstrued as a card-carrying conservative, lambasting icons of the conservative cause. My kids came to enjoy his verbal bombast and hyper-salivated diatribes.

During any of Savage's shows, you'd be treated to Brooklyn-accented Yiddish words, which are an incisive education, unarticulated elsewhere in such concise form. Savage commonly used the word **shtick**. Variants of this word are *schtick* or *shtik*. This noun usually involves a performance bit or a repetitious behavior relied upon, i.e., a canned act.

This Yiddish term draws from High German *stücke*, meaning "a segment or piece." Or in Old English, *stycce* means "a lump, bit, or piece." How these tributaries came into Yiddish to mean "an act"—as in a vaudeville stunt or a continually repeated presentation, is perhaps the hocus pocus that makes colloquialism what it is.

VERBAL BOMBAST AND PIANO LESSONS

Shtick is descriptive of what politicians and media talking heads do. They whip out their stock speeches, complete with cliché anodyne and threadbare buzzwords, and they work crowds with this prepackaged tripe. And while Michael Savage's snarky appraisal is meant to focus you on the banal approach of political showmen (gender neutral), he tends to rely on his own shtick on a regular basis. There is nothing like a pot calling the kettle black.

The word shtick is apt for much of what we see and hear today. It identifies a common proneness, even outside of politics, where people roll out a decrepit act to both wow and dupe. A shtick can be anything from what the Three Stooges did for decades to what political candidates and people with agendas do today.

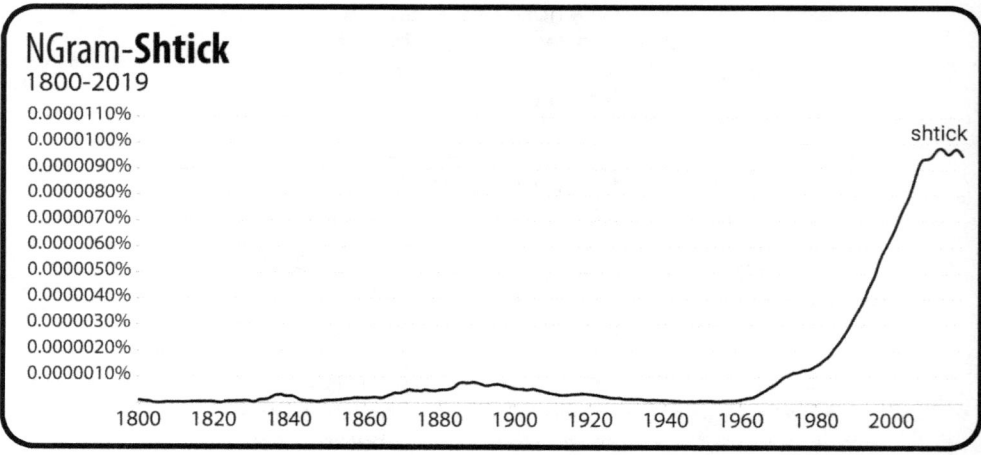

DOES YIDDISH ALWAYS INSULT?

`Gunning-Fog Index: 10.5`

It is excellent when you can be direct in another language and not be frowned upon or vilified for it in the present company. The years 2001 – 2006 were instructive years for me on many levels. As mentioned before, I used to dutifully take my children to music lessons.

Once a week, we'd make the long drive to Omaha and back. Part of our family's evening back and forth was Dr. Michael Savage on his former talk show. Some might cringe at this admission. However, I saw Savage, primarily as an entertainer. He is funnier than a rubber crutch.

As a Brooklyn Jew, Savage's demeanor and wit have always been an appendage of how he communicates. Jewish entertainers seem to enjoy putting out their cultural esoterica. Some do it to school audiences on the finer points of Yiddish, like Don Rickles in his Dec. 1, 2014 appearance on Jimmy Kimmel. Rickles rattles off some Yiddish lingo to set the stage to tell everybody what it means.

Savage doesn't put on airs. He just levels the Yiddish as if it were a pistol. If you want to understand the details, you'll look it up. In Savage's case, context and delivery gave me a pretty good idea about meaning. In any case, Savage, at one point (maybe every few days), used the word **schmendrick**, which was a word I had not heard before.

ʃmɛndrɪk

The word schmendrick is a noun that can be spelled a couple ways. An early, everyday public use of the term was in a 19th century operetta, *Schmendrick, or the Comical Wedding* by Abraham Goldfaden. This embodiment was based on a much older play from Romania where a character named *Schmendrik*, a clueless mama's boy, allegorically elucidates the reality of what some considered an "inappropriate" wedding.

DOES YIDDISH ALWAYS INSULT?

Schmendrik became a regular Yiddish word in part because of these two works.

This word initially had many uses. But today it means a stupid person, a nincompoop, and a fool. This word pulls no punches. Schmendrick is not an inescapably unkind word. It is an articulation of reality. This doesn't mean we use it without discretion.

Savage's use is talking about what people do that makes them foolish or stupid. We can admonish people not to be a schmendrick, which is not to say they are but instead to encourage them not to persist and be found undeniably foolish and stupid. I am not promoting a semantical game, just practical use of words—even ones that could be seen as negative.

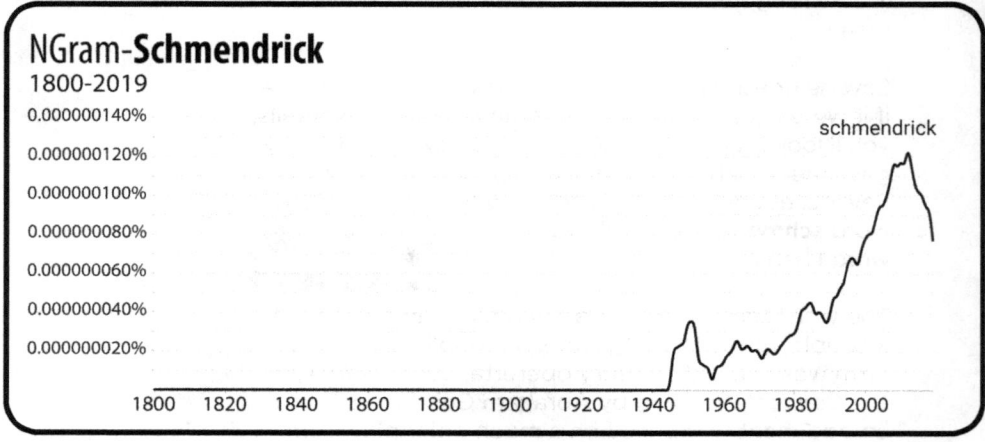

THE DIALECTICS OF ANTITHESIS

`Gunning-Fog Index: 11.55`

Over the years, a significant amount of my shaping came through the understanding and thinking of others, which I gained by reading. I've been extremely picky about my reading because I don't want to waste my time and mind on unnecessary material.

I see people on sites like Goodreads and LibraryThing who voraciously read 400-plus-page novels and fiction material. I just can't bring myself to read that type of content when there are so many practical things to learn that are real. I didn't discover reading, as an enjoyable activity, until I was in junior high. Since high school, very little of my reading has involved fiction material.

It's not that I am against fiction work; it's just that I've invested in non-fiction subject-type reading that, for me, is a retreat and special place. Even so, I have been choosy. One subject I enjoy considering is the relationship of the church community with the state. There are so many ideals in this regard, and I am intrigued with a very edgy perspective.

One of my favorite authors is Jacques Ellul. Having said as much, I totally disagree with him on a few specific areas: pacifism and Anarchism. I have read eight of his 40+ volumes and find his thinking clear, and his handling of complex subjects are reasonably easy to wrap one's head around. The vocabulary in his work is astounding as well. Take, for instance, **antithesis**. I ran across this word in *The Subversion of Christianity*, which I read in 2002.

ăn-tĭth´ĭ-sĭs

Antithesis is a wonderful word. It rolls off the tongue and effortlessly lays out an impactful meaning. This noun is from the late Latin era, meaning, in most basic terms, "opposition." This word has many uses relating to rhetorical applications and a philosophical concept called dialectic process in context antithesis.

THE DIALECTICS OF ANTITHESIS

Antithesis figures into dialectics, yet it has other meanings that have great application for writing and speaking. The adjectival form of the word *antithetical* means "against reason or practical reality." For example, it is antithetical to think that legalized drugs will lower crime rates. In simplistic terms, yes, there will not be as many convictions for drug dealing and trafficking. However, what about crimes caused by dependency and being under the influence? Antithesis can denote oppositional thinking, processes, work, or policies.

Thus, in practical terms, a word like antithesis notes a reality—passive, active, or oblivious—that can negatively affect people or progress. We can call attention to this fact by using this word instead of many other words to say the same thing.

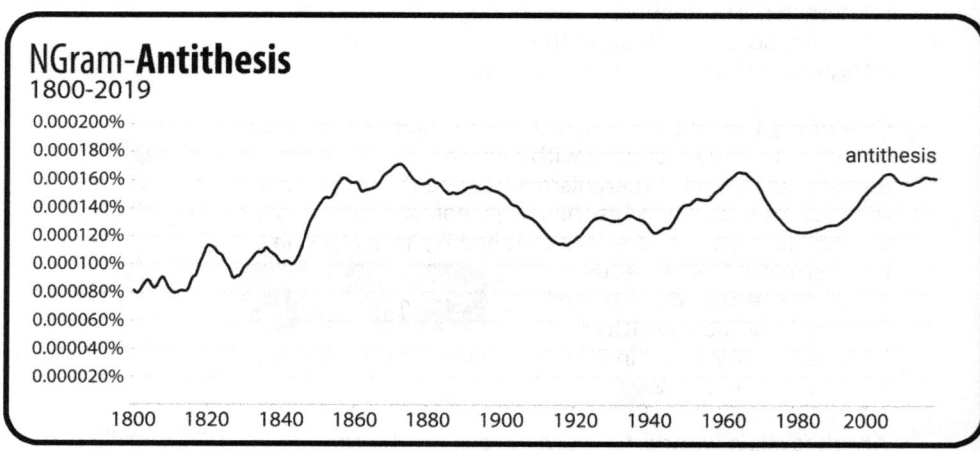

A GREAT RESPONSIBILITY

`Gunning-Fog Index: 13.67`

Of all the words I've come to use, the exact time or story when all terms entered my awareness or usage sometimes escapes me. I like to read general and ecclesiastical history and subject studies concerning the Bible. It is likely that within my reading interests is the place where the next word occurred for me.

For instance, reading historical accounts provides a broader understanding of a period, person, or event. Usually, those who are written about in such material colorfully articulate themselves. When historical accounts involve a particular person from an earlier era, frequently, if they are quoted, this opens up a more expansive vocabulary than what we hear today in everyday usage. If you listen to speeches by FDR, for instance, you'll notice he spoke in what seems to be another dialect. His vocabulary is almost foreign.

I liked the verb **abrogate** from the first time I read it because it is unusual. When I was researching excessively, I likely came across this term in 2003. Abrogate comes from the Latin *abrogātus*, broken down to *ab* and *rogāre*, meaning "to propose a law." In English, the word abrogate means "to nullify or abolish" or when legal or authoritative instruments or proclamations supersede, thus canceling a former standard or formality.

ăb´rə-gāt´

Speaking of religious ideas and concepts, this word takes on an interesting role in putting religious people to the test. Religious people must consider whether history, events, discoveries, or theology can abrogate what the Bible says or how it applies. Or is what the Bible says unabrogatable? And if so, what controls what nullifies the authority religious people give the Bible? These questions constantly conflict with a good portion of the religious crowd. Major historical events have been caused by these questions. The fall-down effect of either answer

A GREAT RESPONSIBILITY

has significant consequences in practical terms, to say nothing of the impact of mass opinion.

The term abrogate is currently connected to treaties, legal documents, laws, and agreements that can be contested because of abrogation or a legal interpretation that can establish abrogation. Abrogation was a significant bone of contention for the American Indian. One day, a treaty was in effect; the next day, something nullified what had been agreed upon just prior; whether a day or year had passed.

I like this word because it warns of potential caprice and lack of circumspection in removing boundaries, established order, or rules that govern and protect everyone. To abrogate anything carries a huge responsibility. I like the warning this word brings to religious discussions.

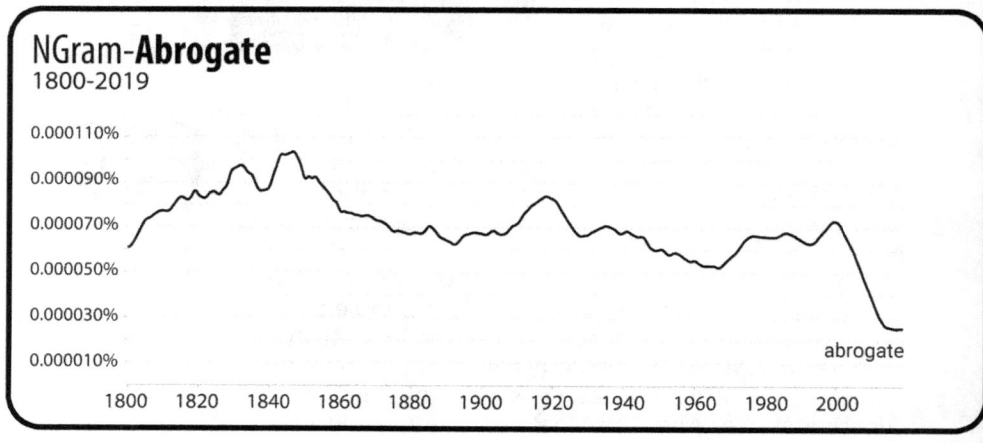

MOVIE VOCABULARY FOR $100

Gunning-Fog Index: 13.12

One of the problems in movies is the underlying agendas of those who make them. I've often wondered if the motion picture industry isn't, in part, a propagandist syndicate. Specific trends point in this direction, and tangible essentia seem to exclude that conclusion from not being logically drawn. In any case, I have a cabinet full of movies I enjoy. Some, though, are mere educational.

One film I watched that is one of those educational/agenda pieces was *Runaway Jury* (2003). The star-studded cast of John Cusack, Gene Hackman, and Dustin Hoffman make the film engrossing. The storyline is about a jury that has been fixed by a special interest group, unbeknownst to the rest of the jury, the lawyers, prosecution or defense, and even the judge.

Hackman is a jury consultant for the defense. His job is to control jury selection to favor the defense's client in a high-stakes, high-profile, and landmark case. Jury selection occurs, installing Cusack—the man with a private agenda. The film is a cat-and-mouse game between all the players: defense, prosecution, the judge, and the two collusionists manipulating the jury.

Once the trial begins, Hackman is clued in that someone else controls the process and outcome. As a pompous hustler, Hackman evokes all means possible to regain control from the "**dilettante**" informant who proposes to upset his end game.

dĭl´ĭ-tänt´

The noun dilettante is an Italian contribution to English. The Italian word *dilettare*, meaning "to delight," comes from the Latin *dilectare*, which has a similar meaning. In English, dilettante means "a peripheral admirer of anything," particularly the arts. An amateur, not educated or experienced in their area of interest, is barely a layman.

MOVIE VOCABULARY FOR $100

Dilettante can also be used as an adjective to describe, e.g., the dilettante businessman.

Dilettante is a powerful word that connotes a factor in today's culture. This word can be perceived as negative, yet it describes or states a reality of relativism within a society. Everybody wants to be seen as established, expert, or unchallengeable in a world of superlative and unbridled progression. Dilettante is a word of discernment, keenness, and evaluation.

Dilettante is also a word of judgment, best used in the past tense. When it is discovered that mediocrity, inexperience, and folly were the cause of a negative situation, *dilettante* or *dilettantism* is the perfect nomenclature of assessment. Labeling someone dilettante, in the present tense, as in Hackman's case, is arrogant conjecture and machoism in speech.

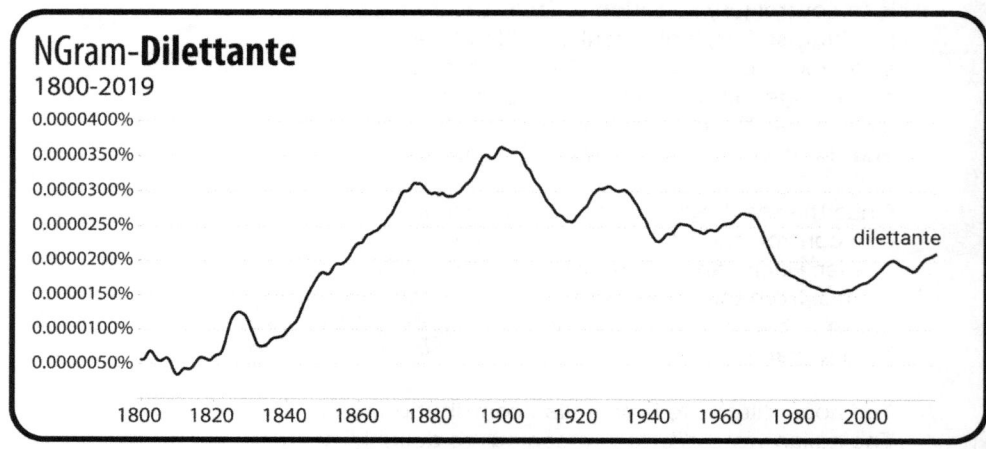

SON OF POSEIDON

`Gunning-Fog Index: 12.26`

The concept of this book is the recall of a specific word and an anecdotal story surrounding its mainstream into my vocabulary. However, there are some great words I have adopted over the years that, for the life of me, I cannot remember where I picked them up.

The word **procrustean** is one of my favorite words. The term has an air to it, yet it is practical and realistically useful for the average bear, such as myself. It is a funny-sounding word that would be distinct if you ever heard someone use it.

prō-krŭs´tē-ən

I might have found this word while researching in 2003. As an amateurish researcher, I commonly look at footnotes in books, check their sources, and do some "due diligence" concerning literary details, which can prove to be a rabbit trail I get sidetracked on. When reading a significant book, I usually bracket interesting passages, write notes in the margins, bend page corners to come back to, and finally record quotes in an Excel file. I am definitely an odd duck in this regard.

And so, too, when I go to write, I will consult a dictionary or thesaurus, grasping to ensure I understand the exact term I mean to use. I could spend significant time reading sources or searching several word definitions to find an even better fit. It is likely in this approach that I came upon the word procrustean.

This adjective came from Greek origins, Greek mythology specifically. The son of Poseidon was Procrustes (or Damastes), "a subduer" who invited passersby to stay with him. As they slept, Procrustes went to work on them to "fit them" to the bed he afforded them. He was known to amputate or stretch things to make someone fit.

SON OF POSEIDON

Procrustean means "producing acquiescence by heavy-handed means." A second definition speaks to a total disregard for individuality or circumstance, ostensibly for the goal of conformity. This word is so contemporary.

Who hasn't been forced by one means or another to conform to an arbitrary ideal? Who hasn't encountered an "enforcer" who uses heavy-handed means to achieve the appearance of unity? Such sounds like a couple churches I went to... I digress.

Procrustean is sure to reinforce, call attention to, or raise awareness for writing or speaking. Even with the high-minded notions of individuality today, there remains a brutish reality of forced compliance or—dare I mention political correctness. In such an environment, the word procrustean is apt for describing the era in which we live.

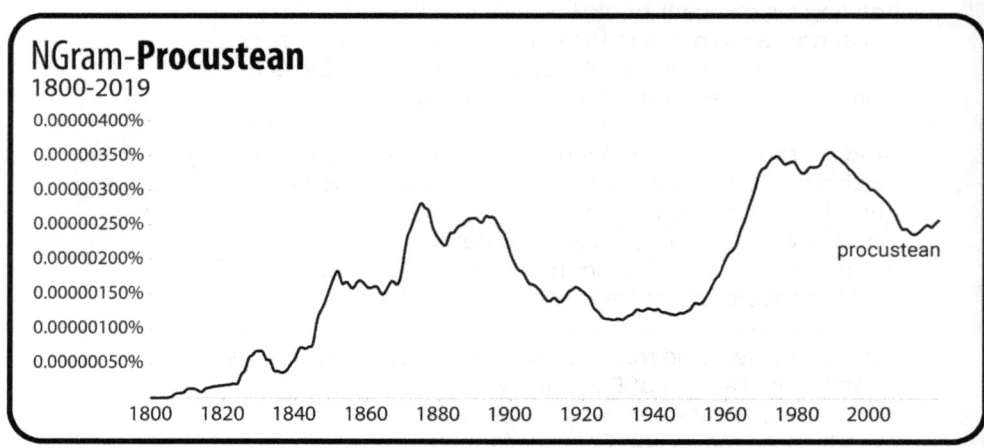

CONTINUING TO SOAK UP UNDERSTANDING

Gunning-Fog Index: 11.16

As I prepared for this book, I began to make lists. As a writer, I check a litany of words to ensure my application is reasonable and correct. I don't know if other writers do this or if they have extreme vocabularies from which they recite and plug and play in their sleep.

Life is learning, and I continue to soak up understanding as if I'd never learned anything. A few years ago, a friend, Joe Cavanaugh III, recommended I take the Gallup/Clifton Strengths Finder Test (now known as the CliftonStrengths assessment). Wow, what a revelation! The test results provide your top five strengths; the last of mine happens to be Learner. As I read the description and went through coaching, it was as if I were listening to God Himself. It was accurate: "People exceptionally talented in the learner theme have a great desire to learn and continuously improve." This explains my lifelong continuous observation of words' meanings and the ability to express myself in an ever-increasing exactitude.

I learned the word **tutelage** around 2003 because I used it in my first book, *The Diluted Church*, which was published in 2005. For several reasons, this word is one of my favorites as well.

tōot´l-ĭj´

Tutelage is a noun with several meanings. It can describe the teaching of a student, the act of guardianship or stewarding of a young person, or the influencing master over a protégé. This word comes from the Latin tutela, meaning "protection or guardian."

This word is undervalued. Current use is low level over a 200-year period. This word is a favorite of mine because it exposes the reality of our "education" in modern society outside of school. Whose tutelage are we under in the blogosphere and the social-media opinion-letting environment these days? How does political correctness bend our minds under its tutelage.

CONTINUING TO SOAK UP UNDERSTANDING

Many don't consider bias or an agenda behind the people they listen to, which informs the presuppositions upon which people think, act and talk. The positive side of tutelage is taking someone under your wing in mentoring. If someone learns from your tutelage and becomes splendid or winsome—everyone would benefit from this kind of tutelage.

Tutelage has a powerful implication. It speaks to the power of teaching and the administration of leaving an impression. Both can be good or bad. It is up to us to consider the character or lack thereof of what we are getting. All is not equal just because it exists.

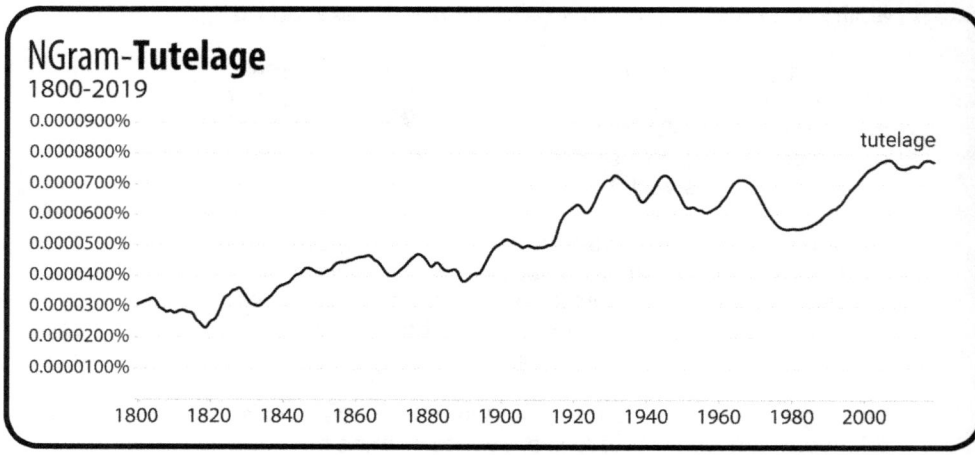

AN ALLEGORY THAT'D STOP A CLOCK

— 2003-04 —

`Gunning-Fog Index: 12.31`

Another type of reading I enjoy immensely is allegory. It is the most challenging form of writing, illustrating an author's mastery of the language. Over the years, I've read several allegories from high school (*Lord of the Flies, Animal Farm*) to religious works (*Pilgrim's Progress*).

For me, the enjoyment of this genre is the level of craft involved in writing them. Thinking through a work while reading it for its intended purpose is engrossing at the deepest level for me.

In 2003-2004, I was finishing my first book, *The Diluted Church*. I was also transitioning from traditional church—Sunday-go-to-meeting—to a more personal faith understood irrespective of creed or institutional conformity. At that time, I was also reading various books and nosing through the footnotes to see referenced sources.

In so doing, I came across the title of another allegory. The author was quite old. Yet, he has stellar notoriety in intelligentsia as being known for fathering modern education. The author's name is John Amos Comenius (1592-1670), known also by his Czech family name, Komensky.

He was the last bishop of a non-Catholic sect called the Unity of the Brethren (*Unitas Fratrum*, a.k.a. the Bohemian Brethren). After being forced out of Moravia, he lived and worked as a religious refugee in Sweden, Lithuania, Transylvania, England, the Netherlands, and Hungary.

His allegory's title was *The Labyrinth of the World -and- The Paradise of the Heart*. I accessed the book through Interlibrary and devoured it like an extravagant pastry. And while doing so, I was treated to a list of words and characters. One character was the word **Ubiquitous**. yōo-bĭk´wĭ-təs

AN ALLEGORY THAT'D STOP A CLOCK

Comenius's allegory was initially written in 1623 in Czech. It was translated widely. However, the earliest English version was in 1901, which plays into the use of ubiquitous in English. A secondary name was used for this same character in this version: Searchall.

Ubiquitous is an adjective that means "seeming to be everywhere." This word comes to English, in the mid-19th century, from the Latin word *ubiquitas*, meaning "everywhere." The word was reasonably obscure until recently. Today, ubiquitous outstrips a more well-known religious term: *omnipresent*, which means the same thing, by a margin of three-to-one according to a Google Ngram search.

I love the word ubiquitous, primarily how the English version of Comenius's work used it. This word has power and notoriety in it. It could be used in a myriad of ways in both speech and written forms. Interestingly enough, I have now seen the word ubiquitous in print four to five times in everyday publications since having adapted *Labyrinth* in 2020.

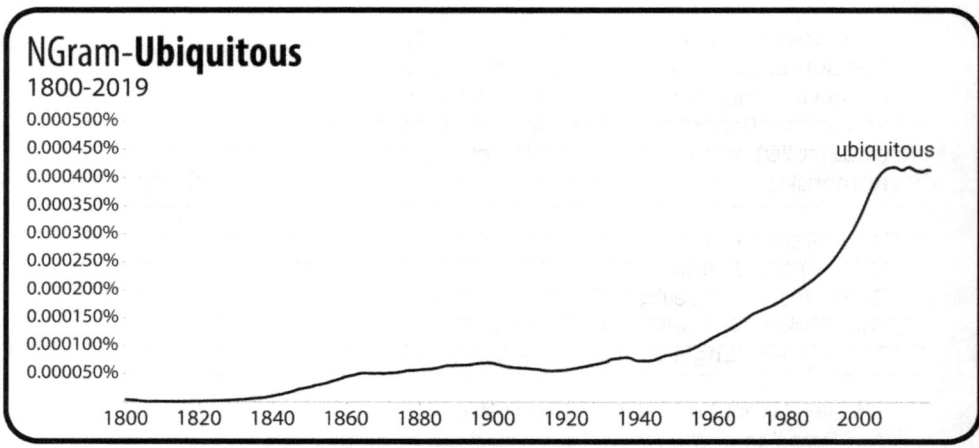

THE SUNNY SIDE OF FRENCH

Gunning-Fog Index: 10.2

Sunny Chsucta (pronounced Shuckta), was a co-worker of mine between 2003 and 2006. She was the first person to give me pause regarding whether vocabulary is primarily provincial or more education-based: the old nature versus nurture conundrum. I've never found any research that would prove one over the other.

Sunny was a little older than I, which may have something to do with her specific vocabulary. She was also an avid reader. So, it is hard to say what was more precipitous to her command of language.

Sunny was a Purchasing Agent, as was I. One part of that job is controlling inventory. Production people want an endless supply at their fingertips, while the purchasing people want low inventory counts that consistently are being expended. Moving stock is far more efficient than piling warehouses from floor to ceiling. The battle between the two extremes continues in almost any manufacturing or supply-chain-supported concern.

I remember Sunny's reaction to Production controlling inventory numbers. Her readied expression was they'd have "**carte blanche**," which was highly negative in her purview. We Purchasing Agents are jittery about losing control of inventory. We live and die on stock levels, availability, turns of inventory, and efficiency. We have another term that is an axiom of our profession: *just in time*, which expresses our objective: to have what just is needed, when it is needed.

kärt bläNsh´

The French noun *carte blanche* has an air of sophistication to it. In the French, this word means "blank document," as in an open checkbook. This exact word in English is almost exclusively idiomatic, meaning full discretionary power or the allowance to do as one chooses without stipulation.

THE SUNNY SIDE OF FRENCH

For a Purchasing Agent, giving anyone in the company carte blanche privileges is like jumping off a cliff into the open air with no parachute or safety harness.

Since carte blanche is an expression with endless application, I have used this word many times since Sunny brought it to my attention. The term is unpretentious. Context often tells its meaning to any would-be listeners.

I was 40-something before I remembered ever hearing this word. I like *carte blanche* because of its novelty and uncommonness. It demands to be heard and understood, which is compelling. *Carte blanche* is a word one doesn't have to use but is not superlatively obnoxious when employed. It is one of those fun words you can throw around in many circumstances. There isn't a gotcha factor to it. People won't turn their noses because you've "big-timed" them with a $500 word for which they haven't a clue.

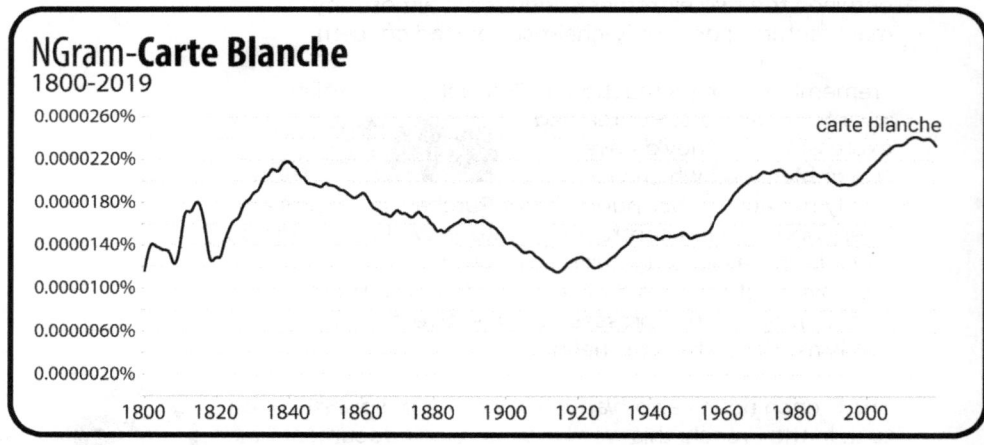

REALITY THAT DOESN'T HAVE TO BE

Gunning-Fog Index: 14.37

Reading Jacques Ellul's work between 2003 and 2009 provided me several good vocabulary words and many pungent and pithy quotes. In my thinking, Ellul's work deals extensively with one topic that remains unknown to the broadest number of people: **dialectics**.

dīə´lektik

Perhaps it is a human naivety to imagine that we won't be, or are not, affected by realities we cannot articulate. Another thing I find astounding is the effort to remain uneducated about what impacts us. The laissez-faire attitude of a so-called enlightened and educated society concerning a word Ellul introduced me to is astounding. Dialectics is not a word unfamiliar in particular crevices of educational officialdom. The problem is its lack of understanding among ordinary people.

Dialectic(s) is a noun arriving in modern English with a litany of endowments: Middle English *dialetik*; Anglo-French *dialetiqe*; Latin *dialectica*; and Greek *dialektikē*. The word has quite a number of applications. It can represent Socratic approaches to detecting false logic. It can migrate into a discussion of the process of change in lyceum social development or degeneration. Dialectic notes tension between opposites that produces a diversion from the status quo.

To be sure, dialectics is fascinating, particularly in that it affects billions of people even though many are unaware. My interest relates to change in which the process and/or tensions between opposites are corollary.

Dialectics is no stranger to social engineers and cultural radicals going back more than a century. The dialectic process states that change (cultural, political, and mores) can be achieved through dialectics. Dialectics is where a thesis (an accepted idea or conclusion) is challenged by an antithesis. The product is synthesis, which is change.

REALITY THAT DOESN'T HAVE TO BE

The synthesis becomes the new reality. As an example, many think Democracy is the be-all-end-all destination. However, in the 20th century, Marxism challenged the viability of Democracy in the hearts of the masses, which fostered a revolution. The 21st century saw the rising specter of socialistic democracy, which is the synthesis between the two.

To the young, the façade of economic equality sounds inviting. Yet, against the background of history, this option has never brought about anything but repression, corruption, reductionism, and ultimately economic collapse.

As we talk, write, and speak, we can mix this term into our contributions and educate people on this undetected reality. We can go on the offensive, uncloaking this common negative. We should note this reality wherever we find it so that it is not the unseen force it is commonly considered to be.

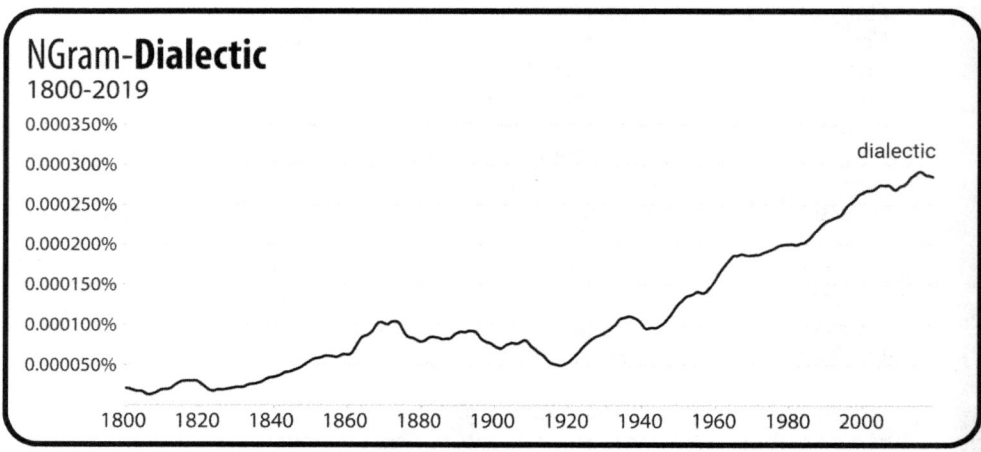

A DRESSED-UP CONUNDRUM

`Gunning-Fog Index: 12.51`

Many words have come into my employ for which I cannot account for my introduction to them. Reading proves to be a rich ground from which to harvest a palatial means of communicating. As a conversationalist and music lover, words also make their entry to my use. Virtually anywhere one can listen to what is said and they can be enriched.

As I've reflected upon this conundrum of where I might have happened upon the word **accouterment**, I haven't even found recent occurrences as the fulcrum around which to wrap my familiarization in an anecdotal story. This word is not exactly a word you run across in the local bar or even in a session of Congress. However, when I prepared the list, and went to write this book, I would use to write this book, accouterment was one of the first words to come to mind. How strange! I would estimate my awareness around 2004 during a period of heavy research.

ə-kōo′trə-mənt

The noun accouterment is illustrative of outfitting, accessories, and/or equipment necessary to carry out a job or that identifies and differentiates one reality from another. For example, a captain has different accouterments on his uniform than a private. One can identify one rank from the other because of the components of dress and uniform between the two. Accoutrement originates from the French word *accoutrer* or *accouter*, meaning "to clothe or equip." It appeared in the 16th century.

Accoutrement's other definition deals with strictly equipping a device, machine, or person in a specific job. Vacuums or cars come equipped in a particular fashion, perhaps for functionality. The shop vacuum could be outfitted for a specific job or market that, without these details, would make the tool inoperable. My Mini Cooper could have been a supercharged, sports version or just

A DRESSED-UP CONUNDRUM

appeared differently with do-dads (accouterments). A firefighter has certain accouterments to do his/her job.

Accouterment is a novel word is a novel word. As a writer and speaker, I like it because it has pizzazz! Why use dull and common words when there are ways to communicate the same thing and more with exuberance and creativity. This word can be used in many ways, both in literal meaning or metaphorical usage.

This word could be used somewhat interchangeably with a word we looked at earlier: *appliqué*. The latter refers more to ornamentation or even unnecessary exterior equipping. However, they have similar meanings, referring to things installed or put on. In the case of accouterments, they are more necessary to the form, fit, and function of something than appliqué might infer.

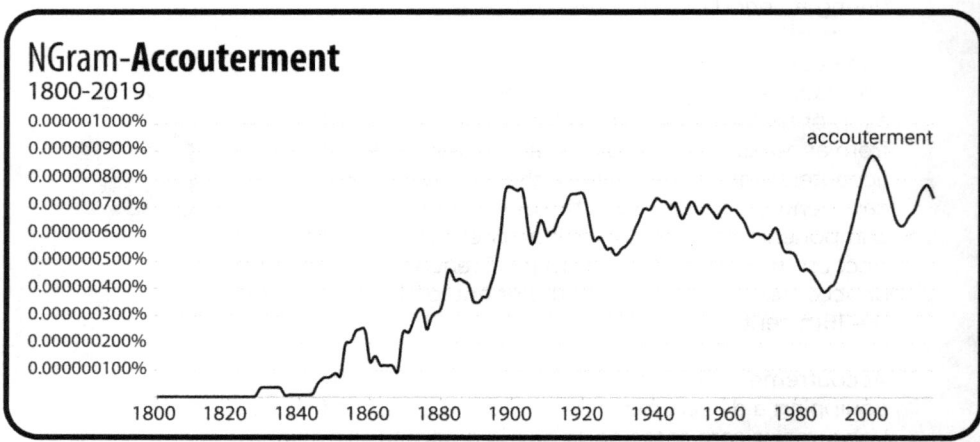

THE EFFUSIVENESS OF ARRANGED WORDS
2004

`Gunning-Fog Index: 10.47`

Many know the story of Morrie Schwartz, more known through the book and movie *Tuesdays with Morrie*. Our family discovered this story in 2004. This heartwarming memoir, first recorded by Mitch Albom, depicts a carefree but brilliant sociology professor whose positive outlook on life was effusive and gripping.

One term Schwartz used was **aphorism**. This noun arrived in the English lexicon through French 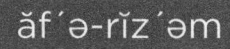 *aphorisme*, which came from the Greek *aphorismos*, which means "a decree or blessing." Simply put, aphorism is a succinct truism or axiomatic principle by which to live or hold oneself to.

Morrie's story was replete with aphorisms: learn to forgive yourselves and others, accept the past as the past without denying it or discarding it, or once you learn how to die, you learn to live. These are beautiful dictums to consider.

Morrie's aphorisms got me to think about what I live by. We live by what we believe, not what we tell others and ourselves all the time.

Some of my aphorisms are:
1. Believing is not a station or objective; it is the point from which we begin to do
2. You live what you really believe; the rest of what you talk about religiously is fecal matter
3. One who refuses to change their opinion proves they love themselves more than they love truth
4. Never argue with an idiot; they will drag you down to their level and beat you with experience

My aphorisms are not winsome like Morrie's. Even so, they are words I live by and measure myself as I consider what others have to offer. As a thinker, I continually reconsider the subtleties that pave what governs cultural behavior

THE EFFUSIVENESS OF ARRANGED WORDS

and ideals that go virtually unnoticed. Aphorisms abound and add to our lives with encouragement, direction, caution, and a level of enlightenment.

Comedy, for me, is a balancing force and the substrate from which a different type of critical thinking arises. Aside from what comes out of their mouths, some comedians are just funny people. Their innate funniness is beyond a stage persona or their trademark. Jonathan Winters and Larry the Cable Guy are two people like this. A guy like George Carlin, his funniness was about getting you to think—if you can get past his crassness.

I have been served notice of being "too serious." And to this dark and seemingly cheerless world in which others think I live, humor and comedy crepuscularly shine into my awareness, providing yet another source of minutia that I can think and laugh about.

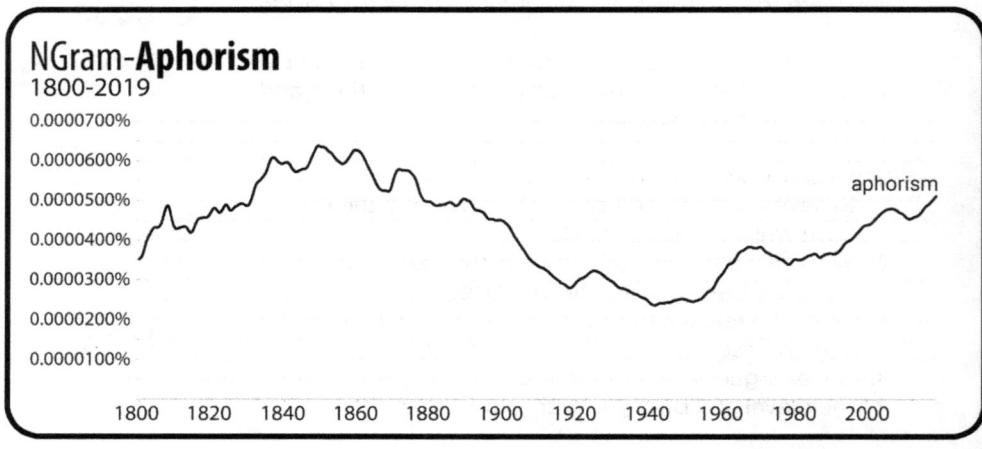

YIDDISH FOR THE MOUTHS OF GOYIM

`Gunning-Fog Index: 12.91`

The contributions of other languages to English are significant and beyond my initial imagination. I started looking at the words I wanted for this anthology and couldn't believe the background and history behind them. Yiddish is just one of likely a hundred contributors.

Scholars say Yiddish started to develop in the 12th century in conjunction with the influx of Jewish migration into central Europe. Some scholars say Yiddish combines German, Aramaic, and ancient Hebrew. Others say it is much older than the 12th century and more based on an infusion of Eurasian languages into Hebrew than German.

Today, Yiddish, for non-Jews, seems more like a collection of idiomatic phrases and colloquialisms than a full-blown language. Yiddish words have a particular distinctiveness. Perhaps it is the unmistakable continental flavor or the punctuative delivery typical in their use. I grew up around many Jewish people. My paternal grandfather, Clayton Price, was a lifelong upholsterer. He once quipped that we (our family) are Jewish by trade. Most of the people we sold to and the textile people we bought from were Jewish, and they were like family. However, I don't recall hearing Yiddish thrown around in these connections. Even so, there are many Yiddish expressions in pop culture and media that I have picked up.

The Oceans movies of the past decade were based on a remake of the Rat Pack's movie Ocean's 11 from 1960. The modern version became a popular series (12 and 13) with an ongoing storyline, achieving significant success. The all-star cast likely had much to do with it, in addition to an audience that loves a continuing tale. One of the characters, Reuben Tishkoff, a washed-up con artist played by Elliott Gould, let go with one of those Yiddish expressions in *Ocean's 12* (2004): **mishigas**.

mĭsh´ə-gäs´

YIDDISH FOR THE MOUTHS OF GOYIM

Mishigas or *meshugas* or *meshaga*, depending on the source you check, comes from the Hebrew word *měshuggā'*, meaning "lunatic or crazy." In this instance, Gould's character used this expression to convey the craziness or predicament that Brad Pitt and George Clooney's characters will drum up.

In the mouth of a non-Jew, terms like mishigas express an air of sophistication. It is not such a flashy term one would be dismissed for pretentiousness. Yet, mishigas illustrates a level of cosmopolitanism for including what is, most times, a culturally provincial word into non-provincial dialogue. Using this word is a nod to Jewish contributions to the texture and substance of society and language.

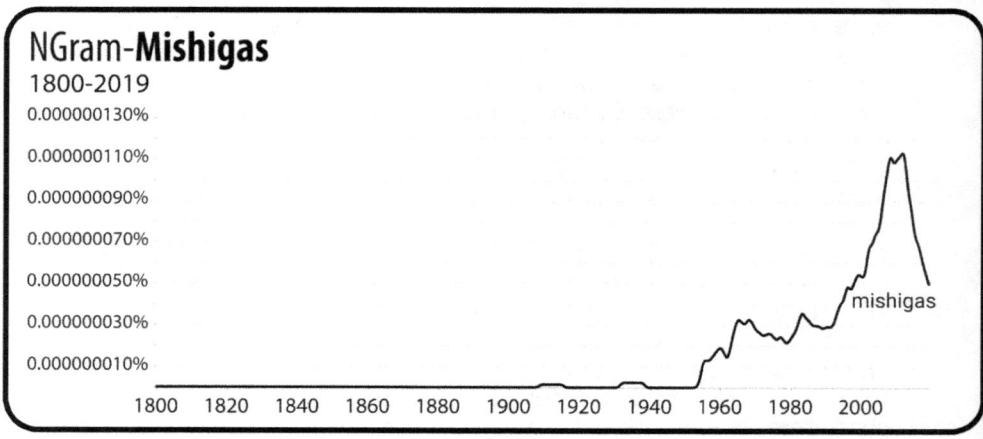

MUSIC ISN'T JUST MUSIC

`Gunning-Fog Index: 9.95`

Since I was young, I've been immersed in music. I remember listening to LPs for hours. My family had tons of music: obscure stuff like Horst Jankowski's all the way to classical standards.

Still, my admiration for music grew. In 2004, I went to the public library and picked up what I considered *an uncommon artist*. I found out Pete Seeger was just unknown to me at that point. The CD, *A Link in the Chain*, is a double-disc compilation of Seeger's folk music—a genre I've come to enjoy. Part of Seeger's performance is commentary, which broadens how he relates to an audience. While giving the backstory to the song "Guantanamera," he used the word **polemics**.

pə-lĕmʹĭks

I had no idea about this word, though context provided a few clues. The root word is, of course, pole, as in a place to stand or point at which to decide. The suffix *"ics"* is a Greek infusion, referring to science or "study of." Thus, polemics is not the study of rhetoric as much as how to use argumentation to confront social evils. This word has several variations: *polemic* (noun), descriptive of what someone is doing; *polemicist* (noun), being one who involves themselves in polemics; and *polemical* (adj.), being illustrative of having the quality of...

Polemics and their variants are descriptive of our world, even though the descriptive word is peculiar. Not a day goes by when we do not see someone making a case for righting some wrong or appealing to the masses to change some erring but longstanding approach.

To understand this word may seem odd. However, the good of it is who I learned it from—a man who is one of our time's greatest polemicists. In 2011, I was in New York State for business. My travel went over the weekend. So,

MUSIC ISN'T JUST MUSIC

on a trek from Nescopeck, PA, to Rouses Point, NY, I drove out of the way 90 miles to see if I could meet Pete Seeger in person.

After some inquiries around Beacon, NY, I parked in the foothills south of town. Seeger puttered between the house and garage with the days' compostables. I was greeted by a gruff, "Who are you?" only to answer that I was a fan from Omaha. Seeger immediately lamented, "Oh, I forget myself." Then, he invited me in for a 45-minute visit. It wasn't 10 minutes before Seeger retrieved a banjo off the wall to pluck through his songbook as we talked. The word polemics now has a personal attachment to it.

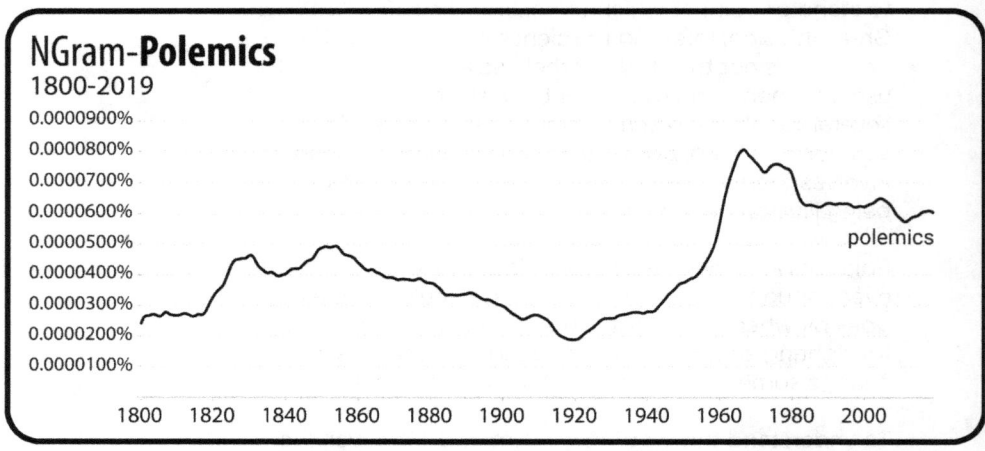

BEAT A DIFFERENT DRUM

Gunning-Fog Index: 10.94

One of the primary jobs I've worked in over the years—perhaps what you could call a career—has been Purchasing in a manufacturing environment. Yet, in a volatile economy, one has to be flexible and crafty to sustain employment. Both the economic volatility and changes in jobs to maintain an income presented me with some unexpected benefits.

From 2003 to 2006, I worked in Lincoln, Nebraska, for a Japanese manufacturing company after a work outage. At this new employer, I was treated to a host of unique individuals who would otherwise be fodder for a list of short stories if I were of the mind to do character sketches. One particular person, Sunny Chsucta—who we met earlier. She sat next to me in the Purchasing Department. She was the veteran Purchasing Agent at this firm. She also was a voracious reader, particularly of science fiction. She was endued with a colorful vocabulary.

Things came up missing during her routine, or perhaps she misplaced stuff... She'd mutter, "Who **absconded** with" whatever it was. I do not recall ever hearing that word before. At first, I didn't take much note of it. But as is my impulse, once some word seizes me, I am duty-bound to find out what it means.

ăb-skŏnd´

I've found this word to be an excellent addition to my regular use because it is unusual. This term is a verb of Latin origin. *"A"* is sometimes a prefix meaning "not" or "to be without," such as in *amoral* or *atypical*. This is a Greek contribution to English. However, in *abscond*, *"ab"* is also like a prefix, which is the Latin form of the same thing. But what about the second syllable? Modern dictionaries do not have an entry.

One source notes *condite*[1] as the contributor to the word abscond, which means "pickle or embalm." There are few

BEAT A DIFFERENT DRUM

other standard references on how this latter word relates to abscond. The proper meaning of abscond "is to take or make disappear so as not to be detected." Maybe "preserving" the stealth and removal of an item could be the connection.

In any case, the word abscond has been used in my vocabulary since 2005 when Sunny Chsucta repeatedly bounced this word to my awareness. I find it a great way to replace *stole*, *thieved*, or the slang term *lifted*. Synonyms give listeners a reason to listen because you're not beating the same drum as everyone else.

[1]Webster's Third International Unabridged Dictionary

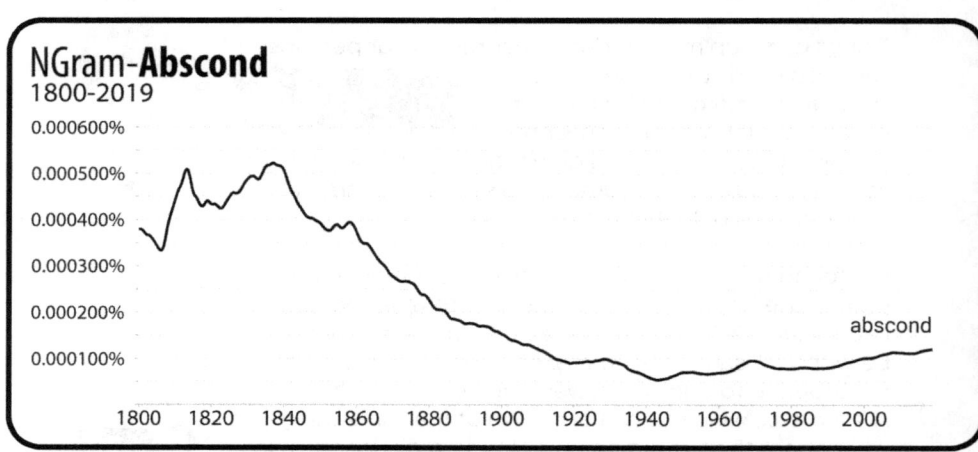

SUPPLEMENTARY SUPPORT

`Gunning-Fog Index: 11.57`

There are some words I learned over the years. I cannot recall a particular anecdotal story about where I made their introduction... Even so, there is a story. As a reader and writer, there is sometimes a seamless conveyance between what is read and heard at one point that becomes used at another.

If that isn't the case here, I bet there is an unconsciousness in the acquisition of content, concepts, and words used to communicate them that we pick up some reticular way. This might be a vestige of our youth where we soak up everything without being able to relate where we took possession, or it might be an ongoing reality.

As I write, words come across my mental ticker. I will commonly consult a source to check and see if the word is proper or figuratively applicable to my intended use. I have found this practice to save embarrassment, which is one reason I use it. On numerous occasions, I've cracked open my second edition of the American Heritage Dictionary, my favorite written source. The number of times when I'm "on the money" with my understanding of a word is staggering. I'm not bragging, this is to say I am blown away.

How does this happen? Is this reality some sixth sense, a complexity of the human brain that gathers content and understanding without conscious observation? Our brains and psyche are far more capable than we understand.

Most of my written work circles the relationship between church and state, an esoteric field in some quarters and a constant battleground in others. It is within this context that the word **ancillary** jumped into my awareness. I can't think of anything I ever wrote or thought before 2005 where I saw this word used. Ancillary is not a common word, though it may be for the "long hairs" of convention.

ăn´sə-lĕr´ē

SUPPLEMENTARY SUPPORT

This adjective is a Latin contribution from *ancillor*, which means "handmaiden, one who helps." And so, it is with the English adaptation of the word ancillary. It is defined as what is helpful or supportive but not primary. We could use the word *auxiliary* or *supplementary*.

Since using the word in my first book, *The Diluted Church*, I've seen it in print a couple of times, and I use it regularly. My son once asked why I use "complicated words," thinking ancillary is one of them. It's simple: *ancillary* replaces the use of several words to say the same thing, which allows for concise talk. Thus, I can be a man of fewer words.

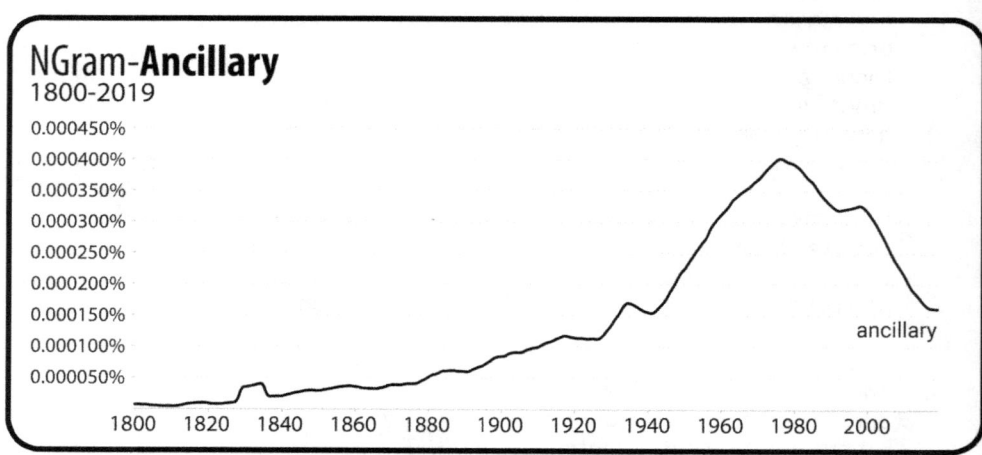

VERBAL FLAMBOYANCE

> Gunning-Fog Index: 9.14

Whenever I hear an unusual word used, my interest is piqued. I could be reading or listening to a medium wherein a word catches my attention. An author I read, Peter Lord, noted that our brain features what is known as the Reticular Activating System (RAS). It's a design of our brain that allows us to focus on something we need to hear above all else or tune out other things deemed unimportant. My RAS must be tuned to words.

As I am wont to do, if you haven't gathered already, I regularly take in movies. One of my favorites of all time is *Oh Brother, Where Art Thou?*, which I saw in 2005. With few exceptions, this film is powerfully crafted on virtually every level. It is well written in the era's local color and the Deep South's locale during the Great Depression.

George Clooney's character, Everett McGill, is in jail for illegally practicing law. He is obsessed not so much with regaining his freedom as he is about preventing his wife from moving on with another suitor. He escapes from a chain gang with two other inmates. He also seems preoccupied with his hair. He describes himself as a Dapper Dan (Deluxe Pomade) man, relating to the pomade he used to slick back his mop. Throughout the trio's travels, McGill takes risks to acquire and use Dapper Dan.

In this side story, concerning hair care products, McGill uses the term **coiffure**, which is not to be confused with *coiffeur*. The former noun is a direct migration from French into English, meaning a person's hairdo, usually fancy. It is unclear why this word came into English as it does not infer nor imply something no other English word communicates.

kwä-fûr´

This word seems totally impractical. However, this is not the case. One day, I had one of those bad hair days. My

VERBAL FLAMBOYANCE

hair looked like an explosion in a haystack. I complained to a coworker about it, kiddingly referring to my "do" as a bouffant—a flamboyant woman's hairstyle from the 1960s. The coworker suggested I get a cut, to which I quipped that I didn't think that was the problem with my coiffure. She smiled wryly at the term, which was the point for which I used it.

Words can be novelties that enrich our ability to entertain, joke, or humor ourselves and others. This word is one I would use in the vein of novelty. My associate chuckled at my response, and laughter is always good medicine.

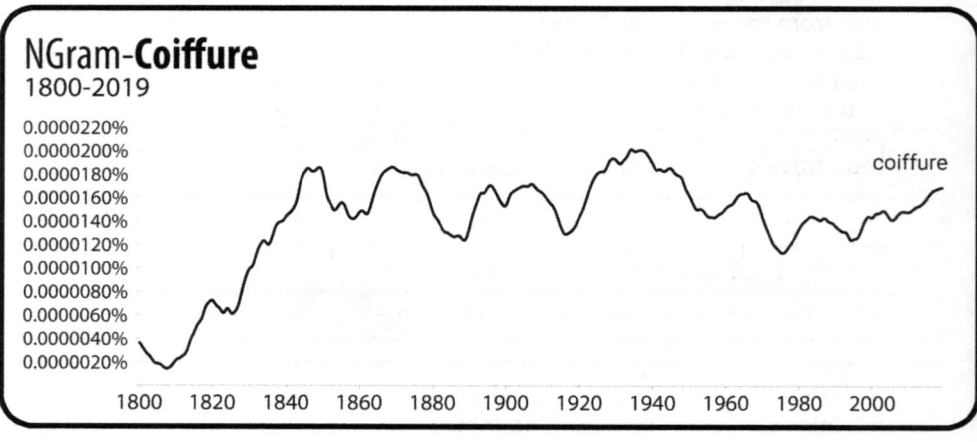

UNSEEN BLINDNESS

`Gunning-Fog Index: 13.34`

In 2005, I published my first book, *The Diluted Church*. In the months following, varying levels of interest in it surfaced, both negative and positive. At one point, I got an unexpected invitation to share the book at a local extension class of Doane University held in Lincoln, Nebraska.

Professor Don Dickerson, a Jesuit priest, invited me to present the perspective behind my book in his class, Religion in American Life. In this class, students were exposed to various views of religion to understand what is available. Most had been exposed to a single view that prejudiced them against all others. This class was not about right or wrong from any perspective but just informational.

In the regular class time, where I was to present, Professor Dickerson first gave his regular content, which facilitated students to absorb a variety of understandings without feeling they were abandoning their own or being put upon to consider other views. During this particular period, Dickerson presented a cautionary note for all people. He used the term **scotoma** as the conceptual mandrel to wrap his point around.

skə-tō´mə

Scotoma is a noun mainly known and applied in the medical and scientific fields. It is a general term often modified by specific adjectives relating to the description of effect or limitation. Scotoma is a Latin and Greek contribution to English. The Greek *skotōmat-skotōma* relates to "darkening" or "to darken."

Medically, this word relates to diminished vision, i.e., blind spots. It's an area in our vision where there is no sight. Our brain provides a "fill" in this area, but we can utterly miss significant details that appear in these areas of our vision and not realize it.

UNSEEN BLINDNESS

As Professor Dickerson noted, Scotomas can relate to mental or logical blindness because of the views we bring to a discussion or situation. These can occur in prejudices, religious beliefs, values, or subjectively adopted notions to which we attach ourselves. In this sense, scotoma is figurative yet just as real as a visional blind spot.

Scotoma isn't precisely the type of word to toss into the soup of everyday dialogue unless you are a professor, physician, or ophthalmologist. However, the concept Professor Dickerson noted is one to keep in mind. Vocabulary can be a form of awareness as much as something we use. Understanding is as much a use of a word as being able to relate it in verbal interaction.

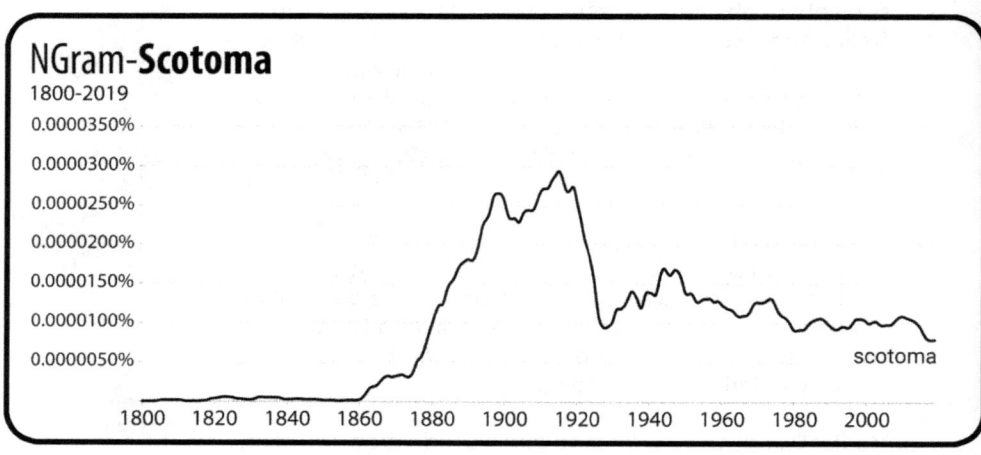

OLD-WORLD MYSTIQUE

> Gunning-Fog Index: 11.8

Many words in English have fallen out of use. It's not because the words are archaic. Perhaps word use falls off because linguistic vogue has moved in a different direction. Or maybe vocabulary shrinks in one respect while expanding in other areas. English is by no means imploding. However, usage is evolving rapidly.

Over the years, and because of my ruts in reading and thinking—history, politics, philosophy, and the like—I've run across an enormous array of words. I've also noticed that works from the first half of the 20th century, which used to be commonplace in style or articulation, are now considered collegiate or scholarly. This is amazing to me. This era of writing is much different than today's accepted standards and ideals.

In the 2010 version of *True Grit*, the dialogue is much different than what we use today. Aside from the formalistic style, word usage, and lack of conjunctions... the dialogue is linguistically more robust and rhythmic and contains a richer vocabulary. There is something captivating about dialogue from earlier eras. *Downton Abbey*, the Masterpiece Theater television drama, is a runaway success. I can't help but think much of its mystique circles around the character interaction, mainly how they speak: the vocabulary and the interplay it fosters.

Some of those "old words" are fun and practical even in our own day. Take, for instance, **trumpery**. It is a determination that something is foolish, fake, or poppycock. This noun originates from Middle English and Old French. The French contributory is *tromperie*, meaning "trickery." For the past 200 years, this word has meant "foolishness" or "lack of substance."

trŭm´pə-rē

According to usages in documents on record, between 1840, when trumpery peaked, compared to 1999, this word suffered a reduction of 95 percent. Yet, the application

OLD-WORLD MYSTIQUE

is not outdated. There are more items today that are foolhardy and insubstantial than in 1840. Therefore, trumpery is just as applicable today as ever.

I discovered the word trumpery in 2005 while reading about John Adams. He was quoted, "Where do we find a precept in the Bible for Creeds, Confessions, Doctrines and Oaths, and whole carloads of other trumpery that we find religion encumbered with these days?"

I like this word, and I drop it in everyday interactions. It is unexpected but not obtuse nor pretentious. While trumpery is a bit archaic, it still has a distinct meaning. Therefore, its use emphasizes whatever is being referred to in a more significant way.

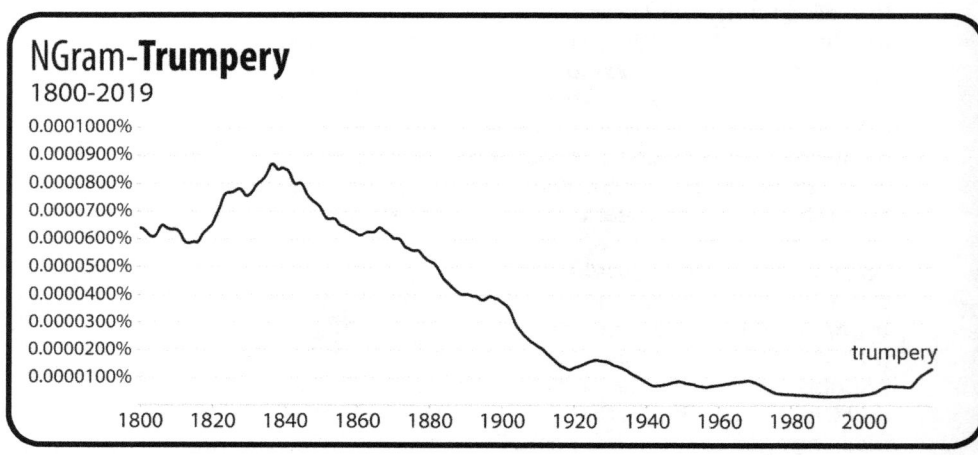

SELF-EVIDENT AT MERE STATEMENT

Gunning-Fog Index: 12.27

Over the years, I have read a sizable percentage of Jacques Ellul's books. Ellul is not well known in the United States. His books deal with all sorts of subjects, from religion and the effects of technology on human society to economics, sociology, and even philosophy. While Ellul is a reasonably easy author to understand and follow, his work isn't precisely primary-school reading. All his work had to be translated into English from French. And in reading eight volumes, I've noticed that specific translators better rendered his work in English than others.

If you were to peruse my library, you would find Ellul's books contain more reader markings than any other books. The reason? His delivery and content are more substantial to my mind than most other authors I've read. Even as an intellectual of the highest order, he made his work approachable for almost anyone. As a cautionary note, I must reiterate that I adamantly disagree with this author's acceptance of anarchism.

In reading about him in 2006, he was described as having an **axiomatic** style. Left over notes from reading about his work and my preparations for this book corroborate this attribution, though I cannot quote a chapter-and-verse source. Axiomatic is an engaging word because it represents a dying reality in today's society, in my experience.

ăk´sē-ə-măt´ĭk

The adjective *axiomatic* comes from the Greek word *axiōmatikos*: meaning "honorable." The root word *axiom* means "a statement or maxim widely accepted to be true or valuable." The suffix "ic" means "of or relating to." In short, axiomatic means "self-evident or something that can be accepted as accurate at mere statement." **Example:** every purpose serves a cause.

In today's society, relativism has not ruined what is axiomatic. It has clouded the simplicity of truth from

SELF-EVIDENT AT MERE STATEMENT

being acceptable. Truth is true no matter the perspective or means used to interpret what is observable. Questioning everything has become vogue. Today, it is rationally permissible to offer the smallest red herring in the effort to change everything. I call this rising specter exceptionism. There seems to be a tentativeness or timidity toward being axiomatic.

Reading a guy like Jacques Ellul, who was 50 years ahead of his time, is refreshing. His thought and delivery style are easy to grasp, without all the caveats and mental contortions of a sycophantic relativist or conflicted philosopher.

It seems fewer and fewer people are sure of anything anymore. Ellul is an example of an axiomatic approach that isn't wrong. One can be confident and not be arrogant or uninformed.

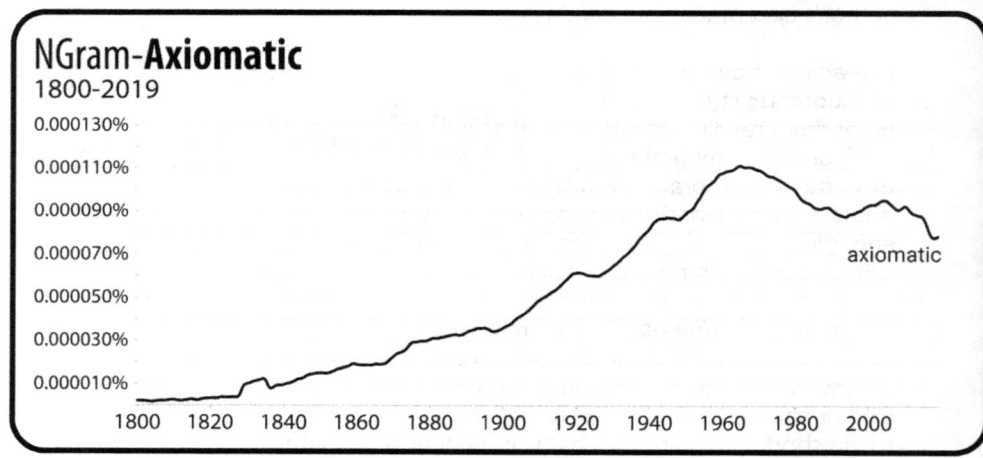

WHAT A POOKA NEVER SAID

Gunning-Fog Index: 11.17

Growing up, I was told a million times that movies were low culture, just a bit above vulgarity. Some used to call the movies "the devil's house." You likely detect the religious prejudice in that sentiment.

Even so, I have since acquired a steady flow of great learning from movies on top of entertainment. One movie I enjoy dramatically is *Harvey*, filmed in 1950. Jimmy Stewart stars plays Elwood P. Dowd, an eccentric. He has an imaginary friend, a 6 foot-3-1/2-inch pooka rabbit named Harvey, with whom he regularly confers. His sister, Veta Simmons (played by Josephine Hull), and the staff at a sanatorium try to commit Dowd and verge on "madness" in all the attempts. The movie is reasonably cerebral in subtlety while hilarious.

Veta has two problems: introducing her daughter, Myrtle Mae (played by Victoria Horne), to society and living with the scandal of her brother's seeming insanity. Early in the movie, Veta and her daughter attempt to put on a society party at the house without Dowd knowing so he wouldn't blow it with his imaginary friend.

As the mother and daughter prepare and discuss the uncle, Myrtle Mae presses Veta about Dowd's actions. In turn, Veta dismisses the conversation by confronting Myrtle Mae about the evils of being **didactic**.

dī-dăk´tĭk

I've watched the movie half a dozen times since 2006. Now, didactic always sticks out. Didactic is an adjective derived from the Greek word *didaktikos*, meaning "apt to teach," and *didaskein*, meaning "to teach." *Didactic* is not a common word in use today, but Veta gave a great example. One English definition is descriptive of someone who attempts to teach others in a way that is vexing.

How many do we know that attempt to impress upon others "the correct" way? In today's society, there

WHAT A POOKA NEVER SAID

isn't a day when someone in our lives doesn't express their opinions in a "teaching" manner. I must say this gets to be a boring drill. Thus, understanding one use of the word didactic stands as a warning.

For me, didactic is a word that is instructive on a personal level as I observe the ebb and flow of everyday life. This word is excellent in writing or speech to make the case for less moralizing and browbeating over some point, even though there are other definitions for the word. Words can just as much be a guard and personal warning of what not to be as they can be instructive in what we communicate.

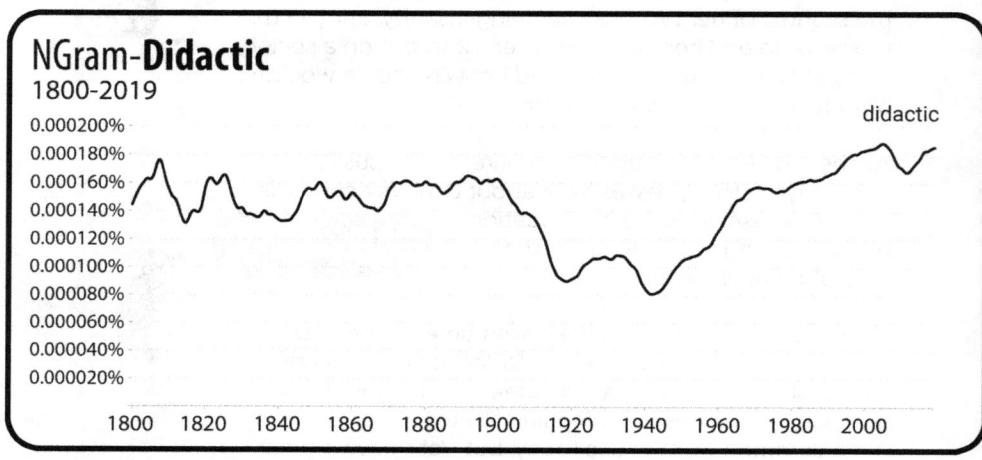

SHATTERING EMPTY VENERATION

Gunning-Fog Index: 11.97

In 2006, a pastor in Colorado named Randy Shupe gave me a mimeograph copy that was a spiral-bound version of the out-of-print book *The Coming Caesars*. This book was impressive on several levels. It was written by a French author, Amaury de Riencourt, an enigma to readers of the past three decades, but colossal in his heyday of the 1950s and '60s.

The book was impressive in the thesis because it provides countless examples of how what happened in Rome politically, on the cultural backdrop of Greece, was and is repeating itself in America, with Europe as the corollary cultural progenitor. He also illustrates a profound knowledge and understanding of America while being a foreigner. He did not treat the presidency with the typical disdain or romantic blindness of a domestic person.

The book was loaded with vocabulary that I was unfamiliar with. One word I picked up was **iconoclastic**. I loved this word from the minute I read it because it bespeaks a reality that can hardly be expressed with half a dozen words.

ī-kŏn´ə-klăst´ĭk

Most recently contributed to English from the Latin word *iconoclastes*—borrowed from Late Greek *eikonoklastes*, (a combination of *eikōn* + *klastēs*), meaning "icon breaker"— we have a word that captures the concept. The adjective iconoclastic infers either the ignoring of traditional beliefs or the destruction of images or ideals.

Sound negative? In reality, it is positive. Who would see Bob Dylan's life's work as negative? Yet, his work, and the wake it caused, were indeed iconoclastic. Check out his lyrics from 1964:
> Come mothers and fathers
> Throughout the land
> And don't criticize

SHATTERING EMPTY VENERATION

What you can't understand
Your sons and your daughters
Are beyond your command
Your old road is rapidly agin'
Please get out of the new one
If you can't lend your hand
For the times they are a-changin'[2]

An iconoclast has a calling on their life to speak out about what others refuse to see or admit. They are as much part of advancement as stalwarts and traditionalists who hold on to actual truth instead of perspectives. An iconoclastic type of person might be flamboyant or odd. They can appear in politics, religion, art, science, literature, and sports. They do not care as much about being seen as being impactful. Frank Lloyd Wright, Stephen Hawking, Dr. Martin Luther King Jr., Nelson Mandela, and Helen Keller are just a few people who are iconoclasts.

There is much need for iconoclastic people today to break up old, tired notions of static feebleness in favor of finding more idealistic answers that work.

[2]*Verse 4, The Times They Are A-Changin', Bob Dylan 1963*

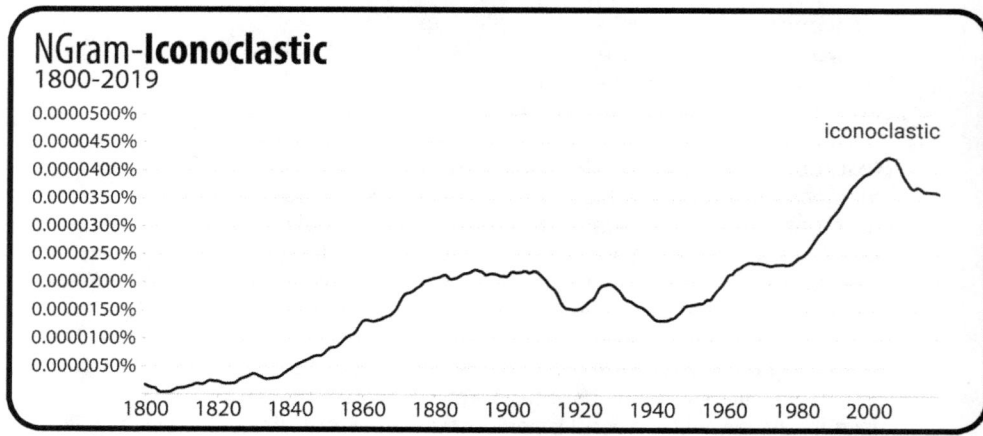

CHALLENGING THE STATUS QUO

Gunning-Fog Index: 10.86

Again, I found encouragement and enrichment in the book *The Coming Caesars*. Some books can be laborious to read, to be bluntly honest. They could contain endless names and details that aren't real. The book could be poorly written or unconvincing, no matter how well written. Other books one can glide through like a hot knife through butter.

For me, *The Coming Caesars* was one of those books that was a clarion call to understand what the author was driving at. I could not put the book down. The narrative concerned history, which I knew well. This book effectively and remarkably connected events of modern America with events and fallout in ancient Rome. The correlations made the point that history is, first of all, cyclical; secondly, we don't seem to learn from it; and finally, we are more than likely to repeat it. In effect, the book is a warning.

The Coming Caesars was clear about the historical events it used to support its thesis. However, it was written 60 years ago. In the history since 1957, I saw how it applied much more to our modern situation than when it was first published, which I found significant. Thus, I republished it in 2013 for a new generation.

One of the many words I was introduced to in this book was **inveigh**. This word is a verb emanating from the Latin *invehi*, which means "to be carried into verbally assault." Originally in the 16th century English, inveigh was spelled *enveigh*. In today's English, inveigh means to communicate to someone vehemently against a problem or issue, either to register non-agreement or to secure change.

ĭn-vā´

Inveigh describes the actions of many today who stand up against brutality and excess from government to religious entities. Spokespeople and leaders inveigh against those seen as serving up inequality or unnecessary force.

CHALLENGING THE STATUS QUO

Political protest can be a means of inveighing against an issue or incident. This word describes going to a company or manager to contend with either a lack of customer service or some sort of failure for which they are responsible. This word can be applied to any situation where the sides are drawn, and an antithesis challenges the status quo.

Inveigh has seen a downturn in usage since the 1850s. It is unclear why this word has fallen out of use. However, it is not antique or out of form. This word seems more practical in written form as a commentary than any other use.

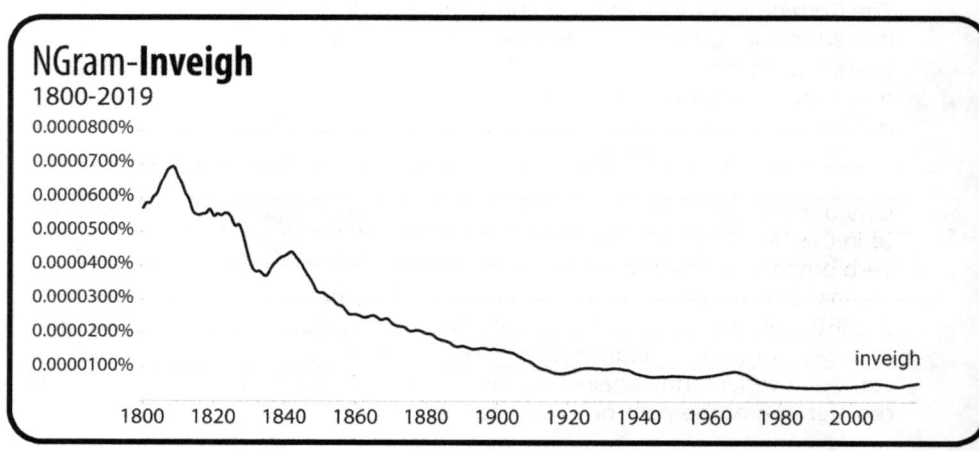

BEATLE WORDS INSTEAD OF MUSIC

Gunning-Fog Index: 12.16

I am a self-professed "Beatles junky." As a young person, I was quite the odd-duck concerning my musical interests. I was a throwback to the coming-of-age era a generation prior to mine. While my contemporaries were freaking out over KISS, Air Supply, and Van Halen, I soaked in the magic and depth of the Beatles. I saw current music as a flashes-in-the-pan or cliché.

The Beatles still wow me 50 years later. I look at them now through the long view of history. They were most definitely musicians and artists of the highest caliber rather than clever wordsmiths or party musicians who were merely lucky in timing.

Since my early enamoration with the Beatles, I've heard, read, and seen a lot in conjunction to them. I saw The Beatles Anthology documentary series, which I watched in 2006. It was a defining collection of Beatles material, even containing prior-to unreleased music. An associated documentary featured footage and interviews—both old and new—that provide a much broader perspective on the artists as part of the collection.

In one installment, John Lennon noted a predisposition of Ringo's, which, prior to this, I was unaware. Ringo had the unfortunate quirk of mixing metaphors, which Lennon noted as **malapropism**.

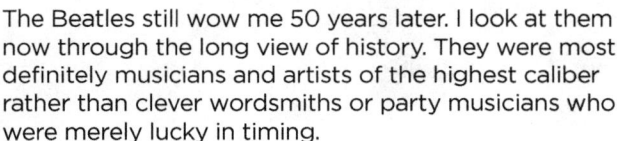

The example Lennon gave related to how Ringo's mannerisms provided the title for a song: "Tomorrow Never Knows." Research as to what was malapropos about Ringo's expression has been inconclusive. However, Lennon's term was the basis for my further education.

Malapropism seems to be a British invention. Most sources point to a character, Miss Malaprop, in the 18th century play *The Rivals* by Richard Brinsley Sheridan. This character continually misused words. However,

BEATLE WORDS INSTEAD OF MUSIC

malapropism likely had other tributaries, namely the French word *apropos*, which means a well-placed word or statement on an occasion. The prefix *"mal"* means "bad or evil." The suffix *"ism"* means "the act or process of." Malapropism, in short, is the practice of saying or using mixed expressions or metaphors or words and expressions incorrectly. Malapropism seems to be an organic development of linguistic rules.

Since entering my use, this word reminds me of what it is called when someone mistakenly says *aviance* instead of *ambiance*—like my wife: purposely dropping this malapropos to drive me nuts. Malapropism reminds me that botching words or phrases is more common than we think. Malapropism is one of those words that we can use, here again, to draw attention to what we are saying because it is not a garden-variety term.

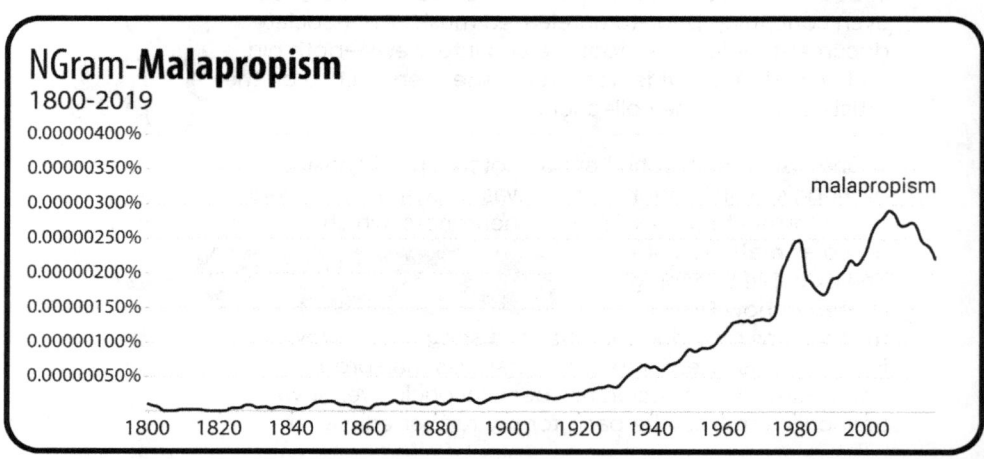

ASCETICISM THAT DOESN'T FOOL ANYONE

Gunning-Fog Index: 13.11

Whenever a movie or pop culture recognizes anything that could be construed as positive towards Christians, then Christians jump on the bandwagon of celebrating that secular culture is "honoring" and "recognizing" their ideal in some sense of inclusiveness. Ludicrous! Over the years, I've seen countless movies where Christians celebrate because they think it lends credibility to their beliefs.

One movie that Christians made much ado over was *Amazing Grace* (2006). I thought the movie was great on the level of scripting, costuming, sets, and casting. However, I was not impressed with the subject matter or how it was handled. The purpose of mentioning the movie is that it provided a charming word to my vocabulary that is practical from time to time.

The character historical figure Lord Tarleton (played by Ciarán Hinds) is a vehement adversary of the abolitionist cause. During an exchange in the House of Lords, Tarleton uses the term **mendicant** to negatively portray the type of people supposedly backing William Wilberforce (played by Ioan Gruffudd). The word mendicant, an adjective in its primary definition, is not a cordial description. However, the term can be used in several ways.

měn´dĭ-kənt

This adjective came to the English from the Latin *mendicus*, meaning "beggar." The anglicized word came into use in the 14th century. In English, it also came to represent the behavior of certain religious operatives, monks, friars, or those who put on as such—whose lives were sustained upon what they were given since they had no personal property. And it was in this vein that Lord Tarleton expended this word toward some of Wilberforce's zealots.

ASCETICISM THAT DOESN'T FOOL ANYONE

Mendicant doesn't have to represent dependent asceticism or street hustler's money grubbing. The term mendicant can be used allegorically to mean something that is not sustainable, or that is unsustained, which continually needs financial propping up. A fictitious example: the employment program of trash sorting could be judged as mendicant because it will never be self-sustaining or subsidy-free.

Mendicant isn't a word that is going to be used often. However, it communicates a concept in a crisp package. Its austerity will command attention. Speech or written material can become dithering or anesthetizing. When we use unfamiliar but well-placed words, it causes people to take note. I've heard it said that we need to be more common in our communication. I couldn't disagree more! If we do not use the words we have, we will not inspire continued learning but rather the law of diminishing returns.

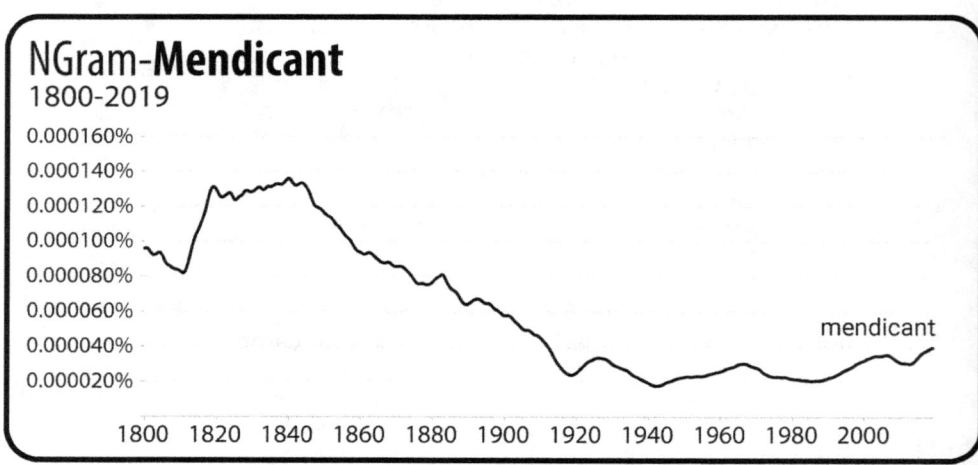

WORDS NOT TO BE CONFUSED WITH DRUGS
2006

`Gunning-Fog Index: 11.14`

In the grand scheme of the English language, there are words, and then there are words. Some of our words become archaic for one reason or another. Today, it seems many words have fallen from the grace of usage. This is a tragedy to me because our language is wealthy and vivid; why retreat to shades of gray?

In my reading of history, philosophy, sociology, and other non-fiction subjects, I am treated to a trove of terms, which in typical use every day you wouldn't hear in a month of Sundays. I enjoy a non-tweet version of communication where sentences are longer and engrossing. Sometimes, I think I was born in the wrong century.

In 2013, I worked to republish an out-of-print book. *The Coming Caesars* is an excellent volume for anyone with an open mind. Amaury de Riencourt, the author, penned the book in a translucent style where you could get his point, but he didn't cloud it with sentimentalism. He is the second French author I've read. In both cases, nothing seems to be lost in translation, nonsensical, or smoothed over. De Riencourt, as well as Jacques Ellul, write in an axiomatic delivery. I don't know if it is a Frenchism or a remarkable coincidence.

I'd read *The Coming Caesars* in 2006 and was impressed with it. As usual, I underlined passages I wanted to quote or research further and circled unknown words. One of the words I discovered in that book was **opprobrium**. This noun is of Latin origin: prefix, "*Ob-*" meaning "against" and the root word *probrum*, meaning "disgraceful act." Transliterated to English, *b* becomes *p*, and the definition becomes strong criticism by a group or peers concerning a disgrace or infamy.

ə-prō´brē-əm

WORDS NOT TO BE CONFUSED WITH DRUGS

The problem with opprobrium is that it sounds like a medical treatment: "I have to get an injection of opprobrium." In some cases, it is easier to be misunderstood with this word than to hit pay dirt. However, that is a risk I am willing to take.

Opprobrium has been outmoded likely because of easier synonyms such as harsh criticism or censure. However, I am inclined to use odd words to punctuate with intensity. This is not a word I use very often because of its nature. However, if I want to refer to censure—which is too familiar these days—or I wish to refer to the disgrace of someone's involvement, opprobrium is a great term.

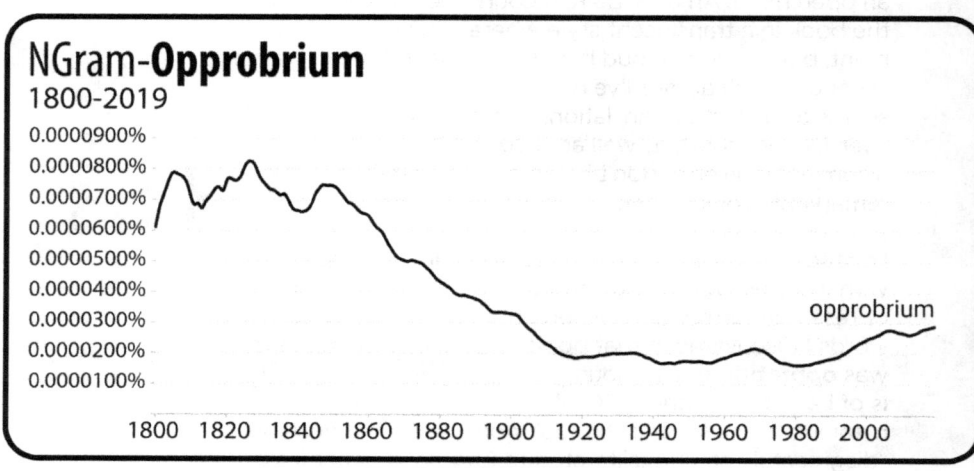

FELLOW EXILES

`Gunning-Fog Index: 13.57`

As you may gather from previous entries, "church" was a large part of my upbringing and imprinting in life. But as time passed, I've acquired a new perspective on what calls itself church. I learned it was not good to ask unrhetorical questions in this venue as it commonly unveils chasms parishioners and leaders don't want revealed. And I am not alluding to atheistic skepticism here.

Little did I realize how many like me left what calls itself church for similar reasons. And when I say many, it is a statistically identifiable reality that has caught the attention of many high-profile social researchers. Many of us exiles find one another outside the institutionalism we formerly admired, wondering, but continuing our journeys.

In 2006, I went to a convention in Wisconsin, Searching Together, where people like me left "the club," as we now refer to it. I met a particular fellow at this gathering: Jay Ferris, a writer from North Carolina. He had a baritone voice akin to Johnny Cash, an infectious grin, and a winsome character that was hard to miss. He was substantive in his presentation in ways that are hard to describe for someone who wasn't there.

In any case, all speakers, of which Jay was one, were required to present for 45 minutes and then face a gauntlet of questions from anyone in attendance: an additional 45-minutes. Later in life, I discovered this approach is a well-worn Anabaptist tradition. The basic approach was that the speaker could not speak with unquestionable authority, a concept that I have come to appreciate. The organizers called this event a dialogue conference.

Jay used a word a couple times during his discourse, which I thought was telling: **persona non grata**. This noun describes someone who has fallen out of grace with a

pər-sō´nə nŏn grä´tə

FELLOW EXILES

group or another person. When someone fails to conform to the wishes of a mutual-admiration society, such as what calls itself church, eventually, this alienation results in a broken relationship; hence, the "erring" person well be viewed as *persona non grata*. The word comes from Latin: *grata* is a derivative connected to where we get the word *grace* from; *persona* and "*non*" need little explanation.

In the everyday use of this word, we often describe ourselves as persona non grata regarding our former social connections. This word is a way not to sound like sour grapes over a situation. It's a way of creatively describing a cold, hard fact that is less deflating on an emotional level.

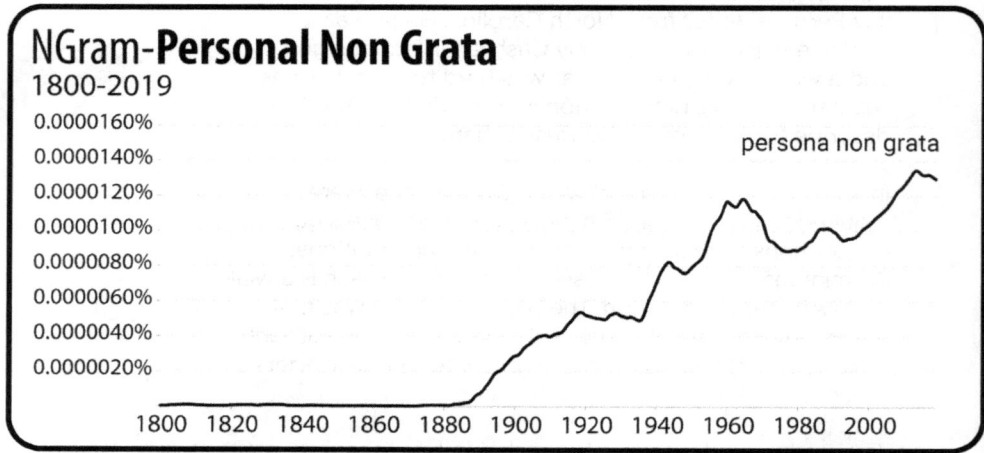

NEW WORDS FROM REGRESSIVE THERAPY
2007

Gunning-Fog Index: 11.93

Over the years, I've known several people who have gone from obscurity to some level of notoriety. Several I know specialize in counseling work with concentrations on different areas of where personal struggles come from and varying ways of dealing with them.

One such person is John Marquez. John is a guy anyone would enjoy. His ability to disarm and make folks feel comfortable is prodigious. The son of a jazz musician, Marquez developed his own brand of treatment and counseling that focused on regressive therapy. While regression therapy is not new, Marquez developed his approach to be practical in small-group or church situations.

Part of regressive therapy focuses on childhood memories. John's focus not only deals with remembering but also on facilitating the little person's trauma or offense to be recalled by the current-day matured person in combination with self-talk between the two.

One gets in touch with their personhood of the past who suffered through some experience to reconcile what that loss caused over the years. Through this process, one forgives and properly grieves to allow the current-day person to walk in mental and emotional freedom from the crippling event.

During one teaching session in 2007, I heard John use a word I was unfamiliar with: **aegis**. I had to look it up because the context did not exactly tell me what it meant. This noun means "power to protect or to support." Coming into English originally from the Greek *aigis*, meaning "goatskin," this word also had literation in Latin. In ancient times, shields were made of animal hides; hence, the applicative in this word of protection.

ē´jĭs

NEW WORDS FROM REGRESSIVE THERAPY

Aegis can have several other meanings or applications. It can mean controlling or conditioning and sponsorship or auspices. This word can be a creative way of saying something that would otherwise alert or offend, as in the case of *controlling*. To some, "controlling" is a negative buzzword. Yet, when doing something under the aegis of intellectual property, it sounds better than being controlled by intellectual property security.

Creativity in communication is vital to maintaining listeners. Sometimes, word choice can significantly assist one in selling an idea. This does not imply that obfuscation or tiptoeing through the tulips is good. It is to say that framing and presentation rely upon not ruffling or alarming people. Today, word choice is a double-edged sword. You can alienate or ingratiate just simply on a single word.

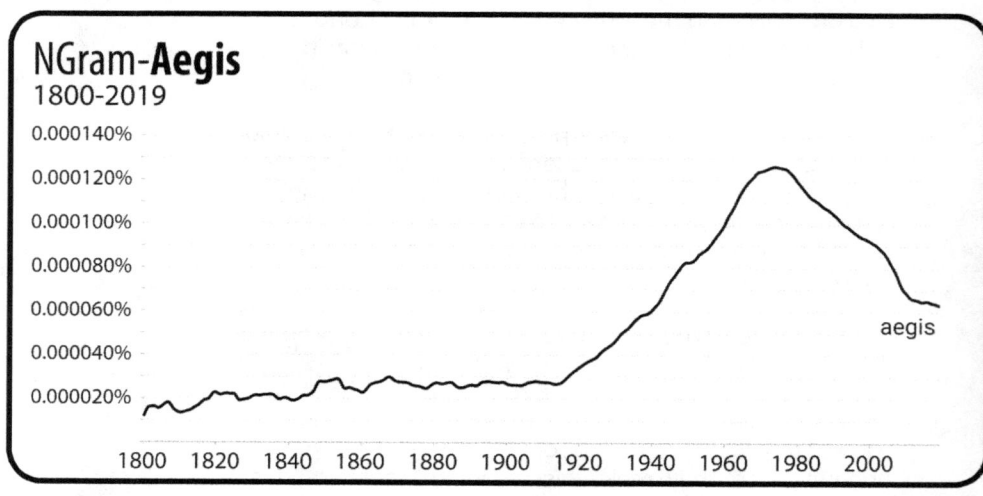

APPROACHING THE LINE OF UNNECESSARINESS
2007

Gunning-Fog Index: 9.54

Fun words are words you can drop in conversation for effect, drama, or to paint a picture. As I've mentioned before, some words are funny to me simply because of the reaction they elicit.

During my days at News Link, which shall be explained shortly. Windshield time—the time sitting behind a windshield while en route to a location—was one of my biggest enemies. Thus, I sought to minimize it by figuring out how to maintain mental sharpness while continuing to make a living.

One of my tactics was listening to things or calling people socially. Listening gets old, too, especially if all there are political commentators or media talking heads. The key was variety. I spent hours talking with my grandfather—Clayton Price—and folks sheerly for the need for variety.

I am an iconoclastic thinker, and to be so, one has to be an effective observer. One has to have broad exposure because how can one be sure they are informed. If a person only listens to one or two sources, who is to say these aren't steeped in agendas? One has to think through what is being said and measure it by a larger perspective—if there is one—to see if whatever is true.

I used to be a religious conservative. Thus, I listen to some of their pundits as well as liberal, anarchist, libertarian, and isolationist notions. One of the great entertainers of our time is Rush Limbaugh. He was funny and articulate, but he was limited to a certain presupposition. While driving in 2007, I occasionally listened to his show for laugh-and-scream value. I could laugh at some of the crazy stuff he said and become enraged over his shortsightedness.

Limbaugh related a story from the 1990s where he got shut off the air in Chicago for making what was thought to be an obscene comment. He talked about a women

APPROACHING THE LINE OF UNNECESSARINESS

"farding in the mirror while driving," which hit the jackpot for my sense of humor.

The word **fard** is a verb with roots in the Anglo-French *farder*, which means "to make up or paint." In English, it merely means to apply makeup—something quite normal, except when driving.

ˈfärd

Farding sounds a lot like *farting*, which introduces just enough ribald to get a rise out of people without going over the line. I've joked with gals I know about going to the restroom to do some farding, followed by spelling out the word. The response is everything from gasps to stitches. This word is surefire for laughs.

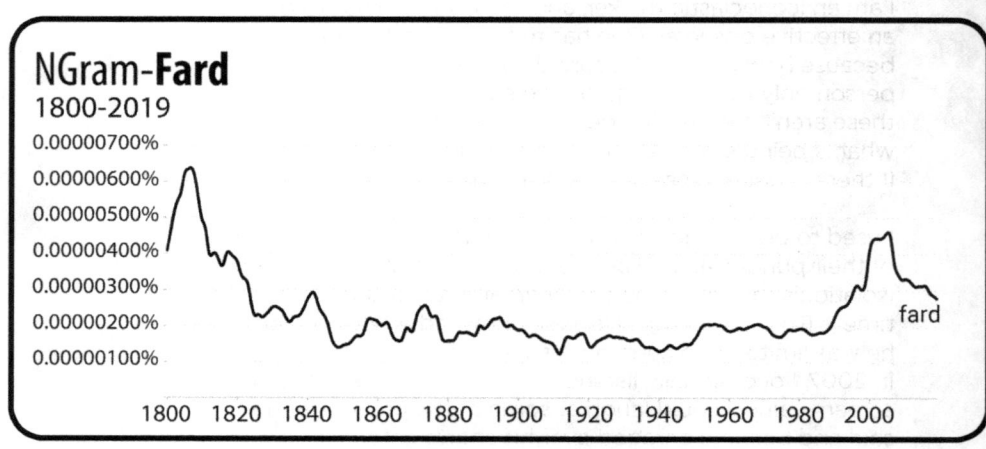

IT RHYMES WITH CALLIOPE
2007

Gunning-Fog Index: 12.64

As mentioned elsewhere I've always enjoyed music. Today's popular music is diverse and wandering. With the advent of indie music, many artists can be accessed and appreciated—unmasked and unmanipulated by record labels and the straightjacket of the music industry.

One particular genre I enjoy is modern folk rock. This genre seems less about the axe-to-grind musicians of the same genre from the 1960s in favor of a quirkier storytelling convention. Often, lyrical subjects embrace historical events or lore plastered on a canvas of rich instrumentation. In this genre, accordions, mandolins, and other instruments create an interesting old-timey sound.

One of my favorite groups is The Decemberists—named after the 1825 Russian Uprising and an unfinished Tolstoy novel. The group of five has cranked out eight albums since 2001. Their sound is vibrant and whimsical, while their lyrics abound in engaging content and uncommon words. One song, "June Hymn," is an ode to the onset of summer. Singer/songwriter Colin Meloy uses the word **panoply** to describe the musicality of a new day.

păn´ə-plē

Panoply is a word in resurgence today. It is nearly as common in use as it was in 1850. This noun is of Greek origin, from the word *panoplia*, which is the combination of the prefix *pan*—meaning "all"—and *hóplon*, meaning "armor, shield and/or weapons." In English, the word means "an impressive array." It means armor or costuming/regalia for an event or even a display of power, such as a military parade.

Panoply is similar to appliqué or accouterment in terms of armor or putting something on for protection. However, panoply more exactly references the degree, extreme, or completeness of armor or protection. It could be used as

IT RHYMES WITH CALLIOPE

a synonym of menagerie about a collection or an assemblage. This word, though resurgent, is telling and widely applicable.

One could use it as Meloy did, which is metaphorically superlative. It could be illustrative of hugeness, an extreme one must face, or one might be encouraged by. Panoply could be heartening or horrifying.

I vaguely remember this word in years gone by. But it didn't make an impression until 2007 when my son introduced us to The Decemberists. Instantly, I was drawn to their music even though they are an acquired taste.

I like the word panoply because it is distinctive. Even though this word has come back into communicative vogue, it still holds a luster and uniqueness on top of saying something big in a succinct way.

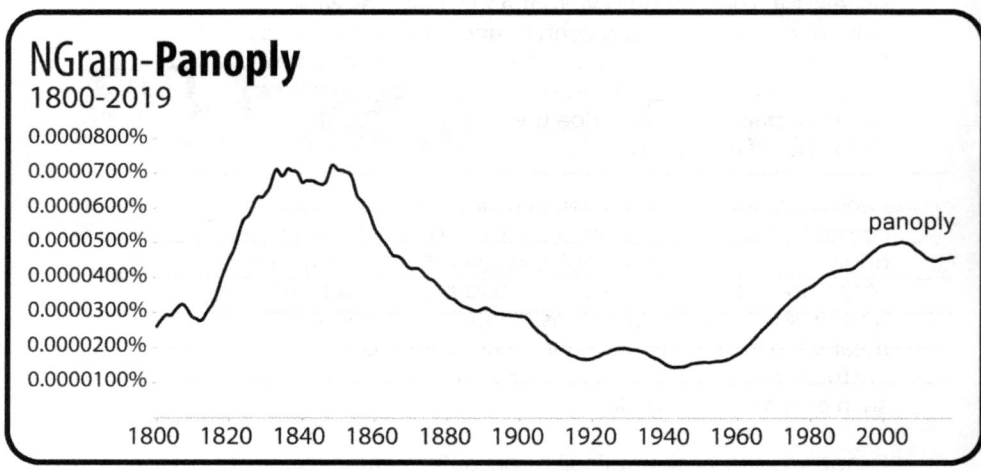

SOME WORDS ARE TOO SUPERLATIVE
— 2007-11 —

> Gunning-Fog Index: 11.81

Another movie provided a novel word I've enjoyed while working myself near to death. I don't think many realize the lexical content one can pick up if one pays attention to movie scripting.

One of the most successful movie series in recent years has been *The Pirates of the Caribbean*. These films are stereotypic caricatures of what we think pirates might have been. Johnny Depp perhaps plays the role of his career as the fictitious Captain Jack Sparrow, who never gets any respect.

Pirates of the Caribbean: Dead Man's Chest (2006) has an English naval ship sailing out to intercept pirates. Its gilded moniker emblazons the port side as the movie pans across the ship amid the action. Its name: **Indefatigable**. This adjective is of ĭn´dĭ-făt´ĭ-gə-bəl French and Latin origins. Its meaning articulates a person's drive and dedication to a confederacy or cause.

Indefatigable finds its basis in the root word *fatigue*, which needs no introduction. Indefatigable is unusual for containing not one but two prefixes and a suffix. The prefix "*in*" means "*not*," and "*de*" means "to reverse or remove." Thus, the word *indefatigable* means "not able to remove the inability wear out": a genuinely superlative term if ever there was one.

During the first couple installments of Pirates, I worked for News Link, a corporate media company whose chief customers are railroads, from 2007 to 2011. The work required a lot of travel. In my last nine months there, I logged more than 52,000 miles by car in addition to air travel.

I prided myself on being "indefatigable" because I commonly worked 12–16 hours most days in the field. The

SOME WORDS ARE TOO SUPERLATIVE

attempt was to cover huge geographic territories and give broad reportage throughout a divisional work group.

Pride may sometimes become the motivation one feeds upon to keep things going. Sad to say, this was me in those days. With my writing partner Kerri Long, who was part-time, we could outproduce any three other employees in our company because we used a different process than others did. By the time I quit, I was clinically worn out. I could no longer keep up that pace, regardless of pride.

Thus, indefatigable is a descriptive that ought to be left to inanimate objects of superior quality or the hopeful will of a group or an ideal. Trying to live up to an unsustainable optimism is the way to beat a path to various results that may be irrecoverable.

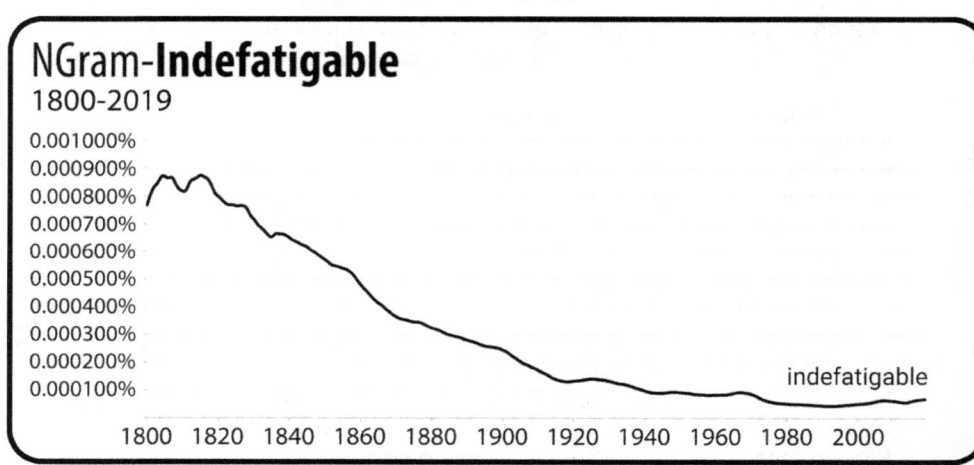

EXACTITUDE AND CREATIVE LICENSE
— 2007-11 —

`Gunning-Fog Index: 11.64`

During my years at News Link, from 2007 to 2011, I met more people than most would in 10 lifetimes. For a talker, that's great because there is no harm or foul in walking up to folks and yammering on in order to acquire the needed content for a corporate newsletter.

News Link had a colorful cadre of people with peculiarities and oddities, which I found, for the most part, entertaining. The company owner, Pete Ringsmuth, was very engaging. He was in his element to impose his level of exactitude with flair and zany improv. Nobody ever worked for any amount of time at News Link without hearing Pete's diatribe about the proper use of *over* versus *more than*—this being just one of his idiosyncratic presentations that spiced up daily production meetings.

Pete was particular because our business was writing and publishing. You've committed history that cannot be changed when you get it wrong in print. If your mistake is the worst kind, you can offend someone and perhaps lose an account. Being correct is paramount.

In 2003, my wife, Pam, and kids saw the first *Pirates of the Caribbean* movie. I learned one word in the first movie that went on to be a regular user for me in everyday conversation: **parley**, which should not be confused with *parlay*.

pär´lē

Parley is a noun originating from the Old French word parlee, meaning "spoken." As the word passed into English, it took on airs of rhetoric. Today's meaning is "negotiating with an enemy concerning terms of armistice or for safe passage." This word can be used figuratively as well.

Because of my artful use of words and Pete's exactitude about them, we were headed for a collision. I commonly saw the material we collected from our accounts as the

EXACTITUDE AND CREATIVE LICENSE

enemy—which needed to be contended with to complete newsletters. I used the word parley figuratively to mean dealing with the material to negotiate our objective.

I remember Pete getting irritated with my usage of parley. He asked me one day, "What does that mean‽" as in, provide a dictionary definition to support my use. Loose-words-sink-big-ships seemed to be his mindset.

Pete's concern shows why creative people need to be careful. While it is allowable to use words figuratively, we may confuse people and even give the impression that we are idiots. This taught me a greater sense of caution. I could justify my approach and use, but then again, Pete had a point for those of us who live and die on written communications.

*Note: The punctuation "‽" is known as an interrobang—an unconventional, novelty punctuation invented in 1962 by Martin K. Speckter. Look it up.

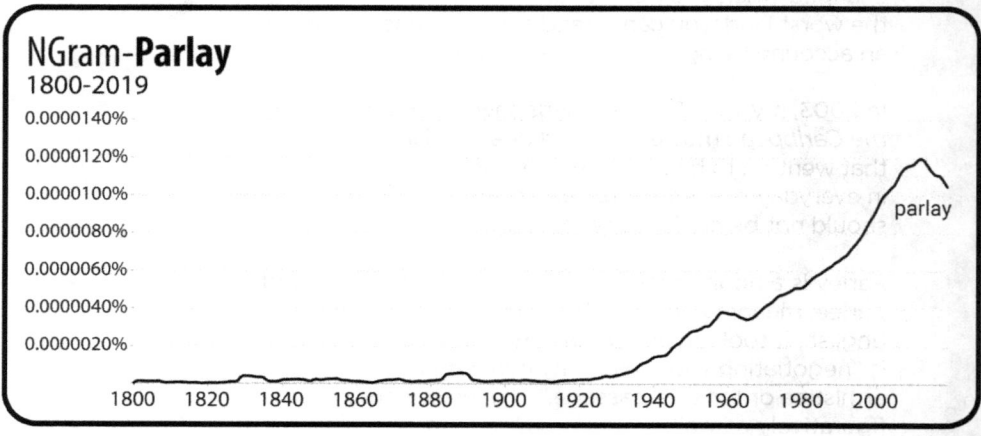

CARTOONS MORE THAN ENTERTAIN
— 2007-11 —

`Gunning-Fog Index: 11.79`

In my years at News Link, I learned much about composition, AP style, railroads, and people. Part of my education involved one fellow who vehemently detested me. Even so, such a person can be learned from. Don Rabbe, a fellow staffer, had robust writing, editing, and organization capabilities. However, he tended to be curmudgeonly. He suffered a major personal blow in life that seems to have left its mark on him. He was obsequious toward those over him, which he felt would go along with his lead and passive-aggressive with those who were either a threat or were junior to him.

Don was a man of vocabulary. He taught biblical languages at his church and was colorful in spoken word. Every day, News Link employees met for an informational meeting. We'd cover AP style details, safety issues, failures in the process that needed to be eliminated, and photography/design tips; all to help us produce a better product. During one of those meetings, Don popped off a term: **milquetoast**. The word was not lost on me.

`mĭlk ´tōst´`

This noun is an American idiom derived from a 1920s comic strip by H. T. Webster titled *The Timid Soul*, which appeared in the New York Tribune. A product of the time, *milk toast*, was apparently Webster's muse. Toasted bread soaked in milk with sugar or cinnamon—soggy, limp, and perhaps bland—reflected in the character Caspar Milquetoast, described as the man who speaks softly and gets hit with a big stick.³ Secondly, the spelling is perhaps a clever phonetic parlance of what everyone knows as milk toast.

The comic strip was not exactly a Charles Schultz/*Peanuts* comic in its cultural reach. However, the expression milquetoast has been in dictionaries since the 1950s. This indicates that the expression became familiar enough in writing and conversation that lexicographers

CARTOONS MORE THAN ENTERTAIN

incorporated it into the dictionary, which broadened the sentiment it represents. The word means "a timid, pushover, spineless person who is easily dominated."

I like the word milquetoast because it is specific. Timidity and tentativeness are exploding trends in society today. Milquetoast describes an increasing number of people who are afraid to launch because of being perceived negatively as "aggressive." Instead of milquetoast being disparaging, I feel this term can be expressed as what-not-to-be. There is a middle ground between utter passivity and opportunistic pugnaciousness. If we use milquetoast tactfully in conversation and writ, we can effectively combat the cultural move toward being overly demure.

[3]http://en.wikipedia.org/wiki/Caspar_Milquetoast

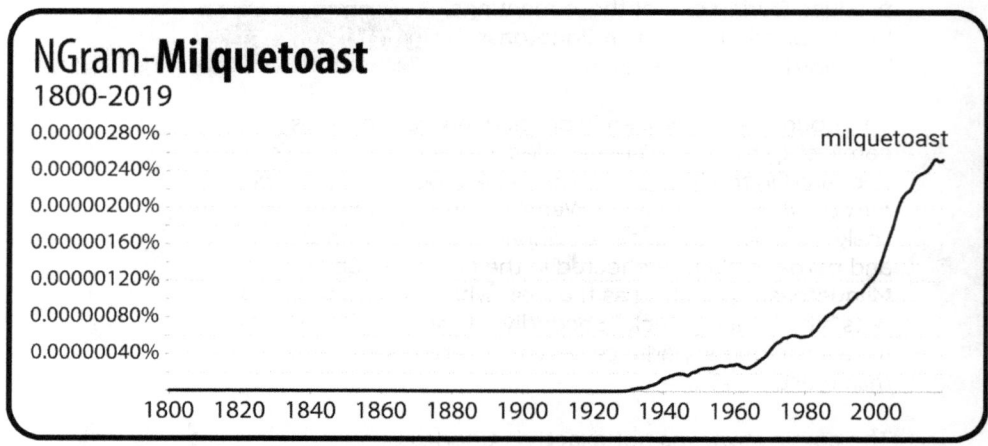

A WELL-SCRIPTED PERIOD PIECE

> Gunning-Fog Index: 11.5

Westerns are a favorite category of movies I enjoy. While John Wayne is an icon in this genre, some other actors and movies are high-water marks for me. One such is the 2008 film Appaloosa, which I saw in the theater, starring Ed Harris, Viggo Mortensen, Jeremy Irons, and Renée Zellweger. This slow-moving flick is entertaining.

Writing is vital to any good period film. This is one measure I look at concerning any movie of that sort. For some unknown reason, a medieval flick where an F-bomb is slipped in is an automatic "F" in my mind. When I watch a film like *Appaloosa* or the modern *True Grit*, I want to be taken back to when speech, life, and thinking were different.

Appaloosa was a total pleaser in this regard. Scripting upheld the era. In one particular case, Harris' character (lawman Virgil Cole) disperses a crowd of angry, outlaw cowboys who swooped into town to free their boss, Jeremy Irons' character (Randall Bragg), who was shanghaied and jailed awaiting a circuit judge. Cole admonishes the mob to skedaddle before an ineluctable thing happens; intimating such would be a game changer.

Again, I had to break out my iPhone to note the word in order to remember to look it up later. The word **ineluctable** is an adjective meaning "unable to be avoided or resisted." It is an old word, originating in the Latin word *ineluctabilis*, from in and *eluctari*, meaning "to struggle clear of." This word is still unclear, but the context of Cole's warning can be understood. If the mob did more than threaten a jailbreak, the "ineluctable thing" would be that the villain Bragg would be dead, and Cole would shoot a bunch of people in the brawl. The word ineluctable could infer fate, the sureness of response, or the natural follow-through of consequence.

ĭn´ĭ-lŭk´tə-bəl

A WELL-SCRIPTED PERIOD PIECE

This word started to ascend public use in the 1880s, coincidentally the period setting of *Appaloosa*. It has continued in applicative use, peaking in 2002 and maintaining a similar status even to today. However, when I researched against six vocabulary/preparation lists totaling 5,000 words, ineluctable or its derivatives did not appear.

Ineluctable is a power word. A professional or person speaking to the public could place this word in their provincial involvements to buttress their appeal. Any opportunist will find application for this word in their involvements. It's a great word because it expresses a reality that would be tough to convey otherwise.

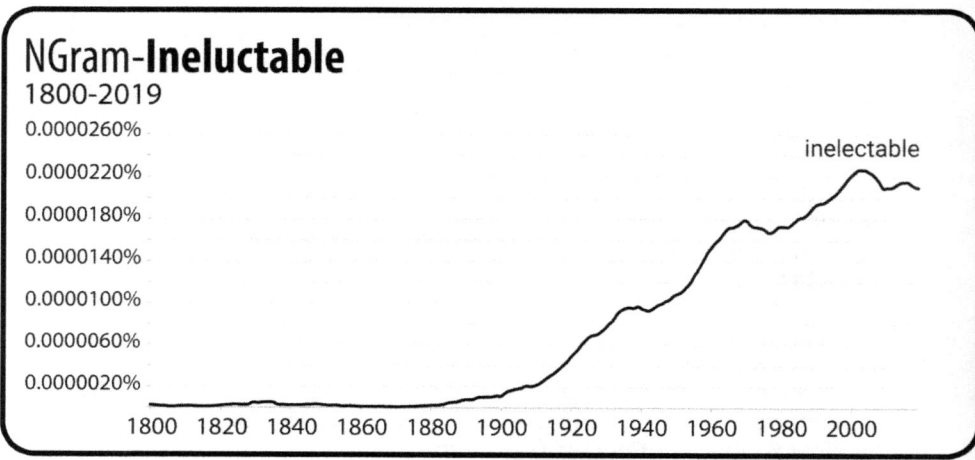

LINEAL VALIDITY
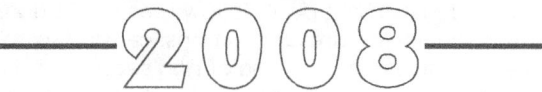

`Gunning-Fog Index: 11.38`

There are words, and then there are words we use as expressions. Over the years, I have been one to use lots of expressions in the way I communicate. Given this propensity, my mind seems geared toward the expressions of others.

Since 2002, a longtime friend, Kyle Knapp, has provided the context of learning one of these words most commonly used as an expression. Kyle is a musician and creative type. His music of choice is folk. This genre tends to be cerebral—it is message-oriented. Thus, like Kyle, those who produce it tend to be sensitive and intellectually directed. And his vocabulary and our interaction provided me a good bit of enrichment, both on the level of understanding and friendship.

Kyle isn't one to drop words just to be noticed. To him, words are a means to make a point that might bring us to ponder. One word I've heard him use since 2008 is **non sequitur**. The word is a noun, a contribution of Latin. It means "nonlinear rationale" or logic that doesn't follow an understandable lineal continuity.

nŏn sĕk´wĭ-tər

Perhaps the most common appearance of this word in modern culture is through the quirky comic strip *Non Sequitur*, which is primarily a social appraisal. Statistically, this word has been on the rise since 1940, surpassing all known appearances in print before that time. However, non sequitur would be an enigma to many people in common use.

As friends, Kyle and I share conversations with connections on Facebook. And I've seen Kyle refer to specific details in thread comments as non sequiturs, meaning an "invalid sequence of thought or conclusion." Such a comment isn't an insult. It's more of an observation.

LINEAL VALIDITY

We all know people who carry on but don't follow reason. Or, their comment is based on disqualifying presuppositions, causing us to wonder how they came to their "conclusion." The use of non sequitur will require tact when talking to people about their content. Most folks get animated when told their explanation doesn't make sense. Such reactions ought to be its own critique. A vociferous response does not establish fact.

One could use the word non sequitur as a device in dialogue as well as an expression to add creativity to what is said. My tendency would be to use this word in observation—"Michael Blumberg's said purpose for attempting to outlaw supersized sugar drinks[4] is a total non sequitur"—rather than saying in accusation, "What you said is non sequitur."

[4]https://www.nytimes.com/2012/05/31/nyregion/bloomberg-plans-a-ban-on-large-sugared-drinks.html

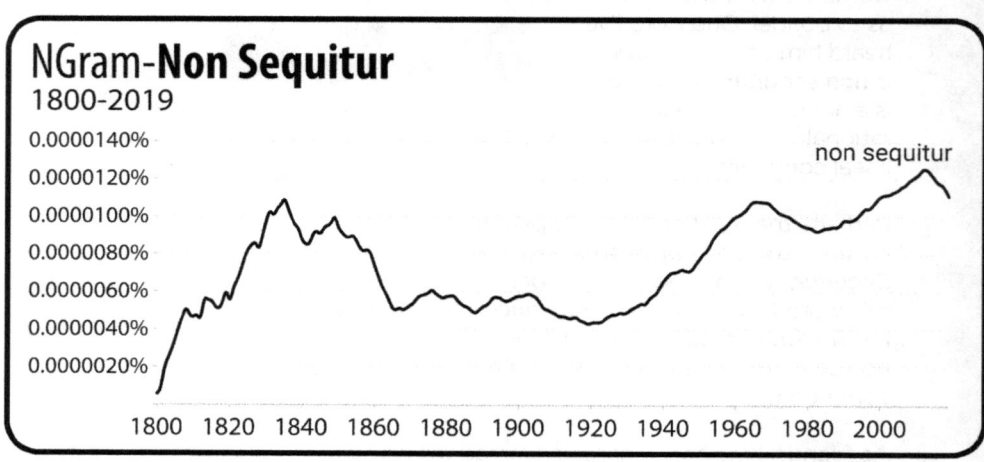

THE PARALLAX OF DIALOGUE AND MOVIES

Gunning-Fog Index: 11.7

On an interim job, I was a salesman for a specialty manufacturing company in Omaha, Nebraska. Finding customers who fit into our niche and capability was challenging. The other part of the challenge is to work with our company to step outside of its own production demands to embrace the production demands of other companies.

This company was owned and operated by James H. Keene III, an elderly gentleman whose life experience and culture are about as diverse as anyone could find in a single individual. Jim was a man of culture and education who could not give up the work-a-day world for retirement. He enjoyed the interaction and challenge of doing new things; it kept him young, even at age 82.

Occasionally, Jim took me to lunch to catch up on my end of the company's happenings and to keep me abreast of oncoming changes. And, of course, our dialogue spanned far more than strictly company involvements. Jim was involved in everything from Omaha opera to the high society of New York City, to even Williamsburg, VA. Thus, our conversation is relatively rich in content.

Coming back from one lunch one day, Jim related the story of a businesswoman in Great Britain showing him around London. He mentioned her using the word **salubrious** sə-lōō´brē-əs in their dialogue. Jim's story wasn't the first time I heard this word. However, I could not exactly place where I had heard this word prior. I thought it might likely be a movie and had a few in mind to check my hunch. I talked with my son and his girlfriend, Stephanie, about my quandary. Stephanie suggested *Last Chance Harvey*, a 2008 movie I'd seen in the theater. My wife and I watched it and sure enough, Stephanie was right.

THE PARALLAX OF DIALOGUE AND MOVIES

Salubrious, an adjective, means "encouraging or bolstering good health and happiness." This word originates in the Latin words *salubris*, akin to *salvus*, meaning "safe, healthy." Salubrious is a word in regression since the 1830s. However, it is by no means arcane. This word is not exactly a term we can use widely anyway because there are other much simpler ways to say the same thing.

A word like salubrious is generally a showstopper. We can throw down a term like this without being seen as pompous. However, our placement must be careful. Jim's story of the businesswoman who used this word was perfect. Public speaking or writing is an excellent medium in which to use such a word.

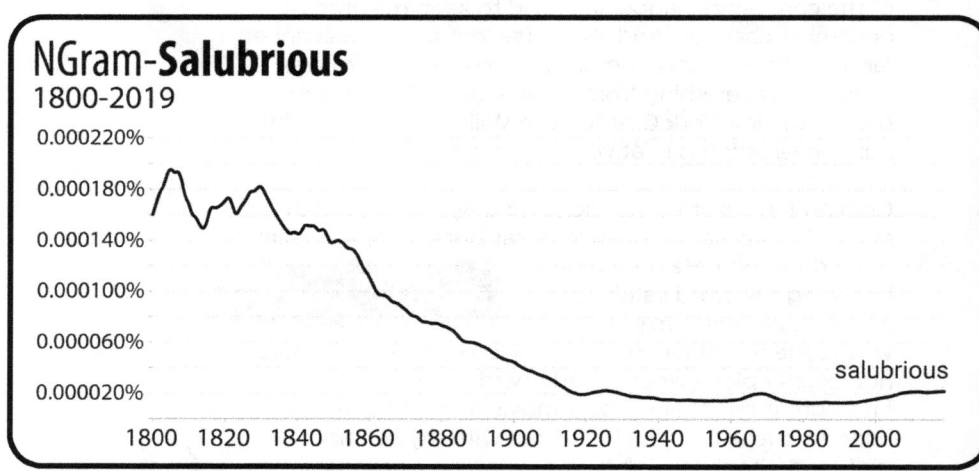

WHEN ONE CARD TAKES DOWN THE HOUSE

Gunning-Fog Index: 12.14

There are few in the Western world who do not have at least some interest in the assassination of John F. Kennedy. You can throw out this subject at a dinner and have a battle royale of opinions. This one event can prompt more raw emotion and opinion than perhaps any other happening in the past two centuries.

To me, the "one lone assassin" story does not seem to support all the verifiable information available concerning the Kennedy's assassination. This event is perhaps the single most illustrative event on how dupable people are, how unfree the American mind is, and how dangerous the people are who are actually running this world. It is not a matter of conspiracy. To me, two realities exist: The first is the way we are taught to think, which is expedient to maintaining easy living; the other is gritty, dirty, and colossally evil, which IF we admit, then we must do something.

No one knows for sure how deep or widespread the Kennedy assassination is, but it seems to implicate a ton of *official* people. The remaining questions form the basis for enough evidence to conclude that the assassination wasn't just some poor shot who was conveniently fingered.

In 2008, I watched one documentary produced by a British firm, ITV, that was particularly interesting concerning the assassination. YouTube has it in a nine-part format. The title is *The Men Who Killed Kennedy*. In the first segment, famed forensic pathologist Dr. Cyril Wecht raises serious questions about the "single-bullet theory"[5] (a.k.a, magic bullet)—the official position of the Warren Commission.

Wecht rejected the official story based on simple evidence, physics, and the fact that steps were taken in Kennedy's autopsy to suppress conflicting evidence or avoid common practices—which muddied the water for

WHEN ONE CARD TAKES DOWN THE HOUSE

further investigation. Wecht states that the magic bullet theory is the **sine qua non** of the Warren Commission report names Oswald.

sĭn ´ĭ kwä nŏn´

Sine qua non is a noun from Latin that means "without which not." In English, the spelling is the same; however, our definition is "an indispensable action, detail, or condition upon which a conclusion rests." This word was mainly a legal term (but-for test)[6], differentiating whether injury or loss is dependent on an act instead of another reason or inexplicability.

[5]https://thehill.com/blogs/blog-briefing-room/4197958-secret-service-agent-raises-questions-about-jfk-magic-bullet-theory/

[6]https://www.law.cornell.edu/wex/but-for_test

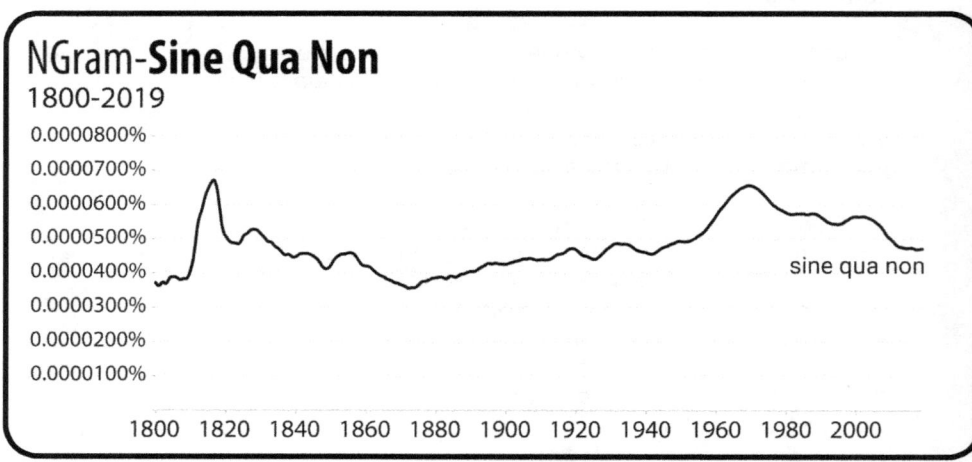

ELOQUENCE: THREE STOOGES' STYLE

`Gunning-Fog Index: 11.43`

The times you least expect to find a nugget of gold are ofttimes when you stumble upon one. Vaudeville, is by now, ancient history as far as entertainment goes. It was marked by the physicality in performance. Performers throwing themselves around, situations purposely running awry, and hair-brain choreography altogether was the confluence that made vaudevillian entertainment hilarious.

Dialogue and scripting are totally secondary to the antics and situations that play out in what became an art form. Yet, if one listens to the content of the stories, there are not only laughs to be had but also an education. The Three Stooges provided me with a word I'll never forget. The time frame in which I would have noticed this detail is sketchy as I watched a lot of Three Stooges material over the years since I was in grade school.

I watched a Three Stooges short, *Half-Wits Holiday*, filmed in 1947, at least six times, most recently in 2008. In any case, it was Curly Howard's last appearance as a Stooge. The short plays out a bet between two psychologists. The wager concerned whether culture is instilled or inherited. The short features the typical slapstick buffoonery, just like every other Stooges bit.

The Stooges entered training for the wagered period of 60 days. Finally, the day comes for the trio to debut into society as "gentlemen." As they enter the social event, Moe assures Dr. Quackenbush, their society tutor, that the fortuitousness of their encounter with him has paid off. Moe uses the word **vicissitudes**, which, for scripting in this particular storyline, was understandable. But such a word coming from the mouth of one of the three biggest fools in comedy—now, that is a comedy!

`və-'s-sə,tüds`

This noun is not a word one will use often, if at all. As a

ELOQUENCE: THREE STOOGES' STYLE

writer of period novels, such as *Pride and Prejudice*, this word would fit in half a dozen times without being odd. Perhaps the use of the word vicissitudes today can only be done comedically, as with the Three Stooges bit, without sounding pretentious.

Vicissitudes came to the English from the French. It has a range of meanings, from "malleability" to "the suddenness of luck in bringing positive change." In the case of the Stooges bit, they employed the word in the second definition.

For me, this word is impractical simply because there is no way to use it unless I take up writing Edwardian society novels. Even so, the way in which I learned this word is not only funny but evidence that education can happen in the most unexpected places.

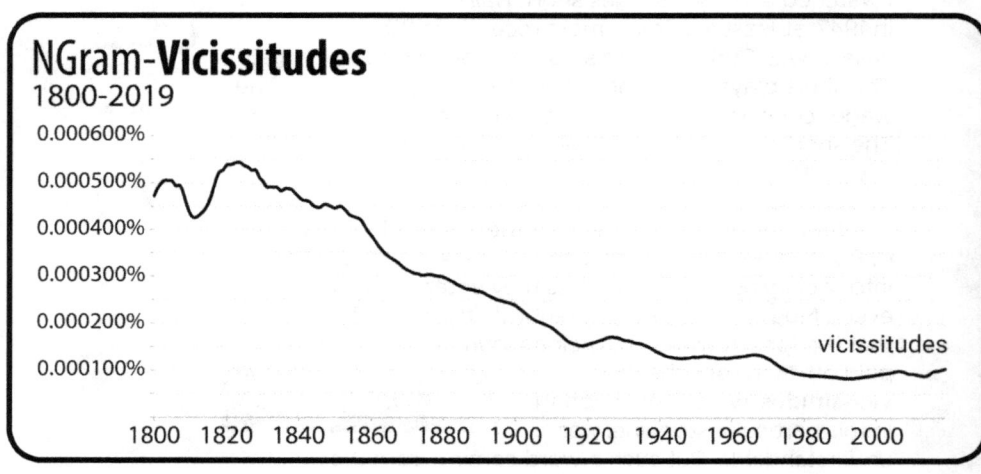

SUBSTANCE OVER IMAGINATION

`Gunning-Fog Index: 10.74`

I believe very much in reading as a percolator for the mind. Those who don't read, a number of whom I have met over the years, are missing out on the enrichment and challenge that can be acquired by reading. My reading habits are up and down depending on what I'm into at the moment. However, reading is never far from my everyday experience and practice.

I read many different things, though I generally stay away from fiction works. It is not that there is anything wrong with fiction. To me, it just isn't real, and what might be learned is far less substantive than non-fiction subjects. Time, the drive to learn, and an aversion to that which is not kept to reality have always been my filters.

In 2009, while searching for something else, I came across a volume titled *The Cynic's Word Book* by Ambrose Bierce. The book is dated 1906. I like reading material of that era because the style of writing and content is much richer than today's standards. Sentences were longer, and word usage was more opulent.

I don't know how I got into *The Cynic's Word Book*—if I was perusing, researching, or getting sidetracked. The title alone was worth my attention because I tend to be cynical. However, the book is more of a Don Rickles cynicism than that of a George Carlin.

In the introduction appeared the word **desultory**. To some, I suppose it may not be extraordinary. However, desultory, in print and publication, has been at its lowest level in 200 years. This adjective is practical, from the Latin word *desilire*, meaning "venture heedlessly." The modern English definition means "lacking purpose, defined objectivity, or zeal; listless or superficial."

dĕs´əl-tôr´ē

Desultory seems to me to be the attitude of a generation these days. The lack of drive, haplessness, and general lack

SUBSTANCE OVER IMAGINATION

of direction in the generation that has just come of age is frightening. Sure, there are bright spots. However, there is a palpable reality of unsureness in the last two generations.

This word is constructive in that it addresses a reality. All of us have been desultory about one thing or another and had down periods where we were lackadaisical. Desultory serves as a warning as much as a classification of description. Negativity comes down to how this word might be used. But it doesn't mean that the word itself is purely demeaning or detrimental.

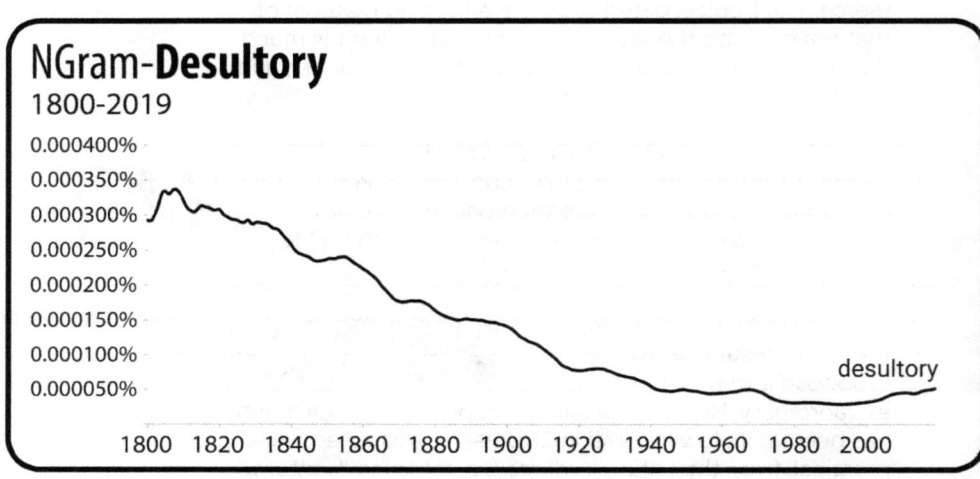

DEFINITELY HARD TO MISS

Gunning-Fog Index: 10.15

I used to work with an interesting group of people at News Link from 2007–2011. I would be remiss if I did not share another anecdotal story concerning one of News Link's funniest employees... Randy Porter was the eldest of the "news gatherers" (folks who went to the field to collect content for newsletters). Randy was the typical field agent gathering and writing his own material for each of his accounts.

Randy is one of those unflappable types. Over the years, he'd worked for regular newspapers and been a writer for most of his adult life. He is a big person, not imposing, but definitely hard to miss. He's also amusing, which is, I suppose, why so many liked him at News Link. He was quick with humor or injecting a conversational obstacle for effect. Randy also took me on a shadowing experience to teach me the ropes for gathering corporate media.

As one of the older guys in the company, he was a responsible, get-it-done-with-no-excuses kind of person. This is a trait I enjoyed about him. He'd bitch and moan about a thing—like anyone else. But he generally seemed like a person who sees life and works in a glass-half-full perspective.

Randy was a talker like I am. I always enjoyed visiting with him about work or whatever was interesting to him. In 2009, Randy returned to the office from one of his trips to drop off his material and check-in, and he'd visit around. I remember on one occasion; he was getting on about something and used the word **indubitably** in a theatrical tone with elongated enunciation... I could count on one hand the number of times I've heard or read that word before or since.

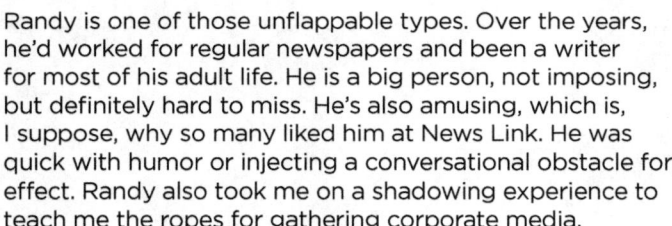

DEFINITELY HARD TO MISS

This word's meaning is not exactly divulged by context. Indubitably is an adverb originating from the Middle English *indubitabyll*, adapted from the Latin *indubitabilis*, meaning "undoubtful." Thus, indubitably means "in a manner of or to a point that cannot be doubted in all certainty." This is another word that is superlative if ever there was one.

You could say undoubtedly, but indubitably, it is much more commanding. Indubitably, it might be seen as more of a Britishism. However, emphasizing our point or being superlative is not out of school. I like this word because it is uncommon. Its highest point in use was in the 1930s. However, it remains in use statistically.

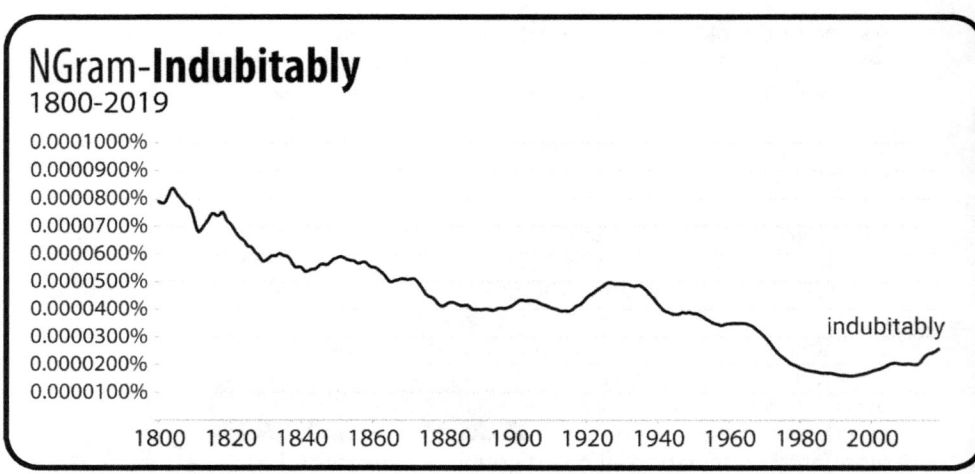

WORDS THAT ARE FAR BETWEEN
2009

`Gunning-Fog Index: 9.64`

In 2009, I traveled all over the country, in 30 states. My job, at the time, was in corporate media for most of the Class 1 railroads in America. After a number of years of heavy travel, I attempted to fill the windshield time with something that would make time pass in a more engaging way. There are significant parts of Kansas, Iowa, and Nebraska that one can only see so many times before insanity begins to creep in. I love the Midwest, but there is only so much one can take!

One of the devices for zoning out was audiobooks. I'd never liked these too much before because one uses an entirely different side of their brain in listening, over and against reading. I always felt that I would miss details easily or, worse, fall asleep.

I went to our public library and picked up a copy of Frank McCourt's *Teacher Man*. I'd noticed the book years before in Barnes & Noble but had not been interested enough to pick it up. This memoir was engaging. Perhaps it would have been more interesting had I read it in print. Nevertheless, I picked up on the word **mea culpa** through this title. meɪ.əˈkʊl.pə

This word is not odd or necessarily rare. Officials, executives, or potentates resign, issuing their mea culpas all the time. This Latin noun is an admission of fault or a resignation to one's fault in a matter. This word, or expression, apparently originates in a Catholic prayer dating from AD 1100, similar to how McCourt relates it in his book.

How often are we at fault in this life? How many ways are there to admit fault or take responsibility? Nobody likes to admit failure. However, a mea culpa, used with contriteness and sincerity, is a creative way to be graceful. Asking someone if their kind-of non-apology, apology, is

WORDS THAT ARE FAR BETWEEN

a mea culpa is perhaps a way to show grace to others or hem them into a more direct admission.

I don't remember too much of the rest of McCourt's story. It did the job of making the monotony of driving in flyover country much more doable. And it brought life to a word I knew of but never had understood its application. And if that is all I bagged out of McCourt's book, I count it as a win.

If we can be creative in our dialogue, public speech, and social situations, knowing how to admit fault in creative ways has got to be valuable. Admitting fault grows rarer by the day in this society, which is a sad commentary.

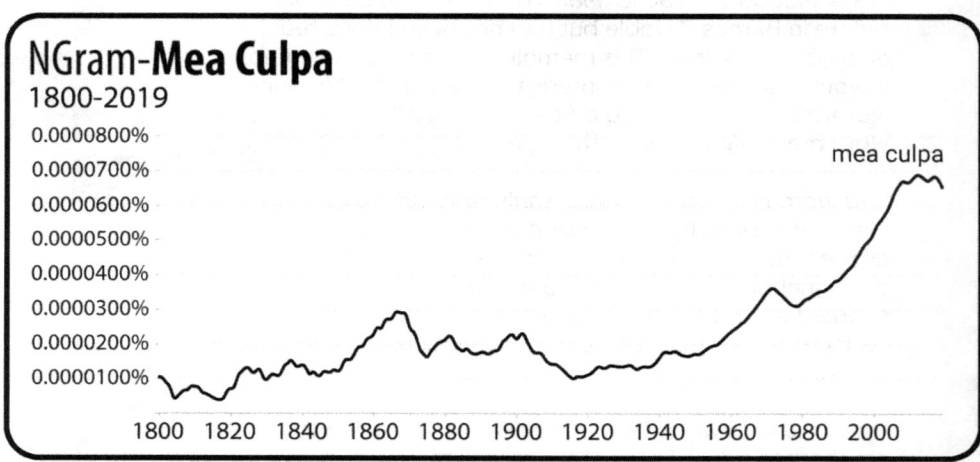

BEYOND WHAT IT IS CALLED

Gunning-Fog Index: 13.95

On numerous occasions, I've wondered what things are called. If misogyny is the appellative of men's general distrust and underlying prejudice against women, what then is the inverse? Time and again, I search for descriptionals for observable tangibilities. Another thought I've considered—beyond "What-is-it-called?"—is, does it still affect me if I don't know how to describe it?

Therefore, the actual description of a thingamajig is tremendously essential. Gravity affected many people before Brahmagupta (598 – 668 CE) elucidated its' phenomenon as *gurutvākarsan*. Part of learning is cognizing what is evident in commonly understood terminology.

I am surprised at the number of people I meet who are oblivious to what's going on around them. What are the effects, or how do you identify "it." Knowing these facts are preeminent in staying away from unnecessarily ineffectual situations.

In 2009, I read *To Preach or Not to Preach* by David C. Norrington. This volume borrowed novelty from Shakespeare's Hamlet to entertain apprehensiveness with regard to traditional conclusions—in the religious community—concerning a core tenet. The book is well-presented and substantial.

Norrington uses the word **sophist**, which was not entirely new to me at that point. This noun comes from the Greek word *sophistēs*, meaning "expert." It migrated into Latin as *sophista*, meaning "rhetorician." In the classic sense, this word refers to philosophers and specialists in presenting a case or cause; however, its secondary meaning includes a pragmatic arguer: those who argue any point, for-or-against, with equal capability.

sŏf´ĭst

BEYOND WHAT IT IS CALLED

Perhaps today, the word sophist more readily describes the latter explanation: a consummate argumentator. Society today seems to be full of people who will argue anything, just to wrangle. Today's sophists aren't usually experts in rhetoric, science, or philosophy. In greatest part today, sophism epitomizes ordinary, everyday people who broach disagreements not to present the best option or an ideal outcome but rather just to win over an opponent, even if it means fallacious reasoning.

In this atmosphere, dialogue turns into combat zones of hubristic, soulless futility. Discussion is often not about right and wrong—objectivity over subjectivity—but rather a battle of who can present a point of view that cannot be vanquished.

Identifying sophism and those who are sophistic in their approach is crucial in avoiding travesty in conversation. Understanding what sophism tends to look like in modern culture is key to not facilitating it or falling for it. Using the term sophist to characterize what is happening as we talk and write will likely educate, which may eventually change this devolution.

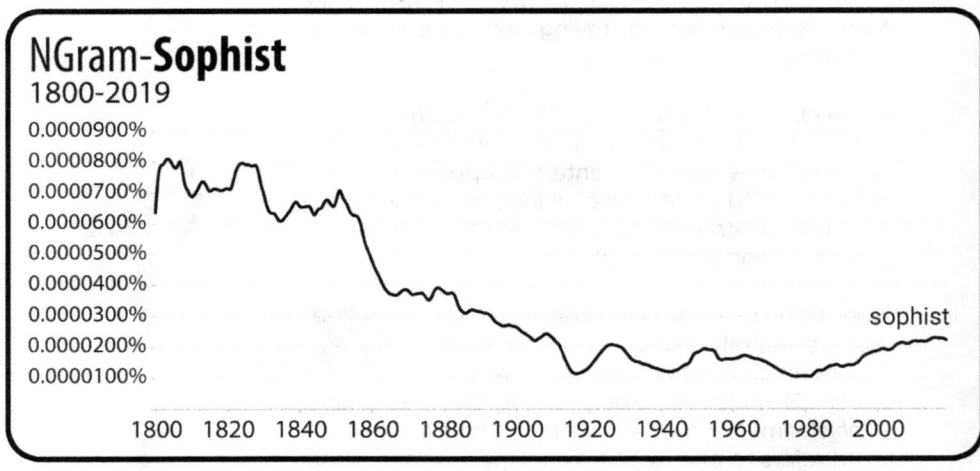

POWERFUL WORDS THAT IMPACT
2010

`Gunning-Fog Index: 12.14`

I have a friend, Steve Bowder, who plays Beatles music in a cover band called Come Together. His approach isn't just to rock out but rather to celebrate the music and memories evoked in an audience by the music. They don't do the typical dress-up and costume changes to represent the evolutions of the Beatles' years. It's not about the Beatles themselves as much as their music.

I've been to several of their performances, which have always been enjoyable. They have a running joke in their performances. As they introduce each song, one of the band members always chimes in, "Oh, this one is my favorites." After a 60-song performance, the bit becomes somewhat tiring, but it's still funny.

The words selected in this book are "favorites" of mine over the years. However, there is an elite few word that are topliners in my mind. Unlike music, in which I could point out specific reasons for determining my favorites, there is no rhyme or reason for those terms that are on my highest admiration list.

One of those extra-special words, in my understanding, is **proclivity**. I've known this word for more than a decade, enjoying its savory use in commonplace conversation. This noun means "a predisposition or predilection toward a predictable act or response." It comes from the Latin word *proclivitas*, from *proclivis*, meaning "sloping, prone."

prō-klĭv´ĭ-tē

Dating from the 16th century, this word is on the rise in usage today, even though it is quite old. It peaked in usage in the 1990s. The last time I remember hearing this word was in the movie *Shutter Island* (2010). Leonardo DiCaprio's character uses this word in his self-deceptive analysis of an alternate world he'd built around him to escape his real life.

POWERFUL WORDS THAT IMPACT

Proclivity is an excellent word in that it describes an inescapable trend of repetition or inclination in a person's tendencies to where it is observable. This establishes a certain level of culpability to one's inclinations rather than an accidental victim-of-circumstance perspective.

Proclivity is an arresting term. It's sure, clear, and enunciatively powerful. It isn't a word one will be dismissed for its use being contrived or audacious. Proclivity is not a low-culture term or modish word. It is a term as fitted to advertising and politics as it would be to culture, acting, or science. It's the perfect storm of the aptness of linguistic apropos that will tell anyone listening that you are well-spoken and represent an appealing acumen.

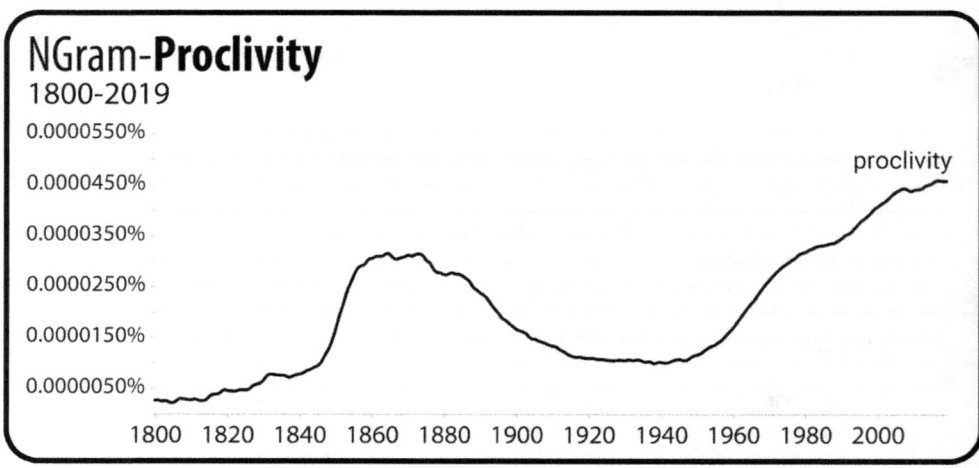

CENSORING IN OTHER WORDS
2010

`Gunning-Fog Index: 12.16`

As a movie buff, I love many films. However, there are very few that I can watch over and over. I can count on one set of my phalanges the number of movies for which there's no limit to the number of times I could watch them.

I suppose this is true because while many films are interesting, they are old hat after their initial screening. So, I got to thinking about why folks can watch *Titanic* a million times or why *Citizen Kane* turns up on many critics' top 10 must-watch lists. I can't speak for others, but I can say that a combination of humor, action, and substance makes some movies timeless.

One of the films on my endless-views list is the *Red* movies (2010 and 2013). I actually like the second one the best. These movies are incredibly entertaining because they pair their action, conspiracy, and whodunit with a heavy dose of tongue-in-cheek comedy.

The movie is about a bunch of retired CIA operatives suddenly being hunted. Bruce Willis's character, Frank Moses, remains in front of the contract killers, who are after him because he is extraordinary in his past and perceptive capability. Meanwhile, his cronies provide information and abet his attempts to discover who is behind it all.

After Frank Moses is shot, the retreating, retired black-ops individuals, played by John Malkovich and Morgan Freeman, meet up with another intelligence-op, Helen Mirren's character, Victoria—to get Moses patched up. Afterward, they sit around discussing the operation that seems to have all of them on a kill list. Discussion of CIA documents reveal why they might be targets. Freeman's character, Joe, announces a list of 12 people, most recently dispatched, except those at Victoria's table and another person who was **redacted**.

rĭ-dăkt´ĭd

CENSORING IN OTHER WORDS

I couldn't ever remember hearing that word before. Redacted is a verb from the Latin word *redāctus*, meaning "to drive back or restore." In English, redacted means "to obscure or edit out sensitive material before publication." Such a word is extremely practical.

When I send out blueprints of my customers to other service providers, I redact my customer's information off of the blueprint so another service provider doesn't get the idea of selling to my customer directly.

Sure, there are other words you could use—*erase, obscure, edit*—that have similar meanings. However, in public or in particular circumstances, the word redacted clarifies your point. You can be more specific in what you say and mean with this word.

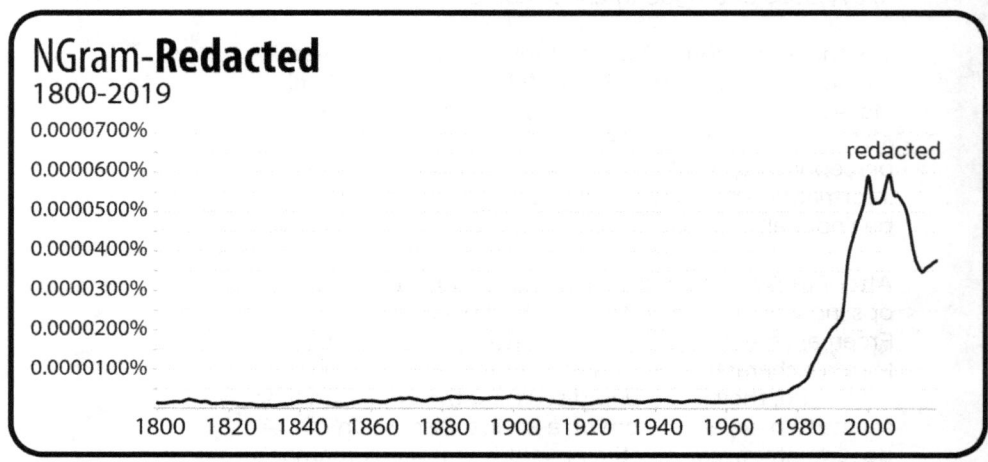

VACCINATING FOR DISEASES IN INTELLECT
2011

Gunning-Fog Index: 11.89

My friend Joe Cavanaugh III is a writer, lecturer, and life coach concerning what he calls *the authentic self*. He's owned businesses and worked for entities such as Gallup. But in recent years, he found his niche in helping others find their—authentic selves—based on his lifetime of interest in discovering the utter uniqueness of each person.

What a fantastic gig! The world in which we live commonly frustrates the uniqueness that each person possesses. The crisis this presents the average person results in many factors, such as broken homes, mental breakdowns, general depression, and suicide. The list of who could be helped in this area is endless.

The only catch is tons of superstars and wannabes vie for influence in this area. Many are opportunists looking to make a fast buck. Joe isn't looking to be the next Jack Canfield or Zig Ziglar. Neither of these people are bad. All this is to say, Joe's focus is totally different.

In 2011, Joe authored a book titled *The Language of Blessing*. This book is about recognizing the specialness of each person and learning to water people's destinies in relationship to their uniqueness, which will expand and positively affect everything in an exponential ripple effect.

At one point in the book, Joe uses the term **inoculate**. Years earlier, I'd heard this word in conjunction with the medical field. However, the word inoculate has wide use beyond medicine. This verb came into our usage from Middle English, meaning "to insert a bud into a plant," i.e., grafting. The Latin word *inoculare*, from in and *oculus*/*eye*, contributed to the earliest English definitions.

ĭ-nŏk´yə-lāt´

While the first definition of inoculate means to vaccinate for disease prevention, the second definition means

VACCINATING FOR DISEASES IN INTELLECT

introducing new ideas to someone, which was Joe's usage. Inoculation can convey or provide a new idea to someone so they won't be weakened to folly or nefarious ideas.

We live in an era where anything means nothing, and everything means something other than what it ever used to. In this environment, good counsel can inoculate against the reductionism of relativistic philosophies. Everything does not fundamentally change because of perspective.

Inoculation is what any good polemicist or teacher ought to be doing. We can't make up people's minds. Still, we can teach—inoculate them—toward practical concepts and a philosophical approach that won't close the mind but will discipline it to detect and avoid lesser ideas for better ones, for wisdom over and against folly.

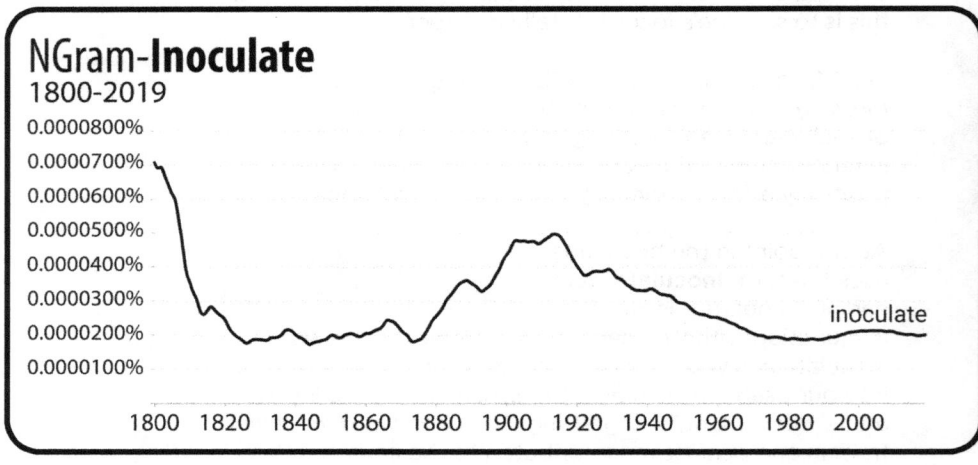

IF ONLY A PILL COULD DO THAT
2011

`Gunning-Fog Index: 11.23`

You'd think after 100 years of motion pictures, Hollywood would run out of ideas. I guess the fact that new movies continue to roll out at a precipitous rate is a testament to human creativity. I think this productivity is particularly true if the motion-picture industry stays away from propaganda and social engineering.

In 2011, the wife and I went to the movie *Limitless*, which we were unsure of—on a prospective level. I was highly impressed with this film. It's a combination of intrigue, high action, and psychological thriller. The cast is first rate with Bradley Cooper (playing Eddie Morra) and Robert De Niro (playing Carlos "Carl" Van Loon). Cooper's character is surrounded by the use of a pill that expands the brain's capacity. He is able to not only climb out of his personal slump but also create a groundswell around himself, which did not go without notice. De Niro's character enters the picture as a calculating Wall Street investment weasel looking for his next big thing.

Morra, still unproven in Van Loon's world, is set to meet this tycoon. In prospective fashion, Morra is informed that Van Loon is capriciously fickle through the use of the word **mercurial**. I'd never heard this word before. Thus, upon getting home, I had to consult my dictionary to further my education. The use of this word in the movie dialogue did not clearly define the word to my satisfaction.

mər-kyo͝or′ē-əl

Mercurial is an adjective with widely varied definitions. The Latin background of this word is *mercuriālis*, which relates to the planet Mercury. This detail colors three of the four English definitions of this term. The element mercury—a.k.a. quicksilver—may be a segue of how this word's definitions veered into describing a person's character or propensity. In English, mercurial has been in use since the early 17th century. This word peaked in the 1880s but has not dropped into oral oblivion.

IF ONLY A PILL COULD DO THAT

I like this word because it is unusual. Mercurial is an engaging term because it's less grandiose than other ways of saying the same thing. As a communicator, this word has been a practical addition to my lexical wheelhouse. To me, it's essential to be able to exert one's self in various settings, and words like mercurial add tremendous depth to how someone communicates.

The occurrence of this personality trait is not uncommon. Over the years, I've encountered a number of personages I would describe as mercurial. I feel this word to be less negative than other synonyms. Thus, it is a word that allows us to express without offending.

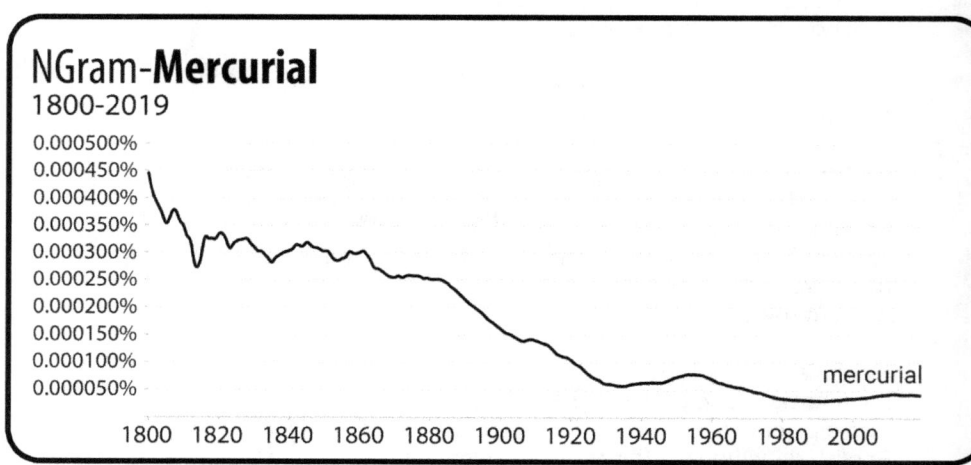

BIG WORDS STILL HAVE PRACTICAL USE
2011

Gunning-Fog Index: 12.02

In 2011, my son Roman once asked me why I use various words as if verbalizations such as I articulate and query with were a pain in the neck. He is not the first to question my sense of verbal bouquet. It is incredible to me that with a dictionary of 470,000 entries,[7] that most people's word usage is as tremendously suppressed as it appears to be.

Sources differ, but some estimate an adult, natural-born English speakers use less than 12 percent of the language, perhaps 42,000 to 48,000.[8] What is the point of words if they are not used? Is an artist suspect for using too many colors or shades in their painting? Imagine Monet's work using only 12 percent of all colors. His work would have been dismissed as rank amateurism. Yet, the written copy in many of today's publications is often at a seventh-grade reading level or below.

Instead of such traditional notions, I am of the mind to write and speak at a higher vocabulary level, but not out of pretension. People never rise to higher competency than to which they have been called. I like words that truncate the need for more verbiage. How is it the acme of foolishness or arrogance to use a single word, which otherwise takes a sentence to replicate the same meaning? And if it isn't folly to speak succinctly, why is there a push to keep a seventh-grade reading level in magazines, advertisements, and media?

The word **perfunctory** is germane to our introduction. This adjective generally describes the society of our day. We communicate in a perfunctory manner, which means to say conversation is carried out with minimal effort and a lack of enthusiasm. Communication has become mindlessly bland, mechanical, and routine-tweeting notwithstanding.

pər-fŭngk'tə-rē

Perfunctory is a great adjective. It came from the Latin *perfunctorius*, which was based on the Latin word

BIG WORDS STILL HAVE PRACTICAL USE

perfungi, meaning "to accomplish or get through with." The English rendering reflects something that is expected, that one has to go through the motions to accomplish.

We all know the perfunctory salutation when we meet the next congressman-elect. We know the perfunctory handwashing necessity before leaving the bathroom. However, perfunctory can imbue positives like the safety that comes through mundane preflight checks and inspections. Perfunctory can refer to the dull and witless. However, it can be entirely positive when referencing regular, routine, and required duties for which we would be less safe by having skipped them.

I use this word quite often in a positive way. Since the prevailing notion of this word is negative, we must be careful not to be misunderstood.

[7]https://www.babbel.com/en/magazine/does-vocabulary-size-matter
[8]https://wordcounter.io/blog/how-many-words-does-the-average-person-know

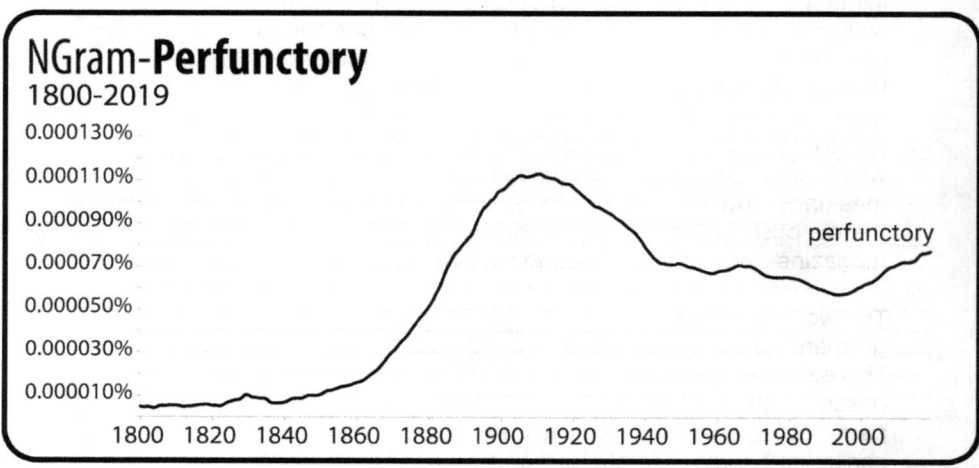

INCONGRUOUS TERMINOLOGY
2012

`Gunning-Fog Index: 10.49`

Television can be mind-numbing because of repetition and predictability. However, some shows buck that trend, offering some engaging content. I remember one such show as a youngster: *Kids Say the Darnedest Things*, hosted by Mr. Affable himself, Art Linkletter.

Linkletter would ask questions or paint a situation for children to respond to, the responses of which is legendary. Children freely offered up everything from double entendre to dirty little secrets without realizing that was what they were doing. They were cute as well as side-bursting. The vignettes of this show are timeless. The show was a hoot because children can surprise us in any number of ways.

My daughter, Genesis, is quite like any young person. She grew up and left home on her own journey. Yet, even children as young as mine serve up capability beyond our imagination. She is similarly motivated and wired as her mom Pam and me are. Her enjoyment of words and literature took her into Jane Austen's *Pride and Prejudice*—a marvel of feminine and literary accomplishment. So, enamored with this story, Genesis toyed with writing a prequel.

For many years, Genesis was a Pharmacy Tech. In 2012, at a psychology course, she came across a term that she and I discussed: **comorbidity**. This word notes a condition in which multiple chronic diseases buffet a patient simultaneously. This term was coined in English during the early 1970s by A.R. Feinstein. The concept of this word is as much a problem in the pharmaceutical realm as medicines for one condition could inflame the other or vice versa.

kō-môr′bĭde-tē

For years, Genesis was my little girl, but her forays in education and profession eclipsed mine, which is gratifying.

INCONGRUOUS TERMINOLOGY

Perhaps all parents want their children to exceed them but are surprised at when and what that might involve.

While comorbidity is a medical/psychological term, I see its use in the figurative sense. The root word *morbid* relates to disease or affliction. If disease can mean trouble, abnormality, or problem, then doesn't it follow that comorbidity could be figuratively descriptive of any number of situations? Could we not say the United States suffered the comorbidity of high inflation and high taxes under the Biden administration's watch? We could correlate any two negatives as comorbids of a victim or a subject.

Many authors use what would seem incongruous terminology—figuratively used words—in a flow for the express purpose of drawing attention to what they are saying. Doing so should be a sparing stunt, as it loses punch if one evokes this device too often. All this is to say, we can be creative with words for a specific purpose.

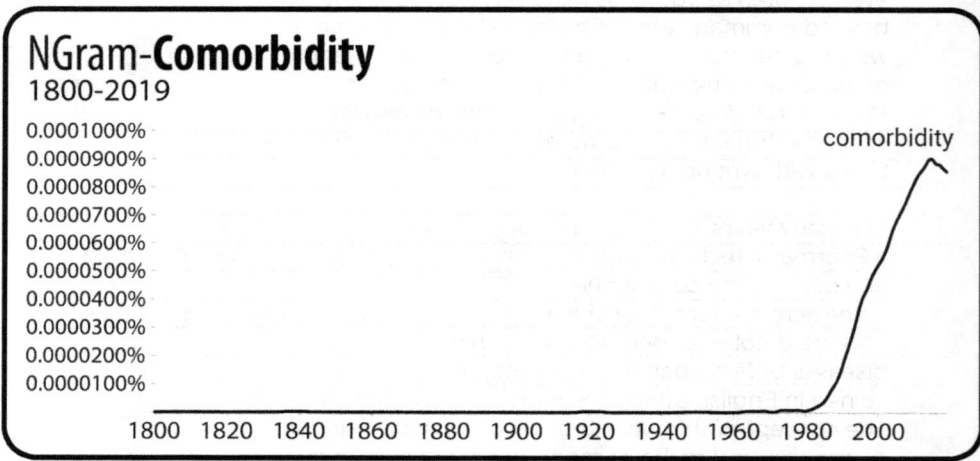

PERIOD STORIES ACCENT CREATIVITY
2012

Gunning-Fog Index: 12.62

Though some of my movie-watching habits, I've become interested in titles my children enjoy. I can't tell you how many times I have seen *Pride and Prejudice* in one version or another. Masterpiece Theater offered a number of productions we've watched because my daughter enjoyed such.

Another one of our crazes was *Downton Abbey*. This wildly successful British mini-series quickly became a family favorite. The whole family waited for the newest season. *Downton* reflected a culture amidst a paradigm shift from an aristocratic caste system, as depicted in *Pride and Prejudice*, in favor of a more egalitarian society. The costuming, script, sets, and production are world-class. The cast and character interaction are resplendent.

For me, part of the draw of these productions is the vocabulary of the scripting. British elocution enriches the dialogue and enjoyment to a higher degree. Unbeknownst to the average American, there are eight major accents in the British Isles.⁹ The uninitiated likely miss the subtleties. However, for the person listening to the words, differences in accent are acute as well as part of the entertainment.

In the fourth season of *Downton Abbey* (2012), the first episode provided

ĭm-pûr´tn-ənt

me the word **impertinent**. I find this word to be ever so British, even though the word is not arcane or eccentric to the American lexicon. The adjective *impertinent* is old, dating from the 14th century. It has Anglo-French origins, preceded by the Latin word *pertinens*. We get the word pertain from the same lexicographic history. The prefix *"im"* came from French influences. In literal terms, this word means "not pertaining to whatever was in discussion." In the simplest of terms, *impertinence* (noun form) is about identifying another person's rudeness.

PERIOD STORIES ACCENT CREATIVITY

The rudeness this word denotes could be anything from imposing oneself on the affairs of others to not abiding by the bounds of propriety: prying, insolence, and interfering. British culture, at least to the American mind, exudes provincial formality. It would be far more common to hear the dismissal of "don't be impertinent" attended by a British accent than to listen to the word used on an ordinary level in the United States. You would more likely hear vulgarity or a lesser form of polite rejection.

The word impertinent has a certain ring to it. Since it is rare in American colloquy, it is inevitable to underscore the point. Most Americans have the horse sense to get the drift of a higher vocabulary. In the case where someone steps over our line, using such words helps to accentuate how something appears to us.

[9]https://www.babbel.com/en/magazine/guide-to-british-accents

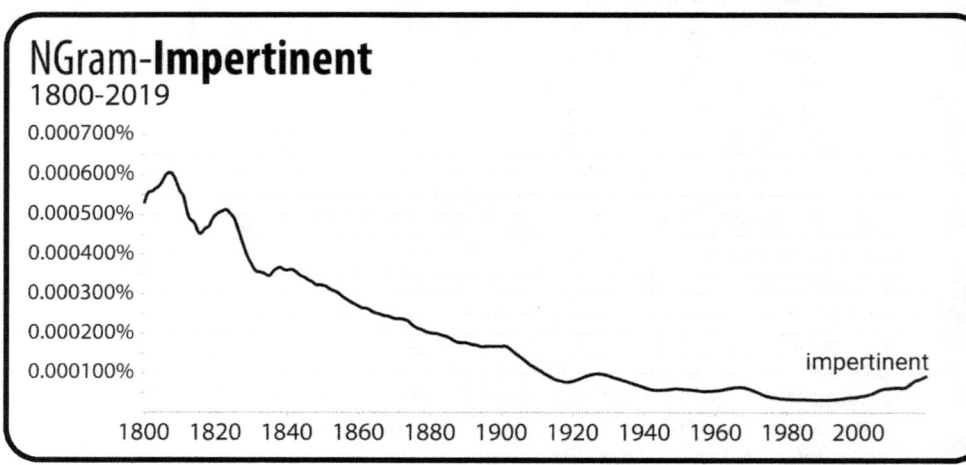

WITH HELP FROM MY FRIENDS
2012

`Gunning-Fog Index: 11.73`

Since 2005, I have been a publisher. I could not find a traditional publisher to take my first book, *The Diluted Church*. So, I started my own entity to handle challenging books like mine that offer significant messages that traditional publishers would not touch with a 10-foot pole.

Part of the process of publishing is editing. There are several ways to go about it. Several styles might be needed in order to edit various types of books. One of my editors, Gary Peterson, became a longtime friend through the editing process. He became a professor of English at two universities in Omaha, Nebraska.

I bounced the idea of this memoir project off him as a confidant. I started to talk to others about potential lists of words I wanted to feature. He saw several French words on my list, which prompted him to tell me of another French word I'd never heard of before: **mot juste**, or most commonly, *la mot juste*.

mō zhüst´

This is similar to another French word: *apropos*, used as an adjective or preposition. However, the latter relates to describing the purposefulness of saying or doing something appropriate, whereas the noun *la mot juste* notes the exact, most fitting word.

French is a language far more exact and diverse in descriptiveness than English. If we correlated English to an axe or chainsaw—cutting instruments—French, by comparison, would be like a scalpel. This is one reason French words migrated into English.

Mot juste is a word one could use in many situations. It could be used negatively to bemoan the lack of exactness of English. Or one might use it to say that an attempt to explain something brought the right mot juste to the subject; perhaps a political cartoon or a comedian's point captures the mot juste of reality. Mot juste can be laid into

WITH HELP FROM MY FRIENDS

conversation at the Rotary Club, or society events that will add character to the repartee.

As with any word unfamiliar to listeners, one can drop a correctly placed word and utterly miss the boat: audience is everything. You don't go to a funeral dressed like you're ready to party. Even so, with a precise word like mot juste, enunciation brings out the flavor and fun of this word in common conversation and serious dialogue. I'm not of the mind to impress or manipulate in speech or ink. Yet, I've always enjoyed mixing it up. As recently as 2012, Gary Peterson extended my capability to do so. It should be fun to listen to others or to be heard for not only what we say but also how we say it.

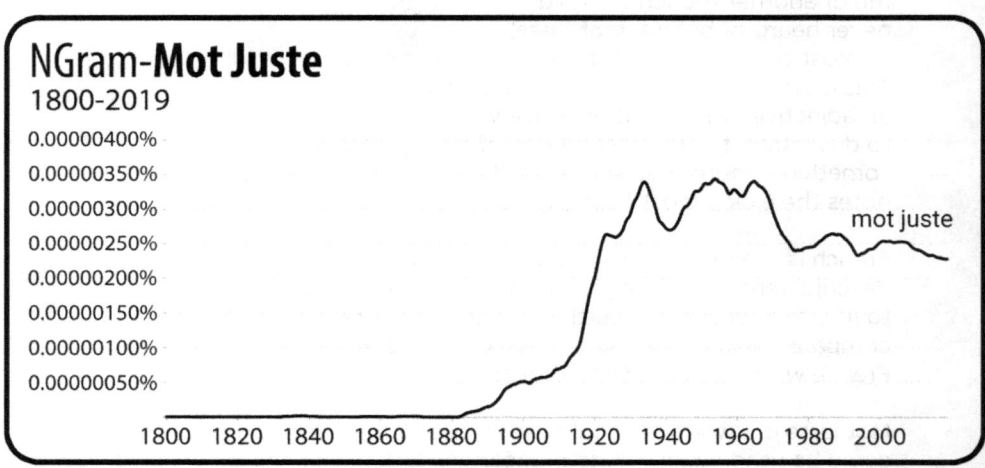

FOOTNOTES AND SCRIPTING

Gunning-Fog Index: 10.5

Sometimes, a unique word might appear to our awareness twice in a short while. One has to consider the odds of stumbling onto a particular word in so quick a succession. Maybe our minds are subliminally aroused by the first occurrence, so we are aware enough by the second occurrence to grasp it. Then again, the inextricable happens all the time.

For years, I have published books for other writers or resurrected old works for re-release. In 2012, I worked an insane number of hours on republishing an out-of-print book, *To Preach or Not to Preach*. This book was written in the 1990s by a now-deceased British author, David C. Norrington. As a typical British author, he had footnotes on footnotes and a bibliography section larger than some chapters. The book also featured a significant vocabulary, by which I was enriched.

Yet, roughly the same period, I watched a movie about the Civil War: *Gods and Generals*. I'm not a Civil War nut, and the movie wasn't earth-shattering, but the same word hit me, like rubbing across a sliver of glass in your finger as you try and find its location for extraction.

The mystery word is **phylarch**. In the *God's and Generals* movie, Stephan Lang, who portrays Stonewall Jackson, at one point says, "I'm your phylarch." In the book *The Twelve Phylarchs*, a note is given to a source referring to this same word as the disciples of Christ (not the denomination).

fī´lärk

Phylarch comes from the Greek. It's a noun with a couple different applications. Contributories are *phyle*, meaning "a Grecian chieftain or ruler." The second tributary is *archi*, a Greek word meaning "highest or most important."

This word could mean anything from a commander in a cavalry unit, such as how it was used in *Gods and Generals*.

FOOTNOTES AND SCRIPTING

Or it could refer to a magistrate of a tribal group. The word could be used in a metaphorical sense to refer to any leader in an organizational structure, such as in the source material I noted.

My feeling is that the purpose of using such a word would be more for creativeness. In writing, one could use this in anything from a gangster novel to a period novel. As an orator, this term could dress up a presentation. In conversation, one could throw this word in conjunction with what they do regarding their position, something to the effect of "I am head phylarch of this committee." One doesn't always have to be straight or serious in how they might use this word.

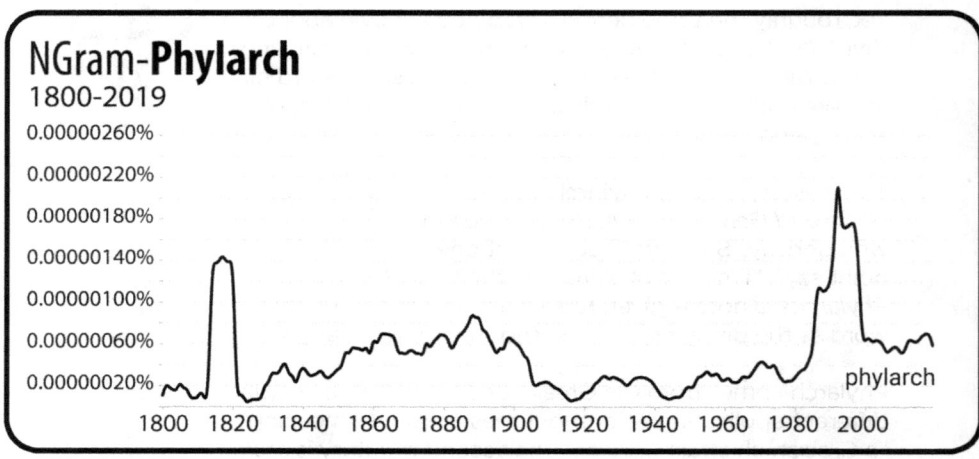

TENSION ALL AROUND CAN BE COMEDIC
2012

Gunning-Fog Index: 10.77

In all of our movie-watching habits, I pass on many titles because they just don't seem appealing at the moment. We've learned over the years that critics' reviews are often unsubstantial. So, we'll see the ones they poo poo, and we bypass many they rave over.

One movie I did not want to see was *Everything Is Illuminated* (2005). There was nothing about this film that jumped out at me. I was not particularly excited about Elijah Wood, who played the main character either. However, in 2012, my son, Roman, cajoled us into watching this film with promises of laughs and humor that would hit our funny bones. It is somewhat gratifying when your children venture beyond you, but they find a way to associate what they discover back to you with an apt fit.

The film was about a current-day descendant of formerly persecuted Jews, who go back to Ukraine to find the woman who saved his grandfather in order to thank her on behalf of the U.S. family. The second story is about an opportunistic family in modern-day Ukraine. They take wealthy Western Jews to see family haunts. The Ukrainian family is highly dysfunctional. Grandpa is supposedly blind but still drives. The grandson seeks to emulate American pop culture, including bedding every girl he can. And the mother and father are emotionally withdrawn but greedy for gain.

There is racial tension, generational tension, and tension between cultures in this movie, all wrapped in copious amounts of humor. The Ukrainian grandson constantly smooths over his grandfather's racist comments by *creatively* translating what was said into English. He mispronounces words and invents new ones. At one point, he uses the English word **proximal**.

prŏkˈsə-məl

TENSION ALL AROUND CAN BE COMEDIC

This word comes from the Latin term *proximus*, meaning "nearest." In English, this adjective means "situated closely to the next point of destination." It is a geological or medical term.

I find it interesting to learn words from a foreign speaker. Why foreign speakers learn and use such different English words than natural-born speakers is a mystery. In any case, being enriched by foreigners helps me express in ways that spice up my communication in practical terms that grab attention, as this same word caught mine.

Proximal is a word we can use in many situations because of its wide application. It is distinctive, which sets apart anyone who uses the word. This word could offer the opportunity to speak further, which presents an advantage when selecting word choice and can be a move of good tactical offense.

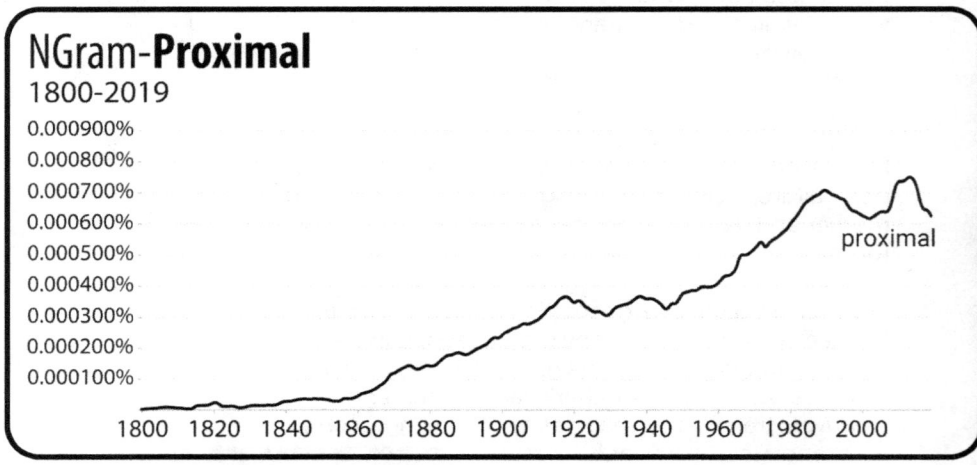

SERIOUS CRITIQUE THAT IS FUNNY
2013

Gunning-Fog Index: 11.21

Sometimes, recognizing a word in one setting reminds me of a prior time when I heard it but didn't take as much note of it. Such is the case with the word in this section. This term will make people blush because it commonly carries the dubiousness of being a below-the-belt reference.

In 2013, I watched a movie my wife could hardly sit through because of its gratuitous and incessant vulgarity. I just accept specific genres are going to be the way they are. Even in a movie chock-full of unnecessarily crude language, there was a diamond in the rough. In *Bad Boys II*, Martin Lawrence plays the comedic straight man who steals the show from his cop partner, played by Will Smith—the rise-above-it-all, self-assured lead man. Lawrence's character suffered a wound (in the first movie) coupled with stress, resulting in the ubiquitous "erectile dysfunction" in modern movies.

At one point, he and Smith's character are in an electronics store talking about various things on their current case, with the store display cameras rolling that coincidentally are close-circuited to every TV in the store. The conversation veers into Lawrence's problem described by the adjective **flaccid**. Store customers erupt in derision and angst at what appears to be homosexual eroticism. Other characters protested the exposure of little kids to such off-color talk. This clip was extremely funny to my sense of humor.

flăs´ĭd

A few years earlier, I read an excellent book by Stanley Hauerwas and William H. Willimon titled *Resident Aliens*. In this book, the authors used the word flaccid in the metaphorical sense to punctuate their perception of what calls itself church: "Christians have given atheists less and less in which to disbelieve! A flaccid church has robbed

SERIOUS CRITIQUE THAT IS FUNNY

atheism of its earlier pretensions of adventure."[10] Wow! I did not remember this reference until I saw *Bad Boys II* and I was researching my records for supportive content.

What is funny to me about this word is the reaction it engenders when dropped in conversation. Americans of virtually any stripe seem to be mortified at the mention of this adjective. The word has many applications, but the general public has it all parked at something below the belt.

Flaccid is a Latin contribution from *flaccidus*. The Latin word carries the same meaning as its English version: "flabby or limp." It could describe anything from celery past its prime to ineffective leadership.

I love the term because of its primary effect on people. Knowing such effects should not stop us from using this word or any other. Correctly placed, it could have a dynamic effect.

[10]*Resident Aliens*, by Hauerwas, Abingdon Press, Pg. 50

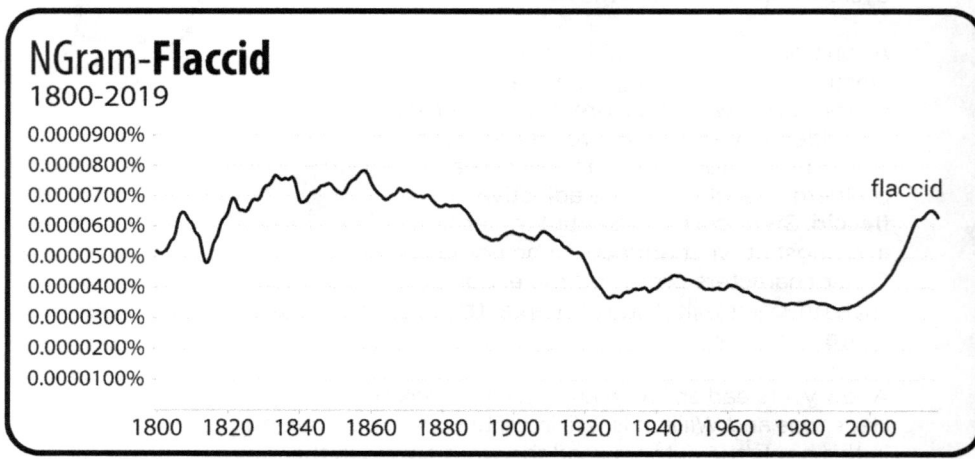

LIGHTING IT UP
ACCORDING TO FRENCH
2013

Gunning-Fog Index: 10.74

One type of reading subject I enjoy most is history. A classic quote about history is that we don't learn from it. Perhaps that is true in one sense. However, I've tended to learn words from history, among other things.

In 2013, I randomly picked up a used copy of *Jesse James: Last Rebel of the Civil War* by T.J. Stiles at a local shop in Omaha's Old Market. I like hardbound copies. Purchasing them used is a great way to save money. The book is a meticulously crafted account of the West's most notorious outlaw. Stiles fashioned a broad canvas, the microcosms of Missouri and Kansas and Missouri's relationship to the rest of the South along with Jesse James's familial situation—to provide background on which to decode fact from myth so that this notorious figure could be treated objectively.

Stiles, an accomplished writer, uses a colorful vocabulary palette. This chronicle is not ostentatious in any way, even though some words used are not likely to occur in any month of Sundays. Even so, the book was enjoyable and engaging on an everyday level. One of the details that comes through this volume is Jesse James's flamboyance in writing.

In the closing sections of this book, Stiles recounts a lackluster robbery of paltry gains the James gang did in Winston, MO. Jesse and Frank, with Robert Woodson, boarded the train—populating the smoking car as a charade for their impending pillage. Two additional gang members embarked on the express car. Once positions were taken, Jesse cut loose with his pistols.

Stiles uses the word **fusillade**, a noun descriptive of a flurry of bullets Jesse let go in commandeering attention and control. Fusillade comes from the French word *fusiller*, meaning "to shoot" or "the shooter." Its

fyo͞osə-läd´

LIGHTING IT UP ACCORDING TO FRENCH

evolution into English is undistinguished beyond that detail. In modern speak, one might say Jesse James laid out a hail of gunfire—arresting control.

Fusillade is more succinct than modern expressions of identical meaning. It is a unique word, which is its novelty. I like fusillade because its enunciation lends toward poignancy. Fusillade can be used allegorically to mean an attack or a verbal barrage in excoriation.

When you use a word such as fusillade, everyone knows you are throwing down big verbal hardware. The objective should be to avoid pretentiousness when using a word like fusillade. This can be done by describing what happened, which will divulge the word's meaning.

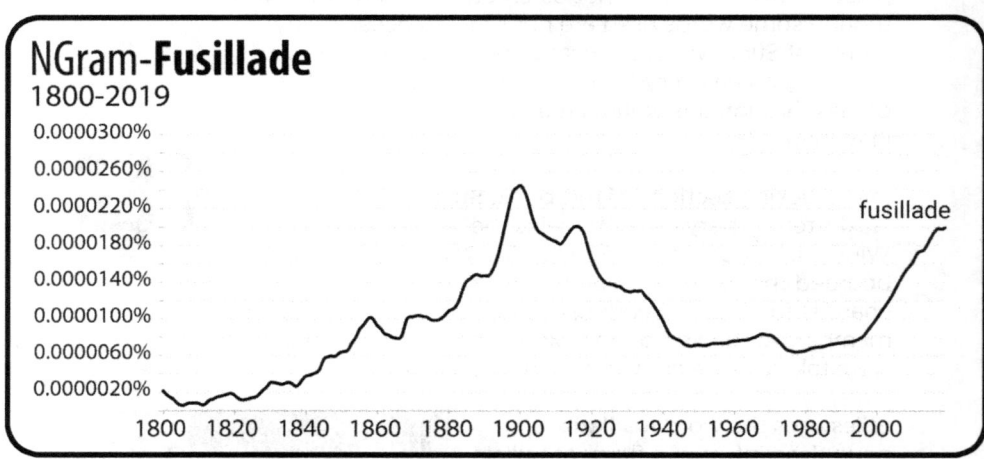

A COMMERCIAL FLOP THAT WAS GREAT
2013

`Gunning-Fog Index: 10.95`

My wife is legally blind. She suffered a vision diminishment from a hereditary condition called Stargardt's disease. This condition most commonly takes hold in later teen years and is undetected for what it really is until all other diagnoses do not address the symptoms. Stargardt's is similar to macular degeneration. Instead of being an aging condition, Stargardt's affects young people.

Because of this issue, movies have become one of our chief forms of enjoyment. We are both cinema aficionados. As such, it is amazing how our perception of a film is versus that of either the public at large or the so-called critics. I can't tell you the number of times we've gone to a movie where our assessment is emphatically opposite of the critics.

One such movie was Disney's version of the *The Lone Ranger* (2013). We loved this movie. Yes, it was a departure from the original Clayton Moore TV series of the 1950s. But then again, who says that a fictitious story has to be continually retold in the same way?

In any case, we've watched *The Lone Ranger* several times, and we enjoy the subplots, quipping, and stitches of comedy strewn throughout the film. It is well told, stereotypically hilarious, and somewhat representative of realities in the Old West as well as creative. The costumes and sets are first-rate.

During one scene, "the Presbyterians" enter the milieu—though they appear more like the Salvation Army, complete with brass band and singing hymns in public. The preacher sets up shop at the edge of a railroad camp. Preaching against sin and vice, he used the word **licentiousness**. This word is a bit archaic in modern times. It was a term common

`lī-sĕn´ shəs.nəs`

A COMMERCIAL FLOP THAT WAS GREAT

in 1805 that dwindled in use (and understanding) to its current lack of pervasiveness since the 1920s.

Licentiousness is, of course, the noun form of the adjective *licentious*. The English got this word from the Latin *licentiosus*, meaning "unbridled, wanton, and volatile." In English, this term refers to something morally offensive, particularly in regard to sexuality. In its lesser meaning, this word means a sharp departure from general rules of acceptable conduct.

Such a word will be sharp in the modern context. The reductionism of morality for the embrace of politically-correct talk is the environment we are surrounded in. One will make a memorable impression in the use of such a word. Knowing such a word will also remind and guard one from being licentious from any perspective.

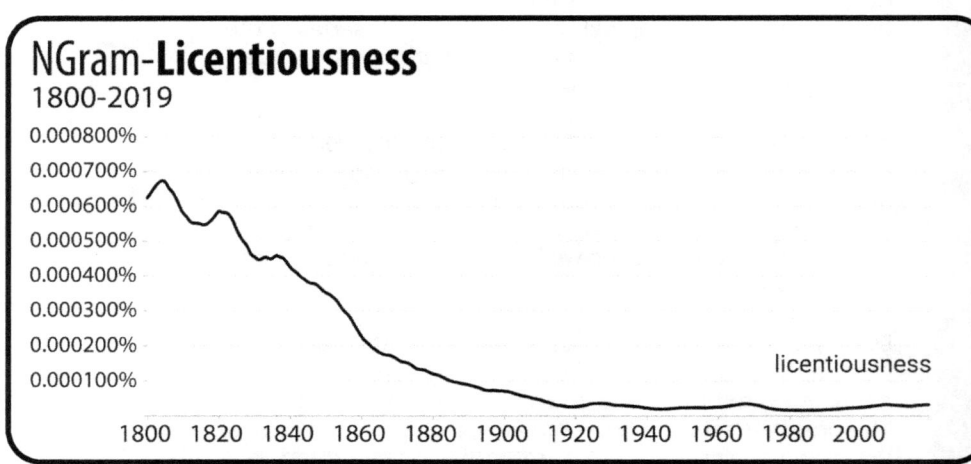

LATE-IN-LIFE IMPACT
2013

`Gunning-Fog Index: 10.77`

In 2013, my wife, Pam, called me at work, telling me, "You have to pick up a DVD on the way home." My wife isn't exactly a spendthrift. Thus, her directive was quite a departure from her usual request for take-out dinner or a Diet Coke on the way home. So, to say the least, I was curious. I did a quick search for availability. Turns out the only place in town that had it was Barnes & Noble. I got home that night to be blown away!

The documentary film *Searching for Sugar Man* is about a thought-to-be failed musician. In 1970 and '71, Sixto Rodriguez recorded back-to-back albums that didn't sell. Fast-forward to 1997, two South African music aficionados are looking for this enigmatic musician. The back story: Rodriguez's music had been pirated and became the musical powerhouse behind South Africa's cultural revolution, ending apartheid. The film documents this unprecedented story. It was so good it won an Oscar in 2013 for Best Documentary.

The film featured a good bit of Rodriguez's second album, *Coming from Reality*. The next day, I was hunting it down to purchase as well. My wife and I enjoy music immensely. This guy's stuff was fresh even though it was 40 years old. Rodriguez is a folk artist of sorts. His music is quirky, verging on psychedelic in some cases. However, his lyrics are on par with Dylan, Cat Stevens, and John Lennon. The second track on this album is titled *"A Most Disgusting Song,"* a talking-song in poetic verse backed by instrumentation. Rodriguez uses the word **ossified**, which grabbed my attention.

ŏs´ə-fīd´

This odd word has great application in everyday life. Ossified is obviously a past-tense verb. It is a Latin-based term, *oss*, originally meaning "bone." This word passed through French influence, which added the suffix *"ifier,"*

LATE-IN-LIFE IMPACT

meaning "the agent of," in this case hardening. Finally, this word came into English in the straight verb sense *ossify*: "to turn into bone or harden: calcify, or make rigid." The word can be used in a metaphoric sense: to become inflexible, unable to change, or opposing change.

Just like a folk artist who accesses cultural and societal realities that shouldn't be, we, too, can use words in our dialogue to make a point. In a metaphoric sense, I have had the unfortunate experience of working for several people who are totally ossified in their management style or perspectives on production models. This delusion can be highly frustrating for the average employee or someone who is motivated the way I am.

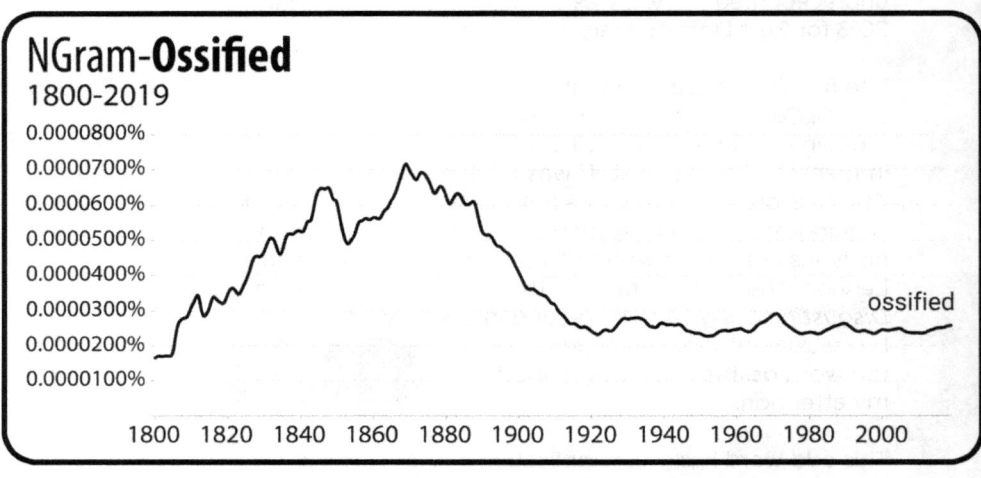

GREEN SPACES SPEAK
2013

Gunning-Fog Index: 8.34

As an avid reader, one comes across all sorts of material. Reading has been both a blessing and a bane to my existence. The blessing is in what I've found through perusal reading. The bane comes from not being able to recall a source at a later point.

I am a strange reader. For one thing, I cannot devour a 400-page book in two days. Secondly, I mark up almost anything I read. I've resorted to such as I become agitated later in the desire to source a bit—a word or the notion for the current project on which I am working. I bend corners and parenthesize areas of interest. I even comment in the margins. I often reduce all such discoveries to an Excel file for potential summons. Even so, many details escape my assiduous efforts.

Where I first saw the word **repose**, I cannot recall. Seems to me it may have been a historical piece, perhaps of the 18th or 19th century. Had the lyrics of *The Star-Spangled Banner* been taught in toto, I would not have been caught later by the word. In preparing for this book, repose made it on a list but in a secondary list. At the time, I had no story of serendipity in which to present it.

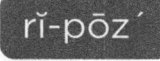

rĭ-pōz´

In November 2013, I visited my folks in El Paso, TX, for the first time in 16 years. Dad took me downtown to a UTEP-sponsored tour about transportation history. El Paso is a railroad town on par with Omaha or Chicago. Even so, I'd never been there throughout all my railroad travels.

This tour became that bit of fortuity I needed regarding the word repose. Close to the end, we came to a green space containing a fountain. And there, designed into the aquatic display, was the quote: "Like water, we are truest to our nature in repose," penned by Cyril Connolly (1903-1974), a British author, editor, and critic.

GREEN SPACES SPEAK

Repose is a verb meaning "to lay in rest and stillness." It originated in Middle English from the Anglo-French term *reposer*. This is a word near extinction in modern use. This word has a poetic peal to it, which perhaps is why it has fallen out of use. This word is a way to say something less complicated than trying to say the same thing in another way.

Repose is a word that can be used in a number of ways. We can be funny or very serious. It is a smart-sounding word without pretension. Additionally, context will tell the average listener what the word means.

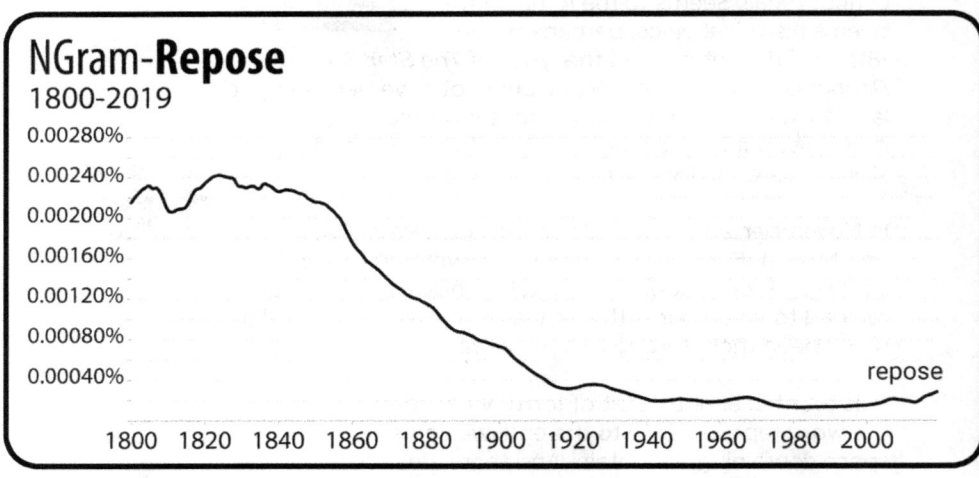

READING TO WAIT PATIENTLY AT SAM'S CLUB
2014

Gunning-Fog Index: 12.66

Since my wife is legally blind, I am commonly tasked with driving her to the store. As my wife shops, I typically busy myself by perusing the movie selection (which no longer exists), spot-reading in some book that piques my interest, or finding a place to sit down, where I usually end up snoozing.

In the year, 2014, I drove "Miss Daisy" to a large membership warehouse to do the weekly shopping. I'd seen the movie selection a hundred times already, so I thought I'd find a spot-read opportunity. I found a new book, *Janis's Intimates: On the Road with Janis Joplin*, by John Byrne Cooke. In my musical interests, I'm a bit of a throwback to an era just before mine, which predisposed my interest in this book.

There is something about '60s music that is engrossing. It was an era of breaking molds, lowering repressive standards, and establishing a new order of entertainment and culture. Janis Joplin was on the cutting edge of America's sexual devolution and the San Francisco rock scene. I can't say I was ever too interested in her music specifically. However, she interests me on the level of being a lead woman in the hard-scrabble days of early rock and roll. I knew how she died, so I turned to the last chapter of Cooke's book to see his take on the aftermath.

In this section, he used a word unfamiliar to me. I quickly took note of it on my iPhone to check up on it in my continuing education. Cooke wrote about how the news of Joplin's passing made it to her immediate intimates, family, and industry connections. He used the word **coterie** to describe part of those connections.

kō´tə-rē

Coterie is a noun meaning "an exclusive group of people who are interested in the same thing, often unified for a purpose." This word originated in the Middle French word

READING TO WAIT PATIENTLY AT SAM'S CLUB

tenants, which drew influence from the Germanic word *hut*, as in an abode or hovel. The implication from the originating languages is of familial, or related connections, or perhaps a small group that could fit in a shack.

This word is of interest to me because it has all the inferences of what church always should have been instead of the impersonal weekend show that it is. Coterie has the feel of warmth, friendly environs, and mutual commitment all rolled into one.

I like this word because it says something special and unique in contrast to today's acceptance of institutionalized shallowness and rugged individualism. It stands for something rare.

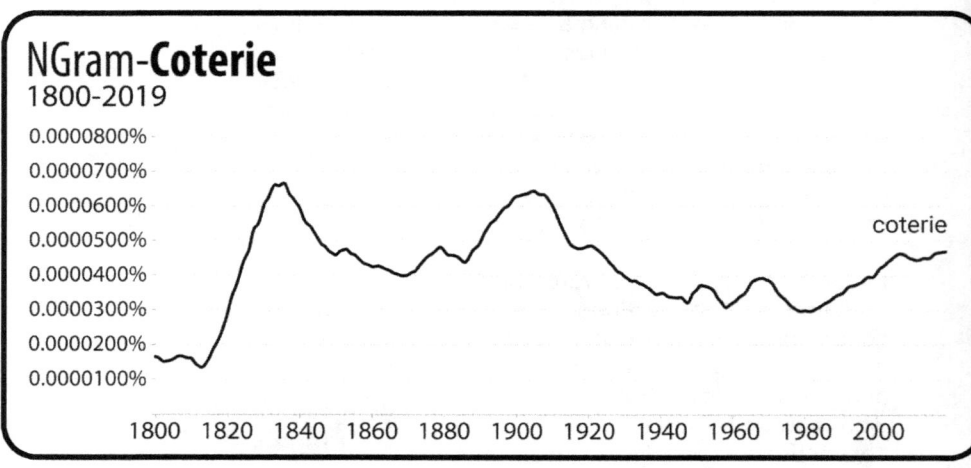

A NICE WORD FOR NEGATIVE IMPLICATIONS
2014

`Gunning-Fog Index: 11.74`

I belong to a large photography group on Facebook here in Nebraska that has more than 428,000 members:* Nebraska Through the Lens (NTTL). Rules are made to keep members from freaking out, which causes drama. In most cases, I agree with the rules. However, in one case, I find "the rule" creates more of a problem. People become obsessive about "the rule."

"The rule" involves train tracks occurring in photos. Train safety is a big issue. In 2014, some "photo takers" in Nebraska posed an entire sports team on some hectic tracks. The result was a shutdown of train traffic, which was unprecedented.

The incident caused pandemonium in the common public and in circles of real photographers who wanted to distance themselves from being misconstrued with the idiots who shut down train traffic. NTTL has become a microcosm regarding this issue and the groundswell surrounding it. Numerous people in the group freaked at the suggestion that someone could be safe and include elements of America's storied history with rolling iron.

I've been around railroads most of my life, even in direct, everyday involvement for more 5.5 years with News Link. I know rail safety, and I know how to take safe risks to get the best photo without endangering my life or anyone else's. Railroad companies can't and won't make an absolute ban on photography around their tracks, nor can they enforce "trespassing" where people typically take photos. Either would be PR suicide, to say nothing of the cost of undertaking said enforcement. Everybody knows rail yards are off-limits, and such is never in question in everyday photography. But instead of educating, a freakish revulsion suggesting total unsafeness in any photograph where there are people in conjunction with railroad tracks in the photo is the most common approach. It is in context to the photography fiasco that one Union

A NICE WORD FOR NEGATIVE IMPLICATIONS

Pacific spokesperson went on local media referencing that specific traffic stoppage in rural Nebraska caused by a photo taker. The spokesperson used the word **interloper** about the person responsible.

ĭn´tər-lō´pər

Interloper is a noun originating in the Dutch word landloper, which means "vagabond." In modern English, the word means "an individual who intrudes in a place or sphere of activity." It's an excellent way of implying trespassing.

We could use this word in a number of ways, both figuratively and indirect meaning. A person could be an interloper in conversation. A neighbor's Zoysia could interlope into our yard, invading our less invasive bluegrass. We can use this word to be diplomatic in our communication.

*Note: This count is as of Nov. 22, 2023

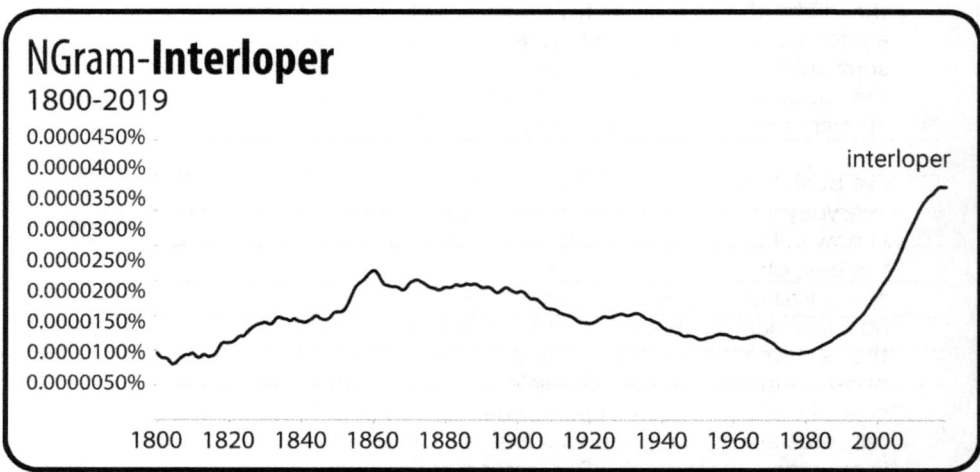

THE UNEXPLAINABLENESS IN FRENCH
2014

Gunning-Fog Index: 9.87

One oddity of my wife and I is that we find entertainment in some TV commercials. What is strange is that my wife commonly mutes commercials, but yet we still discover and enjoy a few of them. The inventiveness of some TV ads or their comedic nature attracts our interest.

Sometimes, my wife used to call me at work to tell me about some commercial. For me, I think the interest started back in the "Where's-the-beef" spots Wendy's ran back in the 1980s. There have been countless great ads since then that are cute, inventive, and hilarious.

One Sonic ad takes the cake! Sonic is not precisely a "high-society" establishment. Yet, in their "Wingman" ad, they put on airs. Sonic's "Two Guys" campaign features Peter Grosz and T.J. Jagodowski yucking it up redneck style. Grosz throws out the culture for Jagodowski to do the straight-man work of stereotypically screwing things up.

In the 2014 Wingman commercial, Grosz floats the term **je ne sais quoi** as their hook, and his sidekick mangles it per their usual  gig. I caught it! I came barreling out to the front room to catch the source.

Je ne sais quoi is a French noun, which is more of an idiomatic phrase in English use. It means "to have a certain something; an indefinable quality, inexplicable, or I don't know what." This is an expression one could be seen as snooty for using. But depending on the delivery and situation, it could be comedic or a serious seasoning to enrich a delivery.

The word is unique to French, dating from the 17th century. In France, it is not unusual, odd, or even exceptional. However, in English use, it's a bit of a device. It's not the type of word one can toss around in various

THE UNEXPLAINABLENESS IN FRENCH

crowds. But in certain arenas, it's a word that will draw attention both to what you are saying and to you.

I like this word because it slows down your listener or reader. It's cause for thought to most, except those who know French as their mother tongue or as a second language. Placed correctly in a mixed-language audience, it will earn you smiles and admiration. For the average bear American, it will give the feel of sophistication and culture.

One could explain the unexplainableness of some modern art pieces by using je ne sais quoi. Many political speeches are je ne sais quoi; they have substance, but many cannot be sure what was said. This is a fun word, but take care of how you use it.

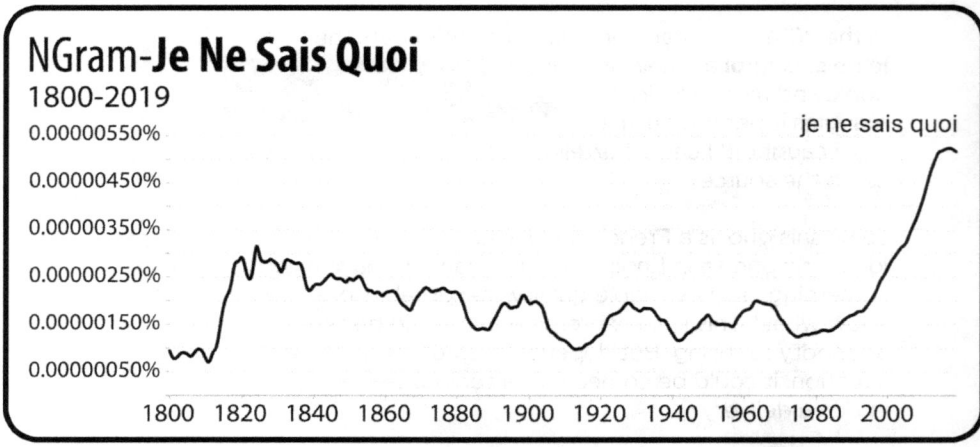

THE MYSTIQUE OF A MYSTIC
——2014——

`Gunning-Fog Index: 12.16`

For some reason, in 2014, I went on a random search for a book concerning Rasputin, the Russian mystic who unwittingly helped bring down the monarchy of Czar Nicholas II. I've wondered about this personage for years. Finally, on a whim, I bought another hardbound book about a historical character and went to town on it.

There are many books about this dark figure. The one I chose was Joseph T. Fuhrmann's book *Rasputin: The Untold Story*. The book was definitely engaging but lacked the first-hand quotes of Rasputin, which I usually prefer in historical accounts.

The story of Rasputin was interesting because there are tremendous myths surrounding him. His life's story is gripping because of its effect in the short term and the far-reaching finality. There are few more tragic stories in history than that which surrounding Rasputin.

Fuhrmann, the author of the account I read, is a consummate scholar and biographer. He wrote with clarity and creativity. Such a biographer can chew through all the minutia that plays into a story and then publish a concise, lineal account that gives readers a sure understanding of a historical personage. Sometimes, there aren't as many direct quotes from the person being featured, which was likely the case with Rasputin.

Part of this account involved some vocabulary gold. One such word Fuhrmann used early in the book concerned aspects of Rasputin's alleged capabilities. The word was **perspicacity**. This noun defines someone's innate ability to give insights not evident to others. This observation does not imply a supernatural peculiarity but rather a simple notation of extreme keenness.

pûr´spĭ-kăs´ĭ-tē

THE MYSTIQUE OF A MYSTIC

This term is another of Latin origin, from the word *perspicax*, meaning "sharp-sighted." In English, it means discernment and shrewdness that have similar meanings. Yet, *perspicacity* seems to be in its own class, utterly differentiated from these other words. Perspicacity is a superlative note. It is like saying extraordinary perception and acuity.

This is a word one to be used more in writ than in speech. It would be hard for context to inform its meaning, and it is unequaled by synonyms. Most synonymic terms give the impression of developed ability, whereas perspicacity seems to be a note of innateness that is exceptional.

There are people with perspicacity. They are not weird or a freak show like Rasputin. Talking about this capacity is to note preeminence. This word is a finer observation instead of a broad generality. Using a word like this showcases a uniqueness in who you are talking about in your own verbal acumen.

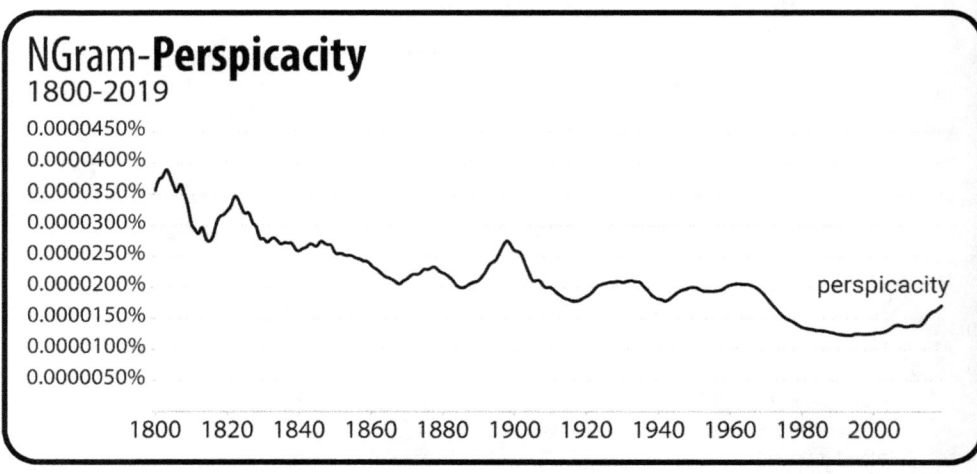

HOW BRITISHISMS ENRICH ENGLISH
2014

Gunning-Fog Index: 11.73

As my wife and I rewatch movies we own, it is incredible the details we catch, to which we seemed oblivious to in prior viewings. I can't tell you how often we talk about a movie where we comment to one another in this regard.

Perhaps the brain can only soak in a limited number of details per sitting. Maybe we are on a different wavelength at various times, so details hit us that would otherwise be smoothed over and go unnoticed.

I watched the movie *Appaloosa* again in 2014. We bought the Blu-ray edition. The film was slow-paced, as I remember. This time, I noticed it was shot in the same town where the modern *3:10 to Yuma* was filmed. I also took note of the actor Timothy Spall, who played Phil Olson, a shop owner and city father in *Appaloosa*.

Spall is a great British character actor, having played everything from Winston Churchill to the voiceover for a mouse in a claymation film. As a city councilman in Appaloosa, he plays a tentative opportunist who asks round questions and circuitously approaches his point. The script allowed this British character some vocabulary more familiar to the British Isles than America, the old Wild West notwithstanding.

Randall Bragg, played by Jeremy Irons, was the story's villain. He lived up to his name, boasting of connections with President Chester A. Arthur, and brashly did as he pleased: a masterful bully. Long story short, Bragg is convicted of a murder and sentenced. However, he escapes justice and cashes in on his connection to the president to acquire a full pardon.

As the townspeople find out about this development, Spall's character responds in a stereotypic fashion, blankly stating, "Evidently, Bragg's claim of association with our president wasn't just **thrasonical**."

thrā-sŏn´ĭ-kəl

HOW BRITISHISMS ENRICH ENGLISH

Thrasonical is an odd adjective. It doesn't have the usual background of a word. It originated from the Latin translation of a Roman comedy, *Eunuchus*, by Terence. In this play, the character Thraso was a braggart soldier. Thrasonical means "resembling the character of Thraso" —being boastful or bragging.

Thrasonical is a word you could have fun with in a social setting. It's a conversation piece because it is sure to cause everyone listening to halt immediately. This is where you can "big-time" others with a tidbit of trivia, and everyone has a laugh. Words don't always have to be serious for what they can communicate. Sometimes, a well-placed word can be an icebreaker or a bit of entertainment.

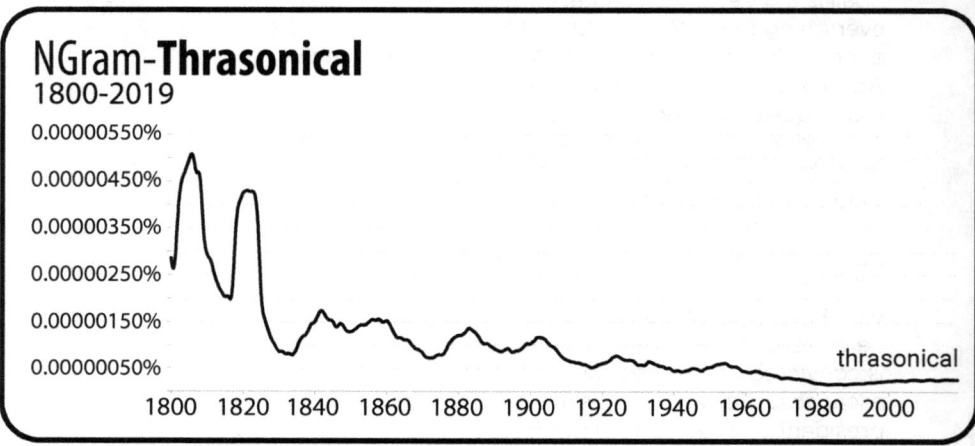

INTERMISSION
WORDS AFTER THE FACT

Afterwords

In recent years, 2020 and beyond, I've come to a period in life where circumstances force one to consider the meaning of life more intently. Initially, I wrote the former sections of this work six to eight years ago as a lark. I'd shelved the project because there were always more important things to do. That is, up until 2020.

My friend Wade Burleson, who wrote the Foreword to this book, asked that I take readers from 2014 to the current day. But first, I must provide a bit of context.

By 2019, I'd been having difficulties at work for several years. I had been able to surmount the perception of incapability. However, the symptoms arose to such a level that I could no longer tell myself it was all in my head—as in my own hyper self-criticalness. I doubted myself on one level but attempted to present that I was as good as the next person. One of the symptoms I'd observed was blackouts at work: I ended up at other people's desks and couldn't figure out how I got there. Another place trouble showed up was when I did some data entry daily. In numerous instances, nothing I checked off on the page resembled what I'd entered into the computer. I could not stay awake or concentrate. I could not retain new tasks or processes and was paranoid that someone would find out. I was a mess!

Work finally approached me. They told me that I must see a doctor. I've always been the type who would not go to the health care professionals unless something is literally falling off. Reluctantly, I went to see my old MD, whom I'd not seen in more than 15 years. The news was not good. After hearing of my symptoms, the doctor administered a Montreal Cognitive Assessment (a.k.a. MoCA test). This test involves an oral recall test of words given to a patient. Then, after a short period, the patient has to repeat the words. These words aren't $500 words no one uses, but mundane,

INTERMISSION—WORDS AFTER THE FACT

everyday words like church, street, football, or Sunday. In the mini-test, I failed royally. I could not remember but a small fraction of the content.

I used to be able to look at a 10-digit phone number and memorize it to the point where I could recite it perfectly two weeks later. Now, I couldn't remember even three digits from looking at it in one program and then trying to type it into my phone to dial. That's sad. The doctor told me that it was his opinion that I was illustrating the symptoms of early onset dementia at just 55. I was sent to a neurologist for a five-and-a-half-hour battery of tests, confirming my condition. Wow!

That was April 2020, a day that will live on in my life as my own "day that will live in infamy." Work fired me forthwith because we live in a "right-to-work state." That means work can fire you for any reason, and there is little recourse. I could do a good bit of the job, but the futzy stuff was a train wreck.

My Response to Seeming Disaster

I have never been the type to take anything sitting down. When life hands you lemons, you aren't supposed to put them in the freezer, so they harden up in order to bean all the idiots in your life. My wife and I went into the "handle-it mode" immediately. I built a lovely 1,200-square-foot house at a lake south of Omaha in 2017. I'd cut 50 trees off the half-acre lot, leaving 23 of the most mature trees in a spread to where we could nest a house. It was picturesque to beat the band! I put a lot of unique stuff into this house. Now, because of health, we had to let it go.

Because of my condition, work, and the scamdemic of Fauci's Chinese lab experiment, we chose to move to Kearney, Nebraska—the edge of nowhere as far as I was concerned. Our children live there. If I were to go south quickly, the kids would step in and help my wife, who is legally blind. What was left of my mind quickly turned to what I could do. I am the type to stay busy with a litany of projects and involvements. It's a family trait on both sides.

A Time for Everything Under Heaven

I quickly settled on a project I'd always wanted to do: adapt a 400-year-old allegory from the very hard-to-read editions over the past 120 years; to a more approachable edition. This title had been something that blew my mind years before, even in its hard-to-read editions. Few books have impacted me in my life than this title.

In my condition, I first wondered if I had the horses to accomplish such a task. I turned to a friend of mine, Wade Burleson, a pastor, historian, and, it would seem, a confidant. I also talked to my doctors, who encouraged the work because it would help keep my mind sharper because of engagement. Wade, always the encourager, blankly responded that he didn't know the title I mentioned and asked for a few sections. I obliged him through email. The next day, he called me, effusive, and told me I "had to do something with this book, as I could not believe it."

I went to work on the project. Some days, I could only spend two hours poring over three editions to adapt to an easier-to-read version before my head was ready to explode. The point of sharing this particular part of this story is that this project would have been impossible without a good vocabulary. Such has been a crowning achievement, especially given my conditions and tremendous hardships. By 2021, we published the most readable edition of John Amos Comenius's epic allegory, *The Labyrinth of the World -and- The Paradise of the Heart*, ever seen in English. We published it not only in print but also in audiobook—for the first time in any language in history—as well as eBook and in both hardbound and softbound. The book is also illustrated.

Transition

The period between 2014 to 2023 was rocky. My reading diminished, then all the busyness, then Labyrinth... I'm now going to share a few more anecdotal stories. These features will be a bit truncated from the cameos of my past writing. I am not nearly as creative these days.

THERE ARE TWO GREAT RULES OF LIFE: NEVER TELL EVERY-THING AT ONCE.

—TIM BENTURI

A REAL-LIFE FORREST GUMP
— 2014-18 —

Gunning-Fog Index: 10.5

I have worked for some real winners over the years. I am not what you'd call a leader. Nor was I ever a follower. My skill sets placed me as second fiddle to several visionaries. I've always seen how to do things faster, easier, cheaper, and better. I've developed a track record of doing so.

Enter James H. Keene, III of Omaha, whom we got to know a bit earlier. I went to work for Jim doing Marketing Management. Jim was aged in years and lived a colorful life, even by Forrest Gump standards. While working for him, I got to hear his stories four times because we traveled together. He went to Cornell '54 and became the number-three man at Peter Kiewit and Sons, Inc. (Kiewit). He ran prestigious projects from the early-warning system in Greenland (1958-61) to the Trans-Alaska Pipeline System—TAPS (1973-1977) to building the Bullwinkle oil platform in the Gulf of Mexico (1985–1988), just to name a few. His stories didn't stop at contracting exploits. He "saved" Omaha Opera and started the Brownville Concert series, which brought big-name acts from New York to an otherwise sleepy hick town in Nebraska. Even in his private life, he and his family were "interviewed" by the Jim Garrison investigators concerning the Kennedy assassination. Jim Keene was everywhere—a veritable Forrest Gump.

Jim always tried to be the "best" person in the room by offering *what he knew* or concerning *whom he knew* as some sort of recognition of his acumen or value. His stories were almost unbelievable, except they checked out. While Jim was a *larger-than-life guy* that might seem over the top. One day, he asked me to go out and **reconnoiter** around about something our present endeavor needed. Since working for Jim, I've heard this word used in old WWII movies.

rē´kə-noi´tər

When Jim used the word reconnoiter, my mind was instantly indicated to this word, but context told me what

A REAL-LIFE FORREST GUMP

it meant. The word originates from the Latin *recognescere*, which migrated into the French *reconnaître*, and shares meaning with the English word recognize. Reconnoiter reached Englishification in the early 19th century.

While there are other words one could use instead of reconnoiter, if one wants to communicate with flair, this word will do the trick. I think this is why Jim used it. He had a predilection for getting attention through his stories, mannerisms, and communication. While the word would be out of place for an Appalachian hillbilly, it would not be out of sorts for the average person and would communicate a level of sophistication.

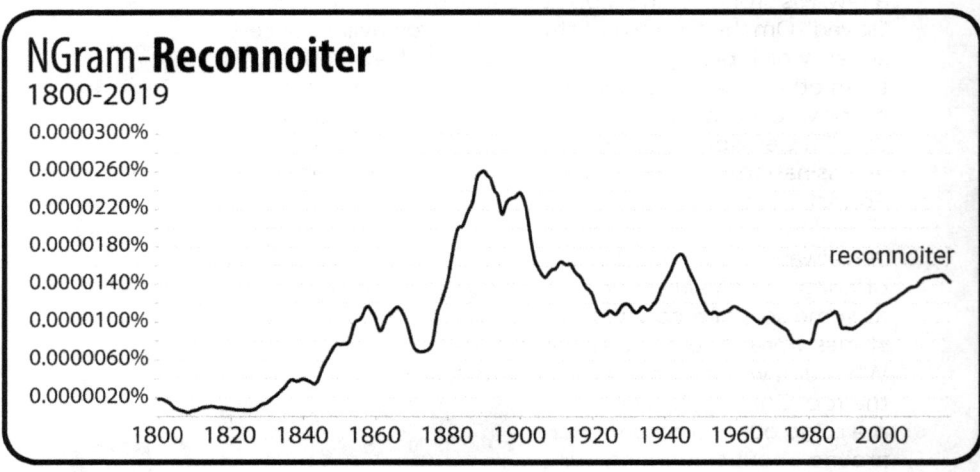

ANOTHER LOOK AT SERVILE TERMINOLOGY
2015

Gunning-Fog Index: 12.92

For more than 12 years, I have been working on a double-volume book concerning the Kingdom of God amongst the kingdoms of men. There are six views on this topic in the streams of the religious universe of Christian thought.

To get a grip on the various ways this topic has been articulated, I read through more than 32 volumes on the subject covering a period of 180 years. While this is not exhaustive, it is an attempt to be comprehensive. Views ranged the gambit. More about these details in the forthcoming books; no spoiler alert is needed.

One of the books in all these studies was titled *Slave of Christ: A New Testament Metaphor for Total Devotion to Christ* by Murray J. Harris. This book is a piercing *tour de force*. Since abolition and the recent scourge of identity politics, believers have had the truth in Murray's book obscured. There are more than 170 references to servile terminology and imagery of "not belonging" in the New Testament, which Murray picked up on in his excellent book.

Murray, of whom I know less than a scintilla, is linguistically capable. He uses the word **epigraphic**, which was new to me. While the term might seem ĕp´ĭ-grăf´ĭk as useless as tits on a boar, it has tremendous meaning and application.

At first, epigraphic could relate to epigraphs—inscriptions, especially on a building or a statue. How dull, right? Wrong! The origins of a word also give greater applicative understanding. Epigraphic came into English circa 1844, from Greek *epigraphē*, meaning "an inscription," and *epigraphein*, meaning "to mark a surface, write or inscribe, to register." An entire group of studies is based on epigraphics: the study of things written in various forms left by ancient civilizations.

ANOTHER LOOK AT SERVILE TERMINOLOGY

While Murray's particular use bears no connection to what I am doing here, in a sense, he was ethnographically studying the use of servile terminology, forgotten terms left in the New Testament in light of what slavery meant in the first century and how it was used metaphorically by New Testament authors. People skate over these terms in our modernity and concentrate on theological minutia and other insignificant details. The effect? It has taken the saber teeth out of the New Testament tiger. In so doing, we miss the most significant end of the message of absolute dedication to God.

Epigraphic is a word of admonition for us to study the little things in the Bible and history that bring greater understanding and dynamic impact to truth in our own day.

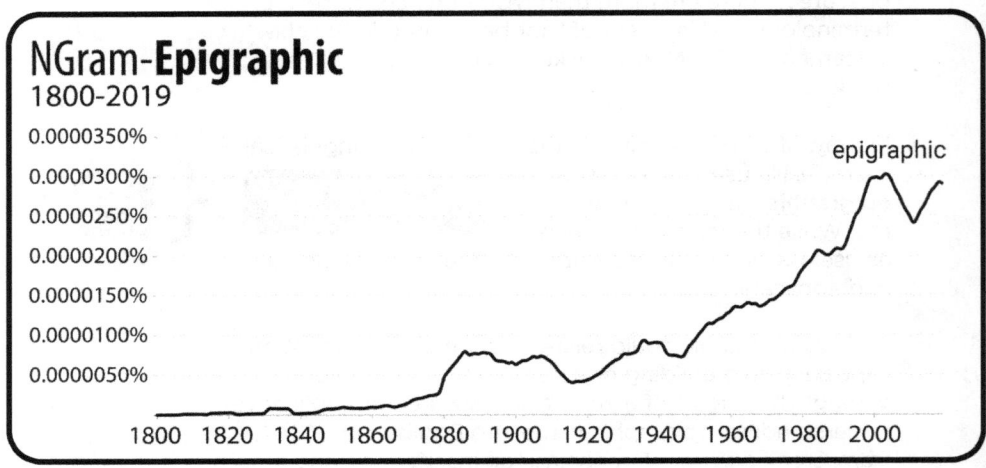

WORDS THAT SLOW READING DOWN
2016

Gunning-Fog Index: 10.2

While I've liked reading over the years, I am not so fond of *big books*. That is books numbering 500 pages or more. I am especially unfond of fictional works where there are 57 characters, and everything has mythical Celtic names or, worse yet, some made-up language and culture. There is nothing wrong with these, of course. However, they have always seemed bromidic and exasperating to my sensibilities. If one has to learn something, it would seem most valuable if it were real.

For some unknown reason, I got to considering Genghis Khan. While he is not a mythical character, his story is of legend far removed from the 21st century and a Western Civilization perspective. Genghis Khan might just as well be mythical because his story is shrouded in contrasting accounts, and his culture is so unfamiliar. However, as a history buff, I am drawn to accounts of its leading personalities.

The volume I bought, titled *Genghis Khan: His Conquests, His Empire, His Legacy*, was a whopping 630 pages. The author, Francis James McLynn FRHistS FRGS, most commonly known as Frank McLynn—is a British biographer, historian, and journalist. He is endued with a gargantuan vocabulary. Since I am an odd-duck, as I read, I circle words I do not grasp. In this largish tome, I ended up circling a whopping 105 words.

Of the many unfamiliar terms, the word **impecunious** grabbed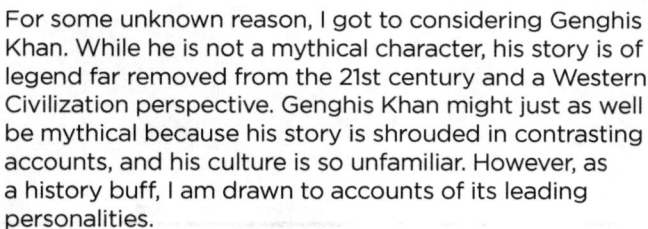
my attention because the context did not exactly divulge its meaning. Inquiring minds, like mine have to know. *Merriam-Webster* did not have my back. Thus, I pivoted to the trusty *Cambridge Dictionary*. Impecunious derived from the Latin, in the 16th century Latin *pecuniosus*—meaning "rich." The English prefix "im" is obvious even to a dolt. Thus, the literal meaning

WORDS THAT SLOW READING DOWN

of impecunious is "penniless" or, idiomatically speaking, someone who is "hard up" without cash.

While being hard up or penniless are common expressions these days, most will think you pretentious to use such a word like impecunious in conversation. Yet, for print, in modern culture, such a use slows the reader down, perhaps to get them to think about what is being said. McLynn weaves this adjective into the story of young Temüjin (the birth name of Genghis Khan) with no hint of pretension. The account was splendidly gripping. I was personally enriched by reading this account, which is the moral of this story.

As a fellow writer, I can see the value of a little-known word like impecunious. Its use is not relegated to some snooty period tale contrasting the rich and poor. I could see this word in a Humphrey Bogart noir movie where he narrates the lead-in to a scene.

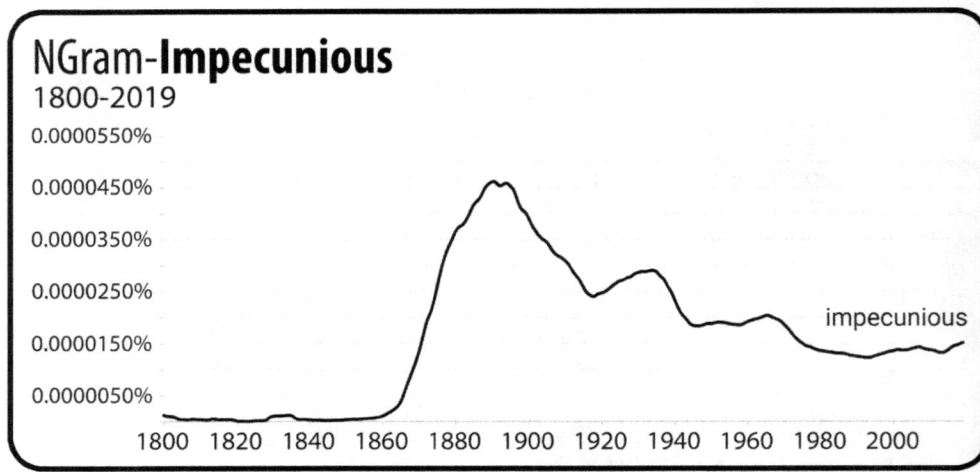

THE IGNORANT VIEW OF COMMUNISM
—— 2017 ——

`Gunning-Fog Index: 12.14`

Occasionally, I'll find some book that enchants me like a cat to *Nepeta cataria* (catnip). Such is the case of *True Believer: Stalin's Last American Spy* by Kati Marton. I loved this book!

True Believer reveals the life of Noel Field (1904–1970), a privileged, highly educated—he graduated from Harvard University in two years—American, a Quaker pacifist who worked for the US State Department and joined the communist underground at the same time (1930s). Field was drawn to communism by the allure of the rhetoric of peace and equality. His childhood was spent listening to America's most intellectual and sophisticated pastors of the period. But his adult life was given to spying, intrigue, betrayal, and murder. When Field was outed by Alger Hiss and Whittaker Chambers in 1948, he fled to Czechoslovakia. In 1949, he and his wife were picked up by KGB-like Czech forces and sent to high-security solitary confinement. He was a known spy for Stalin, yet he was tortured as a "counterspy," all while believing the communist ideal. Field and his wife, Herta, settled in Budapest, still believing in communism, and he died in 1970, well before the fall of communism. Wow, what a crackpot! True believer, as the book title espouses, was no lie.

Author Kati Marton uses the term **agitprop** in this book. This word is fascinating, stemming from Soviet-era concepts and programs. We would do well to learn a bit—the term developed in the 1930s from the Russian word *agitatsiya*, meaning "agitation." In English, *agitprop* relates to political propaganda, or politicization in arts or literature and now media and entertainment. It is a political methodology of agitation and propaganda used to influence and mobilize public opinion. If that isn't happening in America today, I don't know what you'd call it.

`ăj´ĭt-prŏp´`

THE IGNORANT VIEW OF COMMUNISM

Agitprop, or agit-prop as it sometimes appears, is more of a warning to be aware of. The dynamic is alive and well in today's world—like at no other time. Secondly, tons of ignorant and intelligent people are still bought by the come-on of communist/socialist rhetoric. This world will have no peace until the Prince of Peace shows up. In the meantime, if we are following Christ, we will be His peace wherever we go.

This is the meaning of the Kingdom of God, "Your kingdom come. Your will be done, on earth as it is in heaven," Matthew 6:10. The more sold out we are to Christ, the less we would ever be agitprop or manipulated by those using this technique to "level the playing field" an attempt utopia by the device of men.

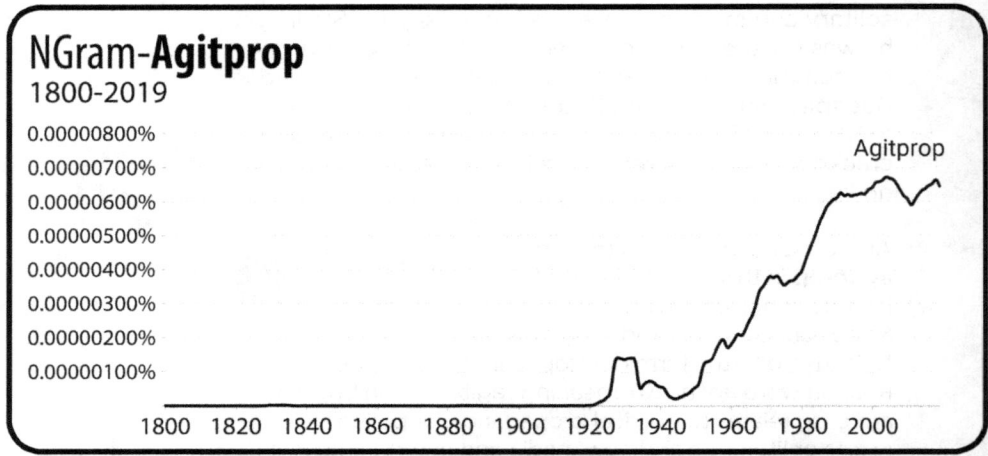

THE MOUSE THAT ROARED
2017

`Gunning-Fog Index: 10.78`

I remember, beginning in 2017, seeing problems health-wise. I took a new job with Siemens. One thing I feared most was learning the new computer system. My boss, Steve Bulter, was very engaging, short, dressed to the nines, and obsessed with image and success. Yet, he had a dual predisposition that could only be described as rage-a-maniac. My undetected health issues brought misunderstanding. He would have me take notes about everything. Using such methods, I'd lose a grasp of 90 percent within five minutes. Notes are meaningless if you lose connection to the subject. Being intensely precocious, this boss noticed the trend and assumed several things. This resulted in vituperations that would get anyone else fired.

The company is a multinational electronics company. I was sent to New Jersey for courses relating to my new area of work, which was fire alarm control systems. This endeavor was so far out of my experience; however, my charming demeanor and positivity spoke volumes to this boss man. The learning curve was steep for anyone; it would be perhaps nine months before I would get my legs under me. Thus, classes, online courses, manuals, and a couple of mentors got me into the field's minutia and set me up to bid quotes for jobs copiously.

I was still in the habit of copying words to databases. The course study in New Jersey used the word **ombudsman**,  which seems about as out of place for electronic-type work as a prostitute at a nun convention. The fact that the company is multinational is perhaps how the word came into the class study. I find that foreigners using English as a third, fourth, or fifth language beyond their mother tongue deal in some of the most obscure English words.

The word ombudsman's earliest antecedent stems from the Danish word *Umbozman*, dating back to the

THE MOUSE THAT ROARED

13th century. It migrated into Swedish, from whence it was adopted into English, as we use it. Initially, the word meant a select royal, civil servant who attended specific complaints brought to the court. It came to mean a person representing an official. Directly in English, this word means an advocate for a consumer, patient, or employee regarding an investigation for settlements from a government or business. It is different than a lawyer.

This is a role I'd never heard of, but one to understand. You could use this word to big-time folks in meetings discussing this type of situation. You will get some looks, but it is powerful if you use the right word in the right place.

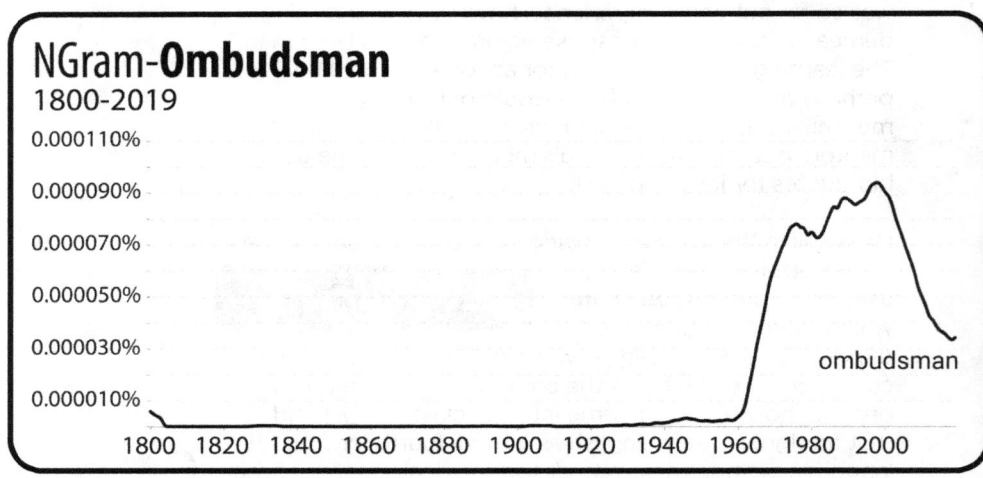

FROM THE MINDS OF BUDDING AUTHORS
2018

Gunning-Fog Index: 9.49

A friend, Jim Backens of Omaha, encouraged me to join him in a local writer's group. He'd been whittling away at writing for years. But more to the point, he was outnumbered—female to male—perhaps six-to-one. He was looking for male camaraderie.

Most of my writing up until then had been non-fiction. However, I was beginning to dabble in writing a dark novel. Jim told me that the group was named, get this—Chuck Rite, which met together monthly to offer encouragement and perspective in writing.

The meetings started with a game of speed writing that we then took turns reading aloud. It was like the game Balderdash, where people who like words could be hysterical, with lots of competition. Then, each attendee brought a written piece of their own, with several copies. The other members would read each other's works. In turn, they offered written responses ranging from suggestions to encouragement.

This put me outside my comfort zone because I might be reading about unicorns or underground creatures, perhaps taking in a treatise or cathartic self-help piece. The subjects or approaches could vary, as did the ability of the writers. Responses were to be encouraging and helpful, both of which were no trouble for me. But some of the subjects— Oy Vey! Words fail me.

One budding author, a typical millennial gal with tats and piercings, had a penchant for tales of yore. She used a word I've never heard: **petrichor**. It sounded like some type of explosive. But my initial guess was wide right of the actual meaning. Her novel was something along the lines of a mythical-type-forest-setting adventure. Upon her use of this word, it was instantly copied into my infamous word-study database.

pĕt´rĭ-kôr´

FROM THE MINDS OF BUDDING AUTHORS

Petrichor is an interesting noun dating from Greek times, yet not appearing in English until the late 1950s. Its roots are πέτρα (pétra), which we usually translate as "rock." Secondly, ἰχώρ (ikhṓr) translates as "blood of the gods." Writers look for ways to describe what is sensory or evident that may not be commonly understood. In this case, petrichor is "the scent of rain." It's widely thought of as a pleasant smell caused by rain on dry ground or when precipitation occurs in a forest, the smell of which hangs in the air.

This word has fantastic distinction. Aside from writing, you can big-time dinner guests or friends with something they won't know.

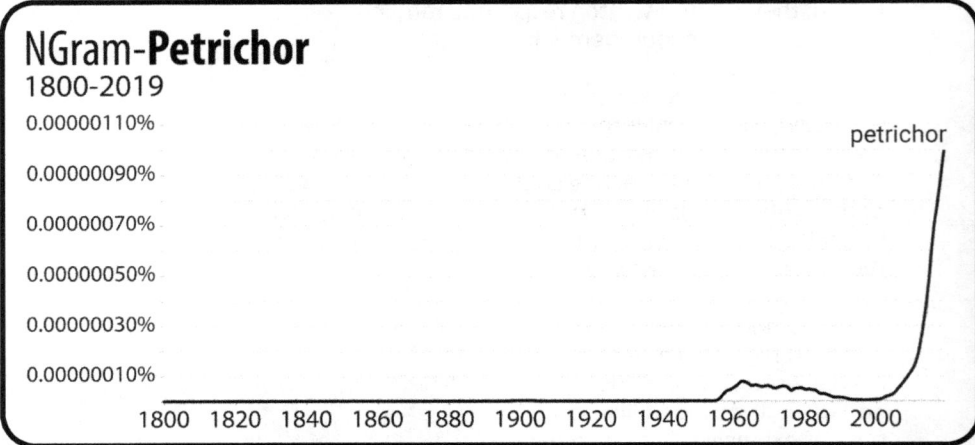

RANDOM FORAY IN THE DICTIONARY
2018

`Gunning-Fog Index: 11.82`

My dear daughter, Genesis, is another logophile, much the same as David Martin and Paul Orner, whom I will get to shortly. Of course, the word fun is a different story with your daughter. The fun often works itself out on board games like Balderdash, which is a total gas for folks like me.

Because of my health issues, we moved to Kearney, Nebraska. My daughter moved there for a year or two. We'd get together with my son, Roman, and his wife, Stephanie, and have one of those infamous Balderdash sessions. At various points, everyone was in stitches over the funny hooey we could all generate concerning a word and the perception of a fake definition.

At other points, we'd argue over words, at which point the dictionary became part of the problem. In one search, we came across the word **uxorious**. I don't recall why we got hung up on this word, but I think it had to do with finding expression in the weird things we observe. This is one of those kinds of words.

ŭk-sôr´ē-əs

The adjective uxorious comes to us from the Latin antecedent *uxor*, meaning "wife." *"Ous,"* as a suffix in English, means "possessing or full of." But this is counterintuitive because uxorious in modern terms means exhibiting excessive and servile fondness for a female spouse or girlfriend. Uxorious could indicate marriage to a domineering wife or expressing an extremely emasculated husband. *Obsequious*, one of my favorite words of all time, is someone acting servile or fawning towards others to gain favor. Uxorious is explicit of a man having a subservient fondness toward a female romantic partner.

Wow, what a word for today's world of gender confusion, role switching, and a lower testosterone count than at any time in history. I'm not implying that patriarchy is good. But we see varying degrees of uxoriousness today. What's

RANDOM FORAY IN THE DICTIONARY

more interesting is that this word, descriptive of a specific type of reality, is at a statistical zero compared to its use in 1800.

What's the upshot for us? Well, you'll lose people using this word in a conversation. However, explaining the term in print or writing it for theater or something acted will bring the word to a broader understanding.

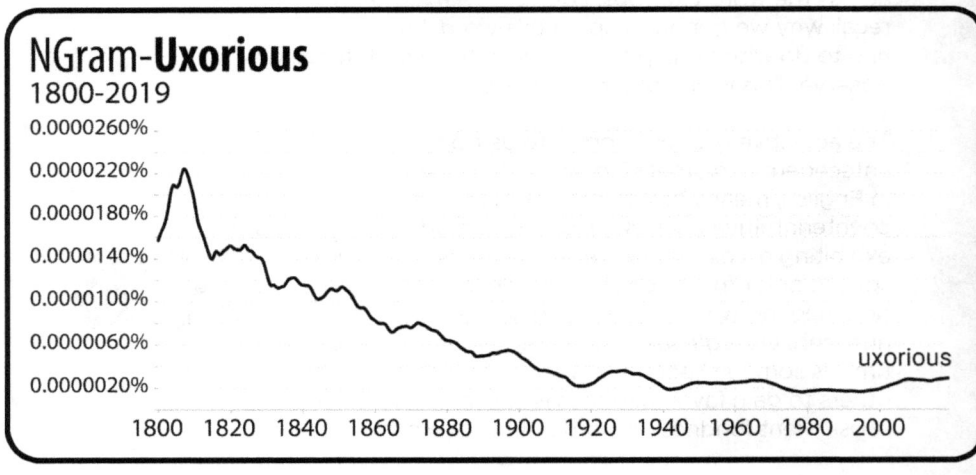

BE AN AUTODIDACT

> Gunning-Fog Index: 11.14

It seems my whole life has been a preparation for a moment. For nearly 16 years, I've been inspired by John Amos Comenius's *The Labyrinth of the World -and- The Paradise of the Heart*, a semi-biographical allegory predating the great *Pilgrim's Progress*. In fact, the former inspired the latter, which is a kick in the head. *Pilgrim's Progress* is the second-best-selling book in history, but nobody has heard of *Labyrinth*. I'd grown up on *Pilgrim's Progress*. But when I read Comenius's book, I was blown out of my socks!

When health took me down, a friend, Dotty Zens, told me, "You don't know that God didn't take you down in order to do this other thing," namely, adapting *Labyrinth* for an easier read. Without going into the whole story, I took three of this title's only four English editions and adapted the reading to a ninth to tenth-grade level from a doctorate-level or a Chaucer-type read. The process took almost two years.

But in my life, I'd worked in several areas: purchasing, importing, publishing, sales, trade shows, mechanical drawing, contracting, and, of course, building a solid vocabulary that all played directly into this production. Without those experiences and preparations, adapting *Labyrinth* would have been more challenging than climbing Mount Everest.

Even so, with an excellent vocabulary, I found an additional need for expression. I was searching for better words, more adept terms; or being more descriptive and detailed than former editions was a crucial part of this effort. I found the word **gourmand** to the precise word I needed in one instance. Former editions used "them" or "some of those" in reference to hedonists reveling in their gorging feast. The plural form of gourmand was the *mot juste*.

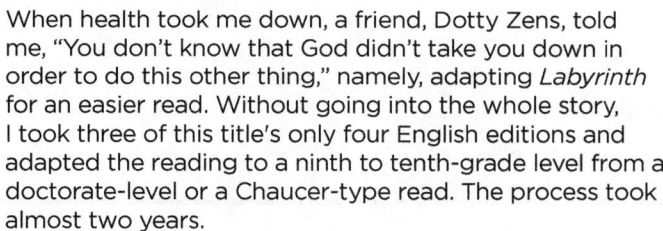

BE AN AUTODIDACT

Our modern English term, goumand, comes from the late 15th century Old French word *gourmaunt*, meaning "glutton." This term should not be confused with *gourmet*, which is the fondness of good eating or what is exquisite in its goodness or taste. The word gourmand peaked in usage in the early 19th century. Yet, it is apt for the book I adapted and quite contemporary to describe an increasing paunch of society these days.

To me, it's a fun or funny word that context defines for a reader. Therefore, it is a great term to toss out there. This vignette illustrates the tenacity of being an autodidact. We can learn if we are determined to find what we're looking for to describe, articulate, and communicate with verve.

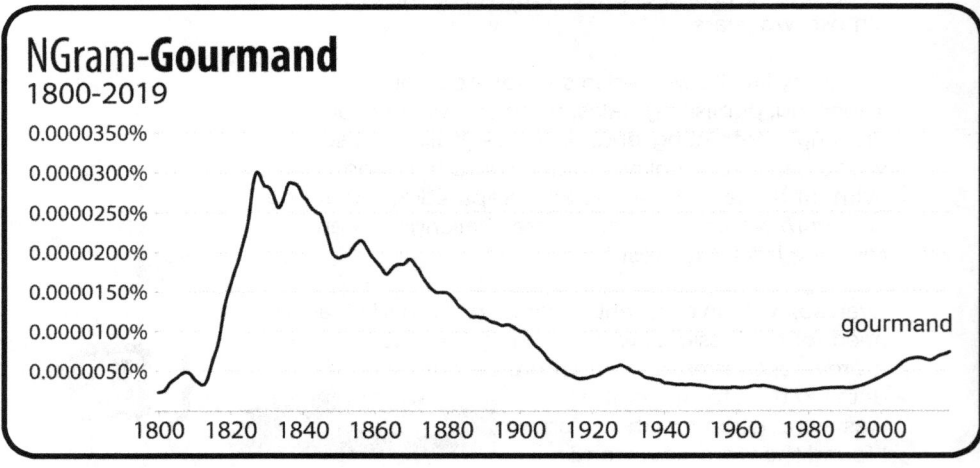

TWO CAN BE RIGHT
2021

`Gunning-Fog Index: 10.14`

Some book reviewers and critics get hung up on spelling, punctuation, or grammatical rules. They will hang you for an end-of-sentence preposition (which is allowable) or passive voice. Or they will find a double spacing or a misspelling and report it with almost anal-retentive glee. While I, as a small publisher, enjoy seeing the goobers in the most professionally, traditionally published works, it merely comforts me that even the big boys miss things.

I was talking with David Martin, an acquaintance I picked up through my forays into the Anabaptist world. He is one of the most congenial people I've ever met. We were talking by phone one day about my work on *The Labyrinth of the World*. I used the word ruminate to describe someone thinking about what he sees in the story. David challenged me that the correct term should be **cogitate**.

kŏj´ĭ-tāt´

David is likely four to five years my junior but 10 years ahead of me in reading. He's not a brainiac, just a Mennonite. They place a high value on reading. I only know one other individual who could match David, in all the folks I know, concerning reading depth. Thus, I had to consider his suggestion.

Like so many other words, I'd never heard this one, either. I'd heard cognition but never thought of relative derivatives. Cogitate was contributed to English from Old French *cogitacion*, much like the word I knew. The Old French was the successor of the Latin *cogitationem*. In literal terms, these words express "turning things over in the mind, motion of thought, to reflect." Rumination or "to ruminate" is based on an animal term, *ruminant*, for hoofed herbivorous grazing or browsing mammals, like cattle, that chew their cud—the plant-based food that ferments in their stomachs.

Ruminate definitely means the same thing today as it did in the 17th century. However, English has a way of words

TWO CAN BE RIGHT

taking on an idiomatic or expression usage. The current Oxford definition of ruminate is "to think deeply about something." The cow/cud thing is secondary.

The upshot is that Mr. Martin was right. And yours truly was correct. Two rights don't make either wrong. Cogitate is a word that will get noticed if you use it in speech or writing. It's not pretentious, just uncommon. For word people, logophiles, like the people I'm surrounded by, these bits enrich our understanding and ability to communicate. It gives us distinction. People will know you by the words you keep.

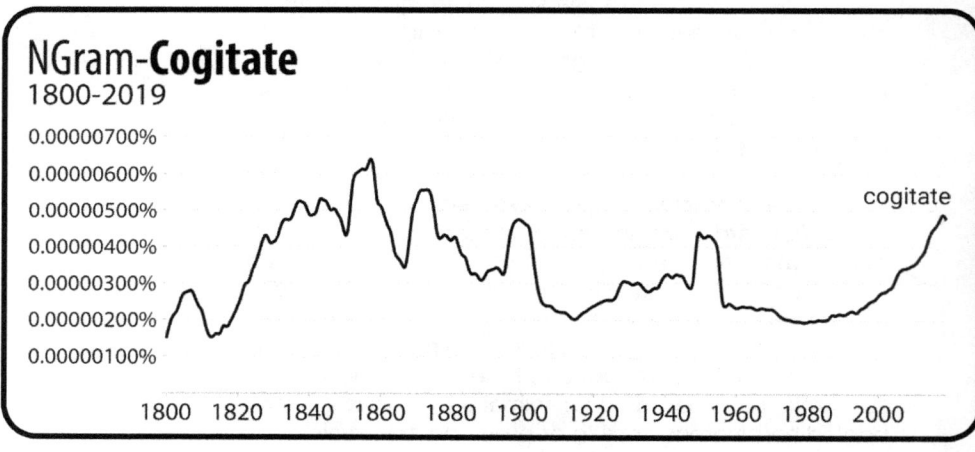

CONVERSATIONS OF BIBLICAL PROPORTION
2023

Gunning-Fog Index: 11.91

David Martin, whom you just met, is the kind of person I visit with quite often. We talk about a range of subjects, some of which are troubling religious concerns. He and I are both migrating in thought and processing our backgrounds to find our own understandings. He is from a very conservative Mennonite background and continues to dress the part. On the other hand, I have also moved far from the religious moorings of my youth. Neither of us would be considered "unbelievers" by the measure of our original associations. But they are not at ease around us.

I've noticed a strange happening can occur when talking to religious people of different backgrounds. If they are insecure, they might say they are "trying to understand you" when in fact they are just measuring you as compared to their own viewpoint. I observe this odd occurrence quite frequently as a vendor at homeschool conventions. People often inquire about the exacts of my religious association or connections. Folks commonly don't listen to what is said but only seem to be searching for similarity in what is expressed as a confirming point or the parroting of buzzwords as the means of connection and trust with someone unfamiliar.

David and I bat these types of subjects around, interspersing with many laughs and jokes. We don't have to have all the answers to be okay. We know we're in the process. The folks who don't know they are in the process present severe challenges to meaningful relationships and connections.

David used the term **Shibboleths** to describe the occurrence we had been talking about. This word

shĭb´ə-lĭth

arose from the Hebrew word shibbólet (שִׁבֹּלֶת) [Strong's H7641]. This noun entered English in the 17th century. In the Old Testament, Judges 12:5-6, one tribe of Israel—the Gileadites—used a known tendency of mispronunciation of

CONVERSATIONS OF BIBLICAL PROPORTION

another tribe of Israel to challenge people escaping from a confrontation as a way to catch Ephraimites, who attempted to appear like the locals.

Shibboleths are a commonly occurring reality used by almost everyone. If you go to Kentucky and do not pronounce the home city of the Kentucky Derby as "Looavul," locals know you're not from there. Many constructs, from sociological concerns to culture, employ this device.

While a word like this is not something you will throw around in conversation, it defines a common precursor that often results in prejudicial attitudes and actions.

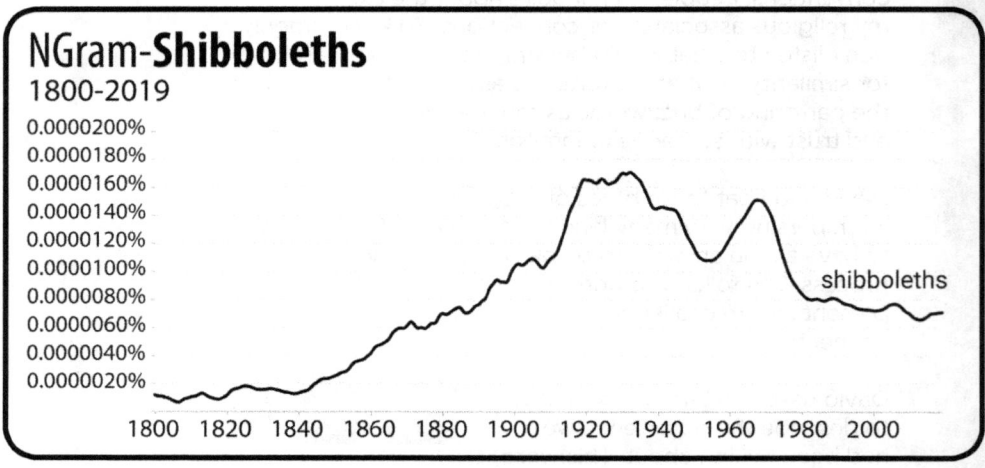

BREAKFAST OVER WORDS
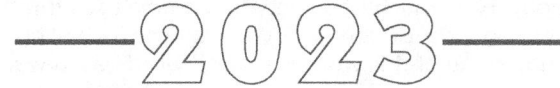

`Gunning-Fog Index: 10.57`

Another of my friends in Chicago, Paul Orner, is also a person of wordplay. Phone calls and in-person visits are always lively and informative. Paul's family, like my own, are empty nesters. He and his wife, Lorraine, travel to Missouri and Kansas frequently.

We've stayed in touch for many years since the early 2000s when we initially met at a Searching Together conference for people of house church persuasion. I enjoy Paul because we can talk about anything, and there is not a minefield of stuff I have to step around in conversation. I have stayed in their home during my travels. On one occasion, Paul was traveling through an area I happened to be passing through. He invited me to a home-cooked breakfast at his Airbnb in the second quarter of 2023.

We sat down over farm-fresh eggs and sausage and carry on with our usual banter. Paul said, "I've got a few new words for you" because he knows my inclinations. One of the words he shared was **inveigle**.
My memory is poor. I discovered I'd   ĭn-vā´gəl
actually run into this term earlier.
While researching through *Genghis Khan: His Conquests, His Empire, His Legacy*, by Frank McLynn book, I see that I'd circled the word back to 2016. But we're going to credit Mr. Orner anyway! The word hit my list because of him and because I can't remember stuff anymore.

The verb inveigle has an interesting background in the Latin element *"ab,"* meaning "separation or departure," and *oculus*, meaning "eye." The combination *aboculus* means "without vision or awareness." Dropping into Anglo-Norman French in the 15th century, the term developed into our English version. The A-NF transliteration was *enveigle* or *aveugler*—"one who blinds someone's perception or scrutiny, one who deludes." In modern English, the word takes on more meaning: to convince by deception, seduction, or flattery to do something.

BREAKFAST OVER WORDS

What a word for today! How much of society and *media* uses this approach in advertisement, propaganda, or content? We live in an inveigling society. Paul's reminding me of this word is a good word—as in warning or awareness.

I can see the use of this word in writing. Since it has grown out of use, not because it's archaic but rather unfamiliar, it will slow down the reader. The inquisitive will avail themselves of a resource if they are worth their salt. In presentations, it will sharpen your appeal because it will pique interest because of the unusualness of the word.

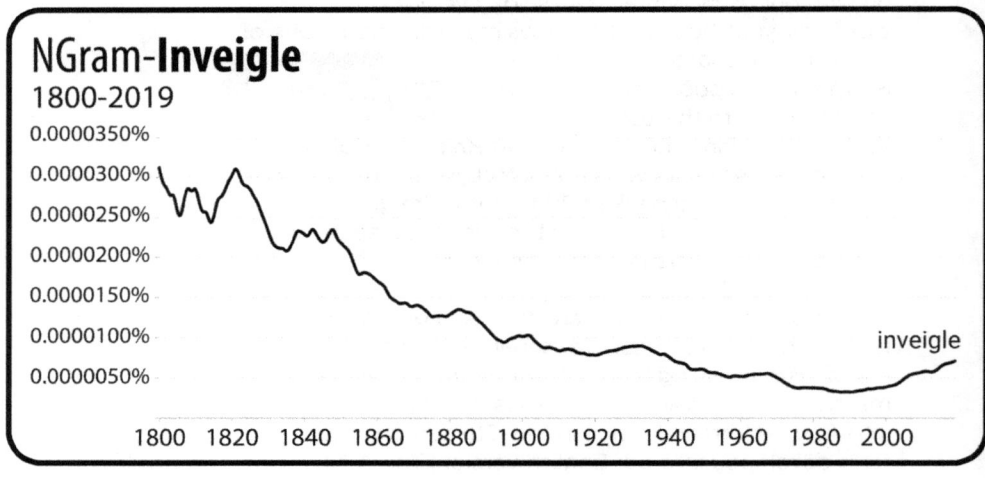

GLOSSARY OF TERMS

This section will define concepts, expressions, or terms you may not be readily familiar with yet. Some are terms I've coined to express a reality I see that I haven't found expression for. Other entries are just uncommon and need further description. My hope is that this section offers more accessibility and education in the way of communication and understanding.

Exceptionism – This reality is where a person finds ways to derail a generalization that would otherwise be true. It is like a "red herring" [something mentioned to divert attention from the subject at hand] only this term embodies people who make a regular and insistent habit of acting in this way. I've seen more of this tendency in recent decades. People insist on finding anything to derail an otherwise natural conclusion by tossing into discussion an exception, therefore toppling the logical deduction. This is a term I have coined and use regularly.

Explosion in a haystack – Growing up, my mother, Karel Ida (Geary) Price, would use this expression to describe how our hair looked in the morning as we rolled out of bed and mowed down into the kitchen for breakfast. Or, if our hair looked bad coming in from play or work in the afternoon she would comment this way. My mother used this expression regularly, and I have continued to do so. It's very descriptive.

Flashes in the pan – This idiom describes someone or something that garnered massive notoriety or attention but only to fade away into obscurity. In the music industry, such are called "one-hit wonders." Flash-in-the-pan derives from flintlock rifles of the 17th century that used a flint strike to set off a small amount of black powder set in a pan at the breech of a gun, which, if set off, would fire the gun. When the gun did not fire, but the powder flashed in the pan, this would be considered a "misfire" because the result of the firing did not happen even though all the other mechanics had worked properly. Thus, a "flash-in-the-pan" came to be used to describe any sudden action that should lead to success that didn't.

Glad-handed – A negative description of a person who warmly greets and shakes hands disingenuously or only to be seen doing it. Politicians are famous for this tendency. This term is never a positive description. It tends towards the derisive, if not plainly negative.

Goyim – This is a Hebrew/Yiddish term carried into English usages. Originally the word was "goy". The plural form, goyim or goys, is a pejorative term to refer to any ethnic outgroup that is not of Jewish heritage. It can also be used by religious Jews and a jib, to another Jew that is not religious or is ignorant of Judaism

Hoity-toity – This idiom expresses one—or a group—who puts on airs, is pretentious, or tries to exhibit or communicate a sense of superiority through snobbish behavior, social graces, or even elocution and fake accent. The superiority can be based on some level of performance, achievement, or level of education. The point is that the person is pronounced when attempting to express themselves in order to demean others or differentiate themselves from what they deem as mere rabble.

Hooey – Is a descriptor of something not true, that doesn't make sense, or that is nonsense that some may believe. Synonyms might be Poppycock, Balderdash, Bunk, or Hokum. The term is definitely slang. However, it is colorful and perhaps has less "low brow" than the other synonyms listed.

In a month of Sundays – This expression, in plain terms, means a terribly long time. A calendar has 28-31 days, which in this expression would be considered "sabbath" and filled with various restrictive religious observances. The term first appeared in 1759. In Puritanical society, Sundays were a long, tedious affair where anything amusing or entertaining was verboten. The expression imagines an interminably long period devoid of anything but dry religious ritual.

Kingdom of God amongst the kingdoms of men – This phrase is something I have coined to express what Jesus and Paul meant by "the kingdom of God" in contrast to how this exact Biblical phrase is misused in Christianity today. Jesus and Paul used the words—Kingdom of God—to mean what God is doing and followers cooperating in it. However, this phrasing has been coopted in modern teaching to mean a bevy of other things utterly devoid of Christ and Paul's usage and meaning. Thus, coining the phrase—Kingdom of God amongst the kingdoms of men—draws back into discussion and understanding the original purpose and application of "the kingdom of God."

Life's like a Box of Chocolates – This phrase was popularized by the 1994 movie Forrest Gump. However, the essence of this notion came from the 1987 novel by Japanese author Haruki Murakami, where the protagonist, Midori Kobayashi, said, "You know, they've got these chocolate assortments… Life is a box of chocolates. I suppose you could call it a philosophy." Forrest Gump's usage is more endearing and undoubtedly popularized the notion into an expression. But what does it mean? An assortment of chocolates presents different tastes and flavors. Unless you have the legend of which one is where it's unknown what you'll get. Some, you make like others, but not as much. However, variety and the unknown are always close when consuming said chocolates.

Lose words sink big ships – This American idiom is reflected in WW II propaganda campaigns, warning of careless talk about privileged information one might know. Many people worked in industries supplying the war effort, and spies were everywhere, eavesdropping on what others were talking about. Military members could be "off duty" but too talkative concerning sensitive information. The idiom carried the thought of consciousness and caution in what one says because of the potential consequences.

Muckety-mucks – A pejorative idiom to refer to people who hold themselves as a cut above everyone else. Often, the implication is arrogance. American colloquial, which is derisive, that average people can refer to folks who have no self-awareness about the way they live and think about themselves in elitism. This expression came from Chinook (native American) jargon, "Muck-a-muck," which referred to important people. The Sacramento's Daily Democratic State Journal in 1856 is thought to be the first official use of this expression. Similar expressions would be bigwigs, big cheese, or pooh-bahs.

Mutual-admiration society – This expression describes a society where people gather in groups with strong feelings and lavish one another with compliments and support in the perspective they hold. The idiom can refer to genuine or ingenuine admirations. It could refer to a workplace, social, or religious situation. The reality is something that the group would never admit but can be objectively observed. Henry David Thoreau and Oliver Wendell Holmes used this expraession as early as 1851.

Oy Vey! – This Yiddish phrase expresses dismay, surprise, or exasperation. There are alternative spellings, or the abbreviated form might be heard as: oy! The expression's evolution came from German but has been modified through Dutch and Swedish influences. I've heard this expression in "Jewish" movies or sitcoms. Having been around many Jewish folks over the years, I've also heard this expression used.

Phi Beta Kappa – While this term has an official definition, referring to a person achieving the highest scholastic distinction in an American university—often being elected to membership in a national honor society. The phrasing can have a strong derisive meaning. A fellow I worked for in Omaha said, "He's not a Phi Beta Kappa," meaning to say the other person is being referred to as not bright. A phrase that can be used to classify the best and to deride is quite a term.

Pot calling the kettle black – This expression is an informal reference to what is known as a Tu quoque fallacy, where a person negates their contention by their own hypocrisy. The person is guilty of the very thing of which they accuse another. When tossed out amid the accuser's testimony or dispute, this derisive retort often quells the intensity of the accuser. The origins of this expression are unknown.

Potty trained at gunpoint – I learned a version of this expression from the 1994 movie Renaissance Man, starring Danny DeVito who played a smart aleck rent-a-teacher. DeVito's character flippantly responded to a drill sergeant DeVito figured to be too uptight. This expression is suggestive of early childhood trauma. It is a subtle slam and questions someone's stableness or perspective.

Pull yourself up by your bootstraps – This is a colloquial expression referring to socioeconomic advancement. It was purposed to be a sarcastic, dismissive comment, thinking it is an impossible accomplishment, because the notion was based on an 1880s reference in a physics primer. Those who have advanced in socioeconomics and are proud of their accomplishments will use this term.

Rage-a-mania(c) – I've coined this term to describe people who freak out over minuscule things or exist in a continuum of rage. Perhaps it refers to Intermittent Explosive Disorder, a DSM classification: repeated, sudden bouts of impulsive, aggressive, violent behavior or angry verbal outbursts. I love my coined term because it doesn't sound pretentious but refers to this growing reality.

Rat Pack – This is a historic cultural term referring to a group of five co-performers in the entertainment industries of Hollywood and Las Vegas during the 1950s and 1960s. Group members were Frank Sinatra, Dean Martin, Sammy Davis, Jr., Joey Bishop, and Peter Lawford. The group made movies together.

Rough and tumble persona – Many times, we'll meet folks, especially men, that put off a "don't mess with me" aura. This is exactly what is meant by this term. It's a way to describe a reality we observe in bullies or gruff individuals or folks that go on spouting the bona fides in terms of grit and toughness.

Scamdemic – This term is one I've heard, and it is totally derisive. Melding "scam" with a pandemic and dropping the "pan," you get the idea. It came into use during the Covid-19 international kerfuffle. It is not without evidence that governments, globalists, and pharmaceutical cartels conspired together to facilitate a global event and offer a "mandatory" solution. Thus, this term has become widely used, and "official sources" try to discredit the notion as a mere "conspiracy theory."

Stargardt (syndrome) – This genetic eye disease affects the macula, similar to Macular Degeneration. This condition usually is not caught or observed until it begins to degenerate a person's eyesight quickly. Both parents have to transmit particular genes to the child affected. It usually skips generations. The condition doesn't take effect until the late teens. Then, it stabilizes in varying degrees of effect. The remaining vision is captured through peripheral receptors; greatly diminishing detailed vision.

Stink eye – This idiom expresses a nasty look. One could just as well use an evil eye or a dirty look. However, these later forms are so pedestrian and well-worn that they have no panache. A friend of mine from Atlanta used it in my presence, and I enjoyed the expressiveness of the term; I have adopted it ever since. According to the Oxford English Dictionary, this term is said to have started among surfers in California.

Sunday-go-to-meeting – This expression means "fitting for Sunday" or Sunday best. It could be used in several ways, both in the negative and positive sense. It originates in the 1830s in the diary of J.R. Motte. I see this as a comical reference, not as it is mainly used. It smacks more of ritual and pretension than a good thing.

Tales of yore – This expression notes olden times, such as ancient times or centuries in the past. "Tales of" is self-explanatory. I find the term jocular and expressive but not negative or derisive.

The final straw – This denotes the finale of a string of unfortunate events that can no longer be tolerated. It is similar to the French world coup de grâce; however, it expresses a more familiar series of events than more dire ones.

Throwback – This might seem like a trolling term (fishing), referring to a small catch. However, it concerns something more suggestive of types or early ancestorial period. For instance, when I came of age in the 1980s, I was aligned with my musical appreciation to that which existed an entire generation before mine. Thus, I would be referred to as a throwback to the 1960s. My peers could not understand me as they either didn't know the music of the '60 or they thought it was an old hat in favor of the vogue of the times.

Tiptoeing through the tulips – This phrase started as a song of romance and rendezvous in the garden for a kiss. It originated in 1929 as a ditty, later made a cult sensation by the whacky 1960s singer Tiny Tim. However, the phrase has become an expression of "skirting the issue." This could embody being diplomatic or obfuscative. This phrase can be seen in the mouth of the Three Stooges or some other comic wanting to give a humorous edge to a comment.

Vaudeville – Is a lost art form of theatre that features a variety of entertainment. Beginning in the 1880s, close to the end of the "Old West." Throughout America and Canada, music halls and stage theatres provided a stage for tropes of singers, dancers, acrobats, and showmen and women ranging from the austere to the bawdy. Cinema of the Old West depicts versions of this form of entertainment. This art form morphed until the motion picture killed it. Isolated "night clubs" now feature more low-class versions of vaudevillesque entertainment such as burlesque.

Victim of circumstance – This phrase represents being a victim of something beyond your control or because of the mistakes of others. Unfortunately, someone can be at the wrong place at the right time. They might be collaterally injured by the inextricable or because of the consequences of the actions of others. The Three Stooges made this phrase commonplace even though the concept is much older.

Worth their salt – Originally, this expression was thought to come from Roman Legion days, when soldiers were paid in salt. The expression means that one is worth one's value in the weight of salt. It is a compliment of value or worth beyond existence and admirable.

INDEX

Actors

Art Linkletter, 177
Ben Stein, 35
Brad Pitt, 08
Bradley Cooper, 173
Bruce Willis, 169
Ciaran Hinds, 131
Clayton Moore, 191
Clint Eastwood, 73
Don Rickles, 85, 159
Dustin Hoffman, 91
Ed Harris, 149
Elliot Gould, 107
Ewan McGregor, 75
F. Murray Abraham, 37
Gene Hackman, 91
George C. Scott, 17
George Carlin, 106, 159
George Clooney, 108
Helen Mirren, 169
Humphrey Bogart, 216
Ioan Gruffudd, 131
Jeremy Irons, 149, 205
Jimmy Kimmel, 85
Jimmy Stewart, 123
John Cusack, 91
John Malkovich, 73, 169
John Wayne, 69, 70, 149
Johnny Depp, 143
Jonathan Winters, 106
Josephine Hull, 123
Judi Dench, 22
Karl Malden, 17
Larry The Cable Guy, 106
Leonard DiCaprio, 167
Martin Lawrence, 187
Morgan Freeman, 169
Peter Grosz, 201
Peter O'Toole, 23
Renee Zellweger, 149
Richard Burton, 23
Robert De Niro, 173
Robins Williams, 51
Russel Crowe, 70
Russell Brand, 70
Stephan Lang, 183
T.J. Jagodowski, 201

The Three Stooges, 84, 157, 158
Timothy Spall, 205
Tom Hulce, 37
Victoria Horne, 123
Viggo Mortensen, 149
Will Smith, 187
Woody Allen, 81

Albums

A Link In the Chain, 109
Beatles Anthology, 129
Coming From Reality, 193

Animals

Black-tipped sharks, 26
Clownfish, 75
Sea Anemones, 75

Art styles

America Folk Art, 58
Impressionism, 58

Attractions

Brownville Concert Series, 211
Chalk Mines, Scotia, NE, 9
Indian Hills Theater, 75
Kentucky Derby, 230
Omaha Opera Company, 153, 211
Pioneer Village, 9

Biographical

A.R. Feinstein, 177
Brahmagupta, 165
Dr. Cyril Wecht, 155
Genghis Khan, 215, 216
Sgt. First-Class Darden, 41

Board game

Balderdash, 221, 223

Books

Animal Farm, 97
Chronicles of Narnia, 44
Gallup/Clinton Strengths Finder, 95
Genhis Khan: His Conquests, His Legacy, 215
Janis's Intimates: On the Road with Janis Joplin, 197
Jesse James: Last Rebel of the Civil War, 189

Lord of the Flies, 97
New Testament, 27, 213, 214
Old Testament, 229
Pilgrim's Progress, 97, 225
Pride and Prejudice, 158, 177, 179
Rasputin: The Untold Story, 203
Resident Aliens, 187, 188
Slave of Christ: A New Testament Metaphor for Total Devotion to Christ, 213
Teacher Man, 163, 164
The Coming Caesars, 5
The Cynic's Word Book, 159
The Diluted Church, 5, 40, 95, 97, 114, 117, 181
The Labyrinth of the World-and-The Paradise of the Heart, 5, 97, 98, 209, 225, 227
The Language of Blessing, 171
The Subversion of Christianity, 87
To Preach or Not to Preach, 165
True Believer: Stalin's Last American Spy, 217

Bosses
James H. Keene III, 153, 211
Pete Ringsmuth, 145
Scott Souter, 79
Steve Bulter, 183, 189

Botanical references
Exotics, 25
Hosta, 26
Irises, 25
Peonies, 25
Roses, 25
Succulents, 25
Tropicals, 25
Zoysia, 200

Cartoons
Timid Soul, 147
Yosemite Sam, 59

Cartoon-Comic Strip
Casper Milquetoast, 147

Characters
Boss Nass, 75
Dr. Quackenbush, 157
Elwood P. Dowd, 123
Ferris Bueller, 35, 49
Frank Moses, 169
Miss Malaprop, 105
Morrie Schwartz, 105
Myrtle Mae, 129
Obi-Wan Kenobi, 75
Peanuts, 147
Phil Olson, 205
Pooka (rabbit), 123, 124
Procrustes (or Damastes), 93
Randall Bragg, 149, 205
Reuben Tishkoff, 107
Sheldon Cooper, 32, 70
Son of Poseidon, 93, 94
Veta Simmons, 123
Virgil Cole, 149
Civil War, 183, 189

Classmates
Chris Clark, 19
Tina Roll, 19

Collateral Vocabulary
Ideating, 63
Nostrums, 6
Acculturated, 13
Acuity, 204
Acumen, 14
Affectation, 40
Aficionados, 191, 193
Amalgamation, 50
Anarchism, 81, 87, 121
Anecdotal, 6, 7, 14, 93, 103, 113, 161, 209
Anesthetizing, 132
Anodyne, 84
Antithetical, 88
Appellative, 165
Appendage, 68, 85
Apropos, 130, 168, 181
Asceticism, 131, 132
Assiduous(ly), 15, 195
Autodidact, 225, 225
Bromidic, 215
Cadre, 145
Calliope, 77
Caricaturization, 141, 142
Castigate, 22
Cheeky, 18
Circumspection, 90

Colloquial, 80
Colloquialism, 13, 73, 83, 107
Convalesced, 38
Copiously, 219
Counterintuitive, 38, 65, 223
Crepuscularly, 106
Culpability, 168
Curmudgeonly, 147
Delirium, 38, 67
Demure, 148
Dithering, 132
Effusive(ness), 105, 106, 209
Egocentric, 17
Elicit, 49, 139
Elocution, 30, 179
Elucidates, 85
Enamoration, 129
Enigma(tic), 125, 151, 193
Epiphenomena, 80
Esoterica, 80, 85
Essentia, 91
Ethnographically, 214
Etymologists, 15
Euphemistically, 60
Exasperating, 215
Excoriation, 190
Exegetic, 43, 44
Exonerate, 38
Exuberance, 20, 104
Façade, 102
Fictitious, 132, 143, 191
Flamboyance, 74, 115, 116, 189
Flamboyant, 47, 57, 74, 116, 126
Fortuitousness, 157
Gargantuan, 215
Gesticulation, 52
Gratuitous, 187
Homogenize, 49
Hovel, 198
Hubristic, 166
Idiomatic, 17, 73, 99, 107, 201, 216, 228
Idiosyncratic, 145
Imbue, 176
Impaled, 25
Incessant, 71, 187
Incognito, 73
Inextricable, 183
Inimitable, 17

Insipid, 12
Interfaithism, 49
Irrecoverable, 144
Kabbalah, 82
Lacerating, 21, 22
Lackadaisical, 160
Logophile(s), 223, (228)
Lyceum, 101
Metaphorically, 23, 52, 64, 142, 214
Meticulously, 189
Metrosexual, 16
Microcosm(s), (189), 199
Milieu, 191
Modish, 168
Modus operandi, 15, 79
Mystique, 119, 120, 203, 204
Nefarious, 28, 172
Noir, 216
Nomenclature, 92
Obfuscation, 138
Obsequious, 147, 223
Onomatopoeia, 24
Opulent, 159
Ostentatious, 189
Palette, 55, 189
Paltry, 189
Pandemonium, 199
Parallax, 153, 154
Patriarchy, 223
Pejorative, 28, 69
Penchant, 19, 61, 65, 221
Percolator, 159
Perusal, 37, 195
Phalanges, 169
Pique(d/s), (115, 197), 232
Poignancy, 190
Polemicist, 109, 172
Pompacious, 83
Postulation, 52
Pragmatic, 23, 79, 165
Precocious, 219
Predilection, 167, 212
Presupposition(s), 139, (35, 96, 152)
Pretentiousness, 108, 190
Progenitor, 125
Pugnaciousness, 148
Quandary, 153
Relativism, 92, 121
Relegated, 21, 216

Rhetorician, 165
Ribald, 140
Rotund, 53
Salutation, 176
Scintilla, 213
Segue, 173
Self-aggrandizement, 70
Simile, 16
Status quo, 101, 127, 128
Sycophantic, 122
Tedious, 22
Theology, 89
Tome, 215
Truncate(d), 175, (209)
Unbeknownst, 91, 179
Veneration, 125, 126
Vicariously, 31
Vituperations, 219
Vociferous, 152
Communism(t), 217, 218

Companies

Barnes & Noble, 163, 193
Disney, 191
Fastenal, 79
Ford, 49
Gallup, 95, 171
Majors SAT, 45
Peter Kiewit and Sons, Inc. (Kiewit), 211
Praxair, 61
Quizlet, 45
Sonic, 201
Union Pacific, 199, 200
United Electric Supply, 57
Verbal Advantage, 45
Wendy's, 201

Companies (where I worked)

Drake-Williams Steel, 60, 61, 63
News Link, 139, 143, 145, 147, 161, 199
Omaha Steel Castings Co., 51, 53
Siemens, 219

Concept

(Kingdom of God) amongst the kingdoms of men, (5), 213, (218)

Cultural references

Rat Pack, 107
Vaudeville, 83, 157

Cinerama, 75
Cinescope, 75
iTunes, 37
Mimeograph, 125
Ultra-right-wing conservatives, 29
VHS Movies, 73

Customers

Alice Cizek, 57
Ellen Hansen, 57

Design Styles

Art Deco, 58
Early Empire, 58
Nanyang Design, 58

Dictionaries

Cambridge Dictionary, 215
Merriam-Webster Dictionary, 75, 215
Second edition American Heritage Dictionary, 113
Webster's Third International Unabridged Dictionary, 112

Diseases

Stargardt (syndrome), 191
Early on-set Dementia, 5, 208

Documentaries

Searching for Sugar Man, 193
The Men Who Killed Kennedy, 155

Expressions

Exceptionism, 122
Explosion in a haystack, 116
Flashes-in-the-pan, 71, 129
Glad-handed, 79
Goyim, 107, 108
Hoity-toity, 6
Hooey, 223
In a month of Sundays, 189
Life's like a Box of Chocolates, 71
Loose-words-sink-big-ships, 146
Muckety-mucks, 39
Mutual-admiration society, 136
Oy Vey!, 221
Phi Beta Kappa, 12
Poppycock, 119
Pot calling the kettle black, 84
Potty trained at gunpoint, 60
Pull-yourself-up-by-your-bootstraps, 19

Rage-a-mania(c), (60), 83, (219)
Rats off a sinking ship, 57
Rough-and-tumble persona, 33
Scamdemic, 208
Skedaddle, 149
Stink eye, 27
Sunday-go-to-meeting, 97
Tales of yore, 211
The final straw, 80
Throwback, 129, 197
Tiptoeing through the tulips, 138
Tomorrow Never Knows, 129
Victim-of-circumstance, 168
Worth their salt, 232
Glass-half-full, 161
Go south, 208
Hard-scrabble, 197
Hoodwinking, 48
Shot the bull, 51
Ace of spades, 15
Axe-to-grind, 141
Below the belt, 187, 188
Black eye, 18
Browbeating, 124
Chock-full, 187
Colorful metaphors, 39, 40
Do-dads, 104
Laissez-faire, 101
Mealymouthed, 31
Quicksilver, 173
Thingamajig, 165
Brainiac, 227
Drama queen, 17, 18
Ebb and flow, 124
Funnier than a rubber crutch, 85
Lowered the boom, 79
Mulled over, 29
Odd-duck, 129, 215
Off-color talk, 187
Politically correct, 9, 16, 28, 66, 192
Rolling iron, 199
Showstopper, 154
Thunderclouds, 57
Tour de force, 213
University of Hard Knocks, 19
Wheelhouse, 174
Where's-the-beef, 201
Work-a-day world, 153
Ace in the hole, 75

Anal-retentive, 227
Battle royale, 155
Unlacquered, 15
MRO, 79

Featured Vocabulary

Abrogate, 89, 90
Abscond, 111, 112
Absolving, 38
Accouterment, 103, 104, 141
Aegis, 137, 138
Agitprop, 217, 218
Anathema, 45, 46
Ancillary, 113, 114
Anthropomorphism, 43, 44, 81, 82
Antithesis, 87, 88, 101, 128
Aphorism, 105, 106
Apoplectic, 59, 60
Appliqué, 40, 104, 141
Axiomatic, 105, 121, 122, 133
Carte blanche, 99, 100
Caterwauling, 23, 24
Charlatan, 47, 48
Circuitous(ly), 61, 62 (205)
Cogitate, 227, 228
Coiffeur, 115
Comorbidity, 177, 178
Coterie, 197, 198
Coups de grâce, 79, 80
Cretin, 13, 14
Desultory, 159, 160
Dialectic(s), 87, 88, 101, 102
Didactic, 123, 124
Dilettante, 91, 92
Eclectic, 57, 58
Epigraphic, 213, 214
Espirit de corps, 41, 42
Ethnocentrism, 20, 55
Fard, 140
Filch, 9, 10
Flaccid, 187, 188
Flatulent, 151, 152
Fop, 15, 16
Fusillade, 189, 190
Genuflect, 53, 54
Gourmand, 225, 226
Histrionic, 71, 72
Huckster, 27, 28
Iconoclastic, 125, 126, 139

Impecunious, 215, 216
Impertinent, 179, 180
Inculcate, 29, 30
Indefatigable, 143, 144
Indubitably, 161, 162
ineluctable, 149, 150
Inoculate, 30, 171, 172
Interloper, 200
Inveigh, 127, 128
Inveigle, 231, 232
Je ne sais quoi, 201, 202
Lambaste, 55, 56
Licentiousness, 191, 192
Malapropism, 129, 130
Mea culpa, 163, 164, 166
Ménagerie, 63, 64, 142
Mendicant, 131, 132
Mercurial, 173, 174
Miasma, 31, 32
Milquetoast, 147, 148
Mishigas, 107, 108
Monolith, 81, 82
Mot juste, 181, 182
Non Sequitur, 151, 152
Ombudsman, 219, 220
Opprobrium, 133, 134
Ossified, 193, 194
Pabulum, 11, 12
Panache, 73, 74
Panoply, 141, 142
Parley, 145, 146
Perfunctory, 175, 176
Persona non grata, 135, 136
Perspicacity, 203, 204
Petrichor, 221, 222
Petulant, 69, 70
Phylarch, 183, 184
Polemics, 109, 110
Polyglot, 65, 66
Prig, 21, 22
Prima donna, 17, 18
Proclivity, 14, 167, 168
Procrustean, 93, 94
Promulgate, 77, 78
Proximal, 185, 186
Reconnoiter, 211, 212
Redacted, 169, 170
Repose, 195, 196
Reverie, 67, 68

Salubrious, 153, 154
Schmendrick, 84, 85
Scotoma, 117, 118
Shibboleths, 229, 230
Shtick, Yiddish, 83, 84
Sine qua non, 156
Sophist(s), 165, 166
Swarthy, 33, 34
Symbiosis, 75, 76
Syncretism, 49, 50
Thrasonical, 205, 206
Trumpery, 119, 120
Tutelage, 95, 96
Ubiquitous, 97, 98, 187
Usurpations, 35, 36
Uxorious, 223
Variegated, 26
Vicissitudes, 157, 158

Focus on the Family, 29

Foreign Word

    Mangekyō, 65

Friends

    David Martin, 223, 227, 229
    Dotty Zens, 225
    Esad and Dijana Taslidzic, 65
    Gary Peterson, 181, 182
    Jay Ferris, 135
    Jim Backens, 211
    Kyle Knapp, 151
    Norbert Nelson, 17
    Paul Orner, 223, 231
    Steve & Gayle Hillmer, 67

Geographic Mentions

    Alaska, 221
    Australia, 63
    Beacon, NY, 110
    Bosnia, 65
    Budapest, 217
    Cerreto (Italy), 47
    Chicago, 139, 195, 231
    Czechoslovakia, 217
    Denmark, 63
    El Paso, TX, 195
    England, 97
    Fort Knox, 39
    Gibbon, NE, 9, 25
    Greenland, 221

Gulf of Mexico, 211
Hungary, 97
Island of Crete, 14
Japan, 42
Kearney, NE, 209, 223
Kentucky, 230
Lincoln, NE, 111, 117
Lithuania, 97
Mexico, 49, 50, 55
Minden, NE, 9
Minneapolis, MN, 33
Moravia, 97
Nescopeck, PA, 110
Netherlands, 97
New York City, 153
North Carolina, 135
Oakland, NE, 35
Old Market (Omaha's), 189, 211
Omaha, NE, 35, 43, 57, 63, 75, 153, 181, 211, 221
Romania, 85
Rouses Point, NY, 110
Salzburg, 37
San Francisco, 197
South Africa, 193
Sweden, 97
Transylvania, 97
Ukraine, 185
Washington, D.C., 39
Williamsburg, VA, 153
Winston, MO, 189

Historical Figures

Alger Hiss, 217
Archbishop of Canterbury, 23
C.S. Lewis, 44
Chester A. Arthur, 205
Czar Nicholas II, 203
Dr. Martin Luther King Jr., 126
Fauci [MD, Anthony S.], 208
FDR, President, 89
Frank Lloyd Wright, 126
General Eisenhower, 18
General George S. Patton, 17, 18
General Omar Bradley, 17
Helen Keller
Writer, 126
Jim Garrison, 211
John Adams, 120
John Amos Comenius, 7, 97, 209, 225
John F. Kennedy, 155
King Henry II, 23
Lord Tarleton, 131
Monet [Claude], 175
Nelson Mandela, 126
Noel Field, 217
President Bush, 83
Prince of Peace, 217
Rasputin, 203, 204
Robert Woodson, 189
Stalin, 217
Stephen Hawking, 126
Stonewall Jackson, 183
Temüjin (Genghis Khan), 215, 216, 231
Thomas Becket, 23
Whittaker Chambers, 217
William Wilberforce, 131

Historical References

1825 Russian Uprising, 141
Battle of the Bulge, 17
Black Death, 32
Blockbuster, 73
Bosnian War, 65
Bullwinkle oil platform, 211
Cholera, 32
CIA, 73, 169
Civil War, 183, 189
Conquistadors, 50
Communism, 217, 218
Dapper Dan, 115
Edwardian society, 158
Great Depression, 115
Gurutvākarsan, 165
KGB, 217
Marxism, 102
Normandy invasion, 18
Socialist(ic), (102), 218
Third Army, 17
Trans-Alaska Pipeline System, 211
WWII, 211

Interrobang, 146

Languages

Anglo-French, 140, 179, 196
Anglo-Norman French, 231
Aramaic, 107

Danish, 219
Dutch, 27, 34, 200
Eurasian, 107
French, 13, 40, 41, 51, 59, 63, 67, 68, 69, 79, 82, 99, 100, 102, 103, 105, 115, 119, 130, 133, 143, 158, 179, 181, 189, 193, 201, 202, 212, 227
French (Middle), 67, 73, 197
French (Old), 119, 145, 226
French Norman, 61
French-Swiss, 14
German (High) [ic], 13, (34), 75, (85), [198]
Greek, 31, 32
Hebrew, 107
High German, 34, 83, 175
Italian, 18, 47, 91
Latin, 12, 26, 29,34, 38, 40, 51, 53, 59, 60, 61, 69, 71, 75, 78, 87, 89, 91, 95, 98, 101, 111, 114, 115, 117, 121, 125, 127, 131, 133, 136, 137, 143, 149, 151, 154, 156, 159, 162, 163, 165, 167, 170, 171, 173, 175, 179, 185, 186, 188, 189, 192, 193, 204, 206, 212, 215, 219, 223, 227, 231
Middle English, 10, 15, 24,67, 73, 101, 119, 162, 171, 196
Old English, 83
Old French, 119, 145, 226, 227
Spanish, 50
Yiddish, 83, 85, 86, 107, 108

Military

2nd of the 6th Cavalry, 39
Bradley M-3, 39
Drill Sgt. 1st Class Darden, 41
M1 Abrams Tanks, 39

Movies

Amadeus, 37
Amazing Grace (2006), 131
Amen!, 17
Antz, 44, 81
Appaloosa, 149, 150, 295
Bad Boys II, 187, 188
Casino Royale, 22
Citizen Kane, 169
Defiance, 17
Everything is Illuminated (2005), 185
Ferris Bueller's Day Off, 35, 49
Forrest Gump, 211, 212
Gods and Generals, 183
Half-Wit Holiday (1946), 157
Harvey, 123
In the Line of Fire, 73
Jungle Book, 44
Last Chance Harvey, 153
Limitless, 173
Lone Ranger (2013), 191
McLintock!, 69, 70
Night of the Generals, 17
Oceans 11, 12 & 13, 107
Oh Brother, Where Art Thou, 107
Outlaw Josey Wales, 115
Patch Adams, 51
Pirates of the Caribbean - Dead Man's Chest, 143, 145
Red (2010 & 2013), 169
Runaway Jury, 91
Shutter Island, 167
Star Wars (Episode 1), 75, 76
Titanic, 169
True Grit, 119, 149
Tuesday with Morrie, 105

Movie/TV Series

Downton Abbey, 119, 179
MRO (Maintenance, Repair, and Operations), 79

Music styles

Dixieland Jazz, 37
Folk Rock, 141
Mariachi, 37

Musicians

Air Supply, 129
Antonio Salieri, 37
Beatles, 129, 167
Bob Dylan, 54, 125, 126, 193
Bruno Mars, 37
Cat Stevens, 193
Claude Debussy, 67
Colin Meloy, 141
Come Together (Cover Band), 167
Floyd Cramer, 37
Green Day, 37
Horst Jankowski, 109
Janis Joplin, 197
John Lennon, 129, 193

Johnny Cash, 135
KISS, 129
Mozart, 37
Paul McCartney, 37
Peter Seeger, 37, 109, 110
Ringo (Starr), 129
Sixto Rodriguez, 193
The Decemberists, 141, 142
Van Halen, 129

Pastors

Elmer H. Murdoch, 27, 28, 31, 32
Gordon Peterson, 33
John Marquez, 137
Randy Shupe, 125
Wade Burleson, 5, 207, 209
William Graham Sumner, 20

Periodicals

New York Tribune, 147
Searching Together, 5, 135, 231

People Groups

Aztecan, 50
Japanese, 29, 42, 65, 111
Jewish, 85, 107, 108
Mayan, 50
Saxon, 23

Personalities

Charles Schultz, 147
Dr. James Dobson, 29
Dr. Michael Savage, 83, 85
Jack Canfield, 171
Michael Blumberg, 152
Rush Limbaugh, 83, 139
Tony Campolo, 29
Zig Zigler, 171

Plays

Eunuchus, 206
Hamlet, 165
The Comical Wedding, 85
The Flatulent Lady, 51
The Rivals, 129

Psychological Terms

Histrionic Personality Disorder, 71
Regressive therapy, 137, 138

Relatives

Clayton Price, 107, 139
David Price, 11
Everett Price, 13
Genesis Price, 83, 177, 223
James Gail Price, 13
Jamie (Price) White, 21
Karel (Geary) Price, 3, 11, 55
Lola & Arthur Mast, 9, 10
Margaret Price, 25
Pam (Price), 17, 29, 65, 75, 81, 145, 177, 193
Philip A. Geary (Uncle Geary), (15, 21), 25,
Roman Price, 83, 175, 185, 223
Ruth (Geary) Mohar, 75
Stephanie Price, 153, 223
Stephen Price, 11

Religious References

Unitas Fratrum, 97
Bohemian Brethren, 97
Ephraimites, 230
Evangelical Free Church, 67
Evangelical(ism), 50
Gileadites, 229
Jesuit Priest, 117
Mennonite, 75, 215
Missionaries, 55, 77
Pacifist, 217
Quaker, 217
Salvation Army, 191
Strong's [Concordance], 229
Unity of the Brethren, 97
Reticular Activating System, 115

Salesmen

Jason Smith, 63
Michael Mennem, 61

Schools

Cornell, 156, 221
Doane University, 117
Harvard, 217
Millard Public Schools, 35
Omaha Bible School, 43, 45, 47, 49
UTEP, 195

Shows

Big Bang Theory, 32, 70
Kids Say the Darnedest Things, 177
Master Piece Theatre, 119, 179
NPR, 83

Social Media
- Blogosphere, 95
- Facebook, 151, 199
- Goodreads, 87
- Google, 7, 98
- LibraryThing, 87
- Nebraska Through the Lens (NTTL), 199
- Socialist(ic), (102), 218

Song Titles
- A Most Disgusting Song, 54
- Bolero, 67
- Guantanamera, 109
- June Hymn, 141
- Peer Gynt, 67
- The Times They Are A-Changin', 126
- Tomorrow Never Knows, 129

Teachers
- Clayton Steele, 35
- Don Dickerson (Professor), 117
- Ms. Mazzara, 19
- Ollie Olson, 49

Workmates
- Dennis Sullivan, 60
- Don Rabbe, 147
- Jay West, 53
- Kerri Long, 144
- Miguel Martinez, 51
- Randy Porter, 161
- Steve Bowder, 167
- Sunny Chsucta, 99, 111, 112

Writers
- Terence, 206
- Abraham Goldfaden, 85
- Amaury De Riencourt, 125, 133
- Ambrose Bierce, 159
- Andrew M. Brown, 70
- Cyril Connelly, 195
- David C. Norrington, 165
- Frank McCourt, 163
- Frank McLynn, 215, 231
- H.T. Webster, 147
- Jacques Ellul, 87, 101, 121, 122, 133
- Jane Austen, 177
- Joe Cavanaugh III, 95, 171
- John Byrne Cooke, 197
- Joseph T. Fuhrmann, 203
- Kati Marton, 217
- Mitch Albom, 105
- Murry J. Harris, 213
- Peter Lord, 115
- Richard Brinsley Sheridan, 129
- Stanley Hauerwas, 187
- T.J. Stiles, 189
- Tolstoy, 141

YWAM (Youth With A Mission), 78

Timothy L. Price worked 30 years in Purchasing/Sales/Inventory Control. During the same career he also published, 26 volumes for other authors as well as his own book in 2005: *The Diluted Church*. Among his publishing is the reissue of two out-of-print books: *To Preach or Not to Preach* (Norrington) and *The Coming Caesars* (De Reincourt). *Labyrinth* took eight months to adapt it from existing English editions.

The hardbound edition of *The Labyrinth of the World and The Paradise of the Heart* is like the softbound edition, however, it is full-color throughout. This is a collector's edition and is not just a book, but a piece of art: The 32-page historical and biographical appendix features 11 color photos of his work and significant items about his importance. The binding is museum quality, with debossed front cover, gold foil spine, and fabric headband.

266 pages
6x9x1.25
ISBN: 978-1737235309
Price: $31.95

Available at www.Labyrinthoftheworld.com, Amazon and other bookstores
Also available in Ebook and Audiobook at dealers world wide

The Diluted Church has been in print for 17 years now. It is as salient today as ever, yet with more urgency than ever. Originally addressed to "the religious right," *The Diluted Church* deals with our perceptions as followers of Christ as to who we really are and how this informs what we do. While the United States continues to degenerate in partisan politics and an off-the-cliff plunge into international Marxism, this book is a breath of fresh air to get us pointed again to true north. When we recover a sense of who we are, we no longer have to be a pawn in a political game. We can be something the political order cannot deny, nor avoid, nor can the pilfer to gain power or disenfranchise for political theatre. We become a force to be reckoned with.

276 pages
6x9x.625
ISBN: 0-97865222-0-9
Price: $18.95

Available at www.Labyrinthoftheworld.com
Also available in both print and Ebook through Amazon

The Coming Caesars is a book 70 years ahead of its time, written by a non-sentimental French author in the 1950s, reflecting how the US Presidency was increasingly overstepping its bounds. Now with the Presidency becoming tyrannical and governance is by committees of special interests and unelected people, the Presidency has become something to fear for being out of control. You're not going to get this understanding from any book I've seen written by a US author.

384 pages
6x9x.79
ISBN: 0-978-19384800-4-1
Price: $22.95

Available at
www.Labyrinthoftheworld.com
Also available in both print and Ebook through Amazon

www.ingramcontent.com/pod-product-compliance
Lightning Source LLC
Chambersburg PA
CBHW071738150426
43191CB00010B/1617